The Public in Peril

This is one of the first books to critique thoroughly the rise of Trumpism and its potential impact, nationally and globally. One of the world's leading social critics, Giroux offers new critiques of Trump and his cabinet choices in the context of longer-term trends, including the rise of right-wing populism, the threat of planetary peril, anti-intellectual fervor, the war on youth, a narrowing political discourse, deepening inequality and disposability, authoritarianism, the crisis of civic culture, the rise of the mass incarceration state, and more. Giroux dissects the diverse forces that led to Trump's rise and points to pathways for resisting his authoritarian instincts. Offering a new language of hope and possibility, Giroux's optimism is rooted especially in the resurgence of progressive politics among youth. Giroux reclaims the centrality of education to politics and boldly articulates a vision in which the radical imagination merges with civic courage as part of a broad-based struggle for a radical democracy. Deep inquiries into fast-changing and pressing issues of our time make this book 'the essential Giroux' that citizens and students must read, debate, and act upon.

Henry A. Giroux is currently the McMaster University Professor for Scholarship in the Public Interest and the Paulo Freire Distinguished Scholar in Critical Pedagogy. His most recent books include *Dangerous Thinking in the Age of the New Authoritarianism* (2015), co-authored with Brad Evans, *Disposable Futures: The Seduction of Violence in the Age of Spectacle* (2015), and *America at War with Itself* (2017).

Critical Interventions: Politics, Culture, and the Promise of Democracy
Edited by Henry A. Giroux, Susan Searls Giroux, and Kenneth J. Saltman

The Public in Peril

Trump and the Menace of American
Authoritarianism

Henry A. Giroux

To Tony,
I would still be a
high school teacher if it
had not been for you.
For a great friend, Teacher,
and comrade.
Much love,
Hy

Routledge
Taylor & Francis Group

NEW YORK AND LONDON

First published 2018
by Routledge
711 Third Avenue, New York, NY 10017

and by Routledge
2 Park Square, Milton Park, Abingdon, Oxon, OX14 4RN

Routledge is an imprint of the Taylor & Francis Group, an informa business

Library of Congress Cataloging-in-Publication Data
A catalog record for this book has been requested

ISBN: 978-1-138-71905-7 (hbk)
ISBN: 978-1-138-71903-3 (pbk)
ISBN: 978-1-315-17323-8 (ebk)

Typeset in Adobe Caslon Pro, Copperplate and Trade Gothic
by Florence Production Ltd, Stoodleigh, Devon, UK

For Muhammad Ali and James Baldwin who taught me how to flip the script and struggle with dignity, courage, and hope

CONTENTS

ACKNOWLEDGMENTS

Many of the ideas that inform this book first surfaced in articles I wrote for *Truthout*, *CounterPunch*, *Knowledge Cultures*, *Monthly Review*, *Symploke*, *Tikkun*, and *Social Identities*. Much of Chapter 1 draws upon "Anti-Politics and the Scourge of Authoritarianism," co-authored with Debaditya Bhattacharya, which appeared in *Social Identities* (August 11, 2016). I am grateful to Maya Schenwar and Alana Price from *Truthout* for their continued support and copious editing talents. I am also indebted to Jeffrey St. Clair at *CounterPunch* and Michael Lerner at *Tikkun* for supporting my work. Thanks to Ken Saltman and Brad Evans for taking the time to engage my work and provide insightful recommendations. Leila Gaind was very helpful with her initial edit of the manuscript. My wife, Susan, has been an enormous help in pushing me to the edges of critique and informed analyses. It has become impossible for me to write anything without having the benefit of her brilliance, editing skills, and love and support. My assistant, Maya Sabados, read every page of this book more than once and was invaluable in her editing, listening, and support. I could not have finished this book without her research and editing skills. A number of people have supported my work over the last decade in spite of the lack of support I have received from institutions that should know better. Many thanks to Oscar Zambrano, Michael Yates, Michael Peters, Donaldo Macedo,

Peter McLaren, Brad Evans, Greg Ruggiero, Robin Goodman, and David Clark. My editor at Routledge, Dean Birkenkamp, has been a friend for longer than I can remember and this book would not have been written without his encouragement. I also want to thank the three unnamed individuals who reviewed this manuscript for their insights and help. I have been blessed with having a number of brilliant students in my classes at McMaster. They may have taught me a lot more than I taught them, and I am forever grateful for that gift.

INTRODUCTION: MILITANT HOPE
IN THE AGE OF AMERICAN
AUTHORITARIANISM

> To be truly radical is to make hope possible rather than despair
> inevitable.
>
> (Raymond Williams)

The United States stands at the endpoint of a long series of attacks on democracy, and the choices faced by the American public today point to the divide between those who are committed to democracy and those who are not. Debates over whether Donald Trump was a fascist or Hillary Clinton was a right-wing warmonger and tool of Wall Street were a tactical diversion. The real questions that should have been debated include: What measures could have been taken to prevent the United States from sliding further into a distinctive form of authoritarianism? And what could have been done to imagine a mode of civic courage and militant hope needed to enable the promise of a democracy as a governing principle? Such questions take on a significant urgency in light of the election of Donald Trump to the presidency. Under such circumstances, not only is the public in peril, it is on the brink of collapse as the economic, political, and cultural institutions necessary for democracy to survive are being aggressively undermined. As Robert Kuttner observes:

It is hard to contemplate the new administration without experiencing alarm bordering on despair: Alarm about the risks of war, the fate of constitutional democracy, the devastation of a century of social progress. Trump's populism was a total fraud. Every single Trump appointment has come from the pool of far-right conservatives, crackpots, and billionaire kleptocrats. More alarming still is the man himself—his vanity, impulsivity, and willful ignorance, combined with an intuitive genius as a demagogue. A petulant fifth-grader with nuclear weapons will now control the awesome power of the U.S. government. One has to nourish the hope that Trump can yet be contained. Above all, that will take passionate and strategic engagement, not just to resist but to win, to discredit him and get him out of office while this is still a democracy. We can feel sick at heart—we would be fools not to—but despair is not an option.[1]

Kuttner rightly mitigates such despair with a call for resistance. Yet, such deep-seated anxiety is not unwarranted given the willingness of contemporary politicians and pundits during the 2016 presidential battle to use themes that echoed alarmingly fascist and totalitarian elements of the past. According to Drucilla Cornell and Stephen D. Seely, Trump's campaign mobilized a movement that was "unambiguously fascist."[2] They write:

We are not using the word "fascist" glibly here. Nor are we referencing only the so-called "alt-right" contingent of his supporters. No, Trump's entire movement is rooted in an ethnic, racial, and linguistic nationalism that sanctions and glorifies violence against designated enemies and outsiders, is animated by a myth of decline and nostalgic renewal and centered on a masculine cult of personality.[3]

Large segments of the American public have been written out of politics over what they view as a failed state and the inability of the basic machinery of government to serve their interests.[4] As market mentalities and moralities tighten their grip on all aspects of society, democratic institutions and public spheres are being downsized, if not altogether disappearing. As these institutions vanish—from public schools to health-care centers—there is also a serious erosion of the discourses of community, justice, equality, public values, and the common good. This grim reality has been called a "failed sociality"—a failure in the power of the civic imagination, political will, and open democracy.[5] As the consolidation of power by the corporate and financial elite empties politics of any substance, the political realm merges elements of Monty Python, Kafka, and Aldous Huxley. Mainstream politics is now dominated by hard-right extremists who have brought to the center of politics a shameful white supremacist ideology, poisonous xenophobic ideas, and the blunt, malicious tenets and practices of Islamophobia.

On the other side of the political spectrum, the Democratic Party operates in the service of the war machine, financial elite, and various registers of the military-industrial-academic-surveillance complex. In the current political climate, centrism and extremism increasingly become indistinguishable. The older political establishment's calls for regime change and war are now supplemented by the discourse of state-sanctioned torture, armed ignorance, and a deep hatred of democracy. One consequence is that both parties have thrown, in different degrees, immigrants, poor minorities of class and color, refugees, the working class, and especially young people under the bus. Neoliberalism, with its full-fledged assault on the welfare state and public goods, the destruction of the manufacturing sector, and a dramatic shift in wealth to the upper 1 percent, has destroyed the faith of millions in democracy, which lost its power to contain the rich in a runaway form of casino capitalism. With the erosion of the social contract and the increasing power of the rich to control both the commanding institutions of society and politics itself, democracy has lost any legitimacy as a counterweight to protect the ever widening sphere of people considered vulnerable and disposable. One consequence has been that the dangerous playbook to neo-fascist appeals has gained more and more credence. In addition, large portions of the American public have turned willingly to Trump's brand of authoritarianism.

Trump's election has produced widespread despair, fear, and anxiety in the most vulnerable, largely confirmed by the fact that "over a thousand hate crimes have been reported since Donald Trump won the U.S. presidential election."[6] Even more foreboding is the fact that not only does Trump inherit the repressive policies and practices that followed 9/11 such as a growing national security state, the National Defense Authorization Act, a permanent war culture, the paramilitarization of the police, widespread intrusive surveillance, and the illegality of drone assassinations, but he has at his disposal the ability to wield a massive degree of executive power. As Kuttner makes clear:

> But one should not minimize the perils. Trump will wield a massive amount of executive power. This is a man with a short fuse and a long enemies list . . . he can use the power of the presidency to conduct vast surveillance, threaten the commercial interests of the free press, selectively prosecute, and further weaken the labor movement while his allies in Congress change the ground rules of federalism to undermine progressive policies of blue states and cities. Trump will float above cadres of conservative professionals with detailed playbooks. They will try to back-load the impact of un-popular policies such as deep cuts in Social Security and Medicare.[7]

The future looks bleak, especially for youth as they are burdened with debt, dead-end jobs, unemployment, and, if you are black and poor, the increasing possibility of being either incarcerated or shot by the police.[8] Trump has redefined government as the enemy of economic and social justice and in doing so has created a number of cabinet positions that will run what might be called ministries of repression and injustice. The United States has become a war culture and immediate massive forms of resistance and civil disobedience are essential if the planet and human life is going to survive.[9] Domestic terrorism defined as intentional and criminal acts of violence by the state against civilian populations has become the new norm in the United States.

The savagery of a war culture and its sundry forms of domestic terrorism was on full display in the United States with the September 13, 2016 shooting of Tyre King in Columbus, Ohio, a 13-year-old child who ran from the police while holding a BB gun. Tyre was "5ft tall and weighed less than 100lbs ... [and was an] eighth-grader [who] played football and other sports, and was in a young scholars program."[10] After this innocent child was killed, there were more shootings of unarmed African Americans in spite of growing public protest against police violence. For example, Keith Lamont Scott, 43, of Charlotte, North Carolina, was shot dead while sitting in his truck while waiting for his son to return home on a bus from school. On May 2, 2017, a Texas police officer in Balch Springs, Texas shot into a car killing 15-year-old Jordan Edwards. These shootings barely scratch the surface of the workings of a police state and the increasing number of assaults waged against poor communities of color. As Nicholas Powers points out,

> The old racial line between "Black" and "White" has been redrawn as the line between criminal and citizen. Up and down the class hierarchy from poor to wealthy, Black people have to dodge violence, from macroaggressions to economic sabotage and from public shaming to physical attacks ... every day another person of color is shot by police, and the hole left inside families are where loved ones used to breathe. The cops not only steal the lives of our children; they steal the lives of everyone who loved them. A part of us freezes, goes numb.[11]

There can be little doubt that America is at war with its own ideals and that war is being waged against minorities of color and class, immigrants, Muslims, and Syrian refugees. Such brutality amounts to acts of domestic terrorism and demands not only massive collective opposition but also a new understanding of the conditions that are causing such sanctioned violence and the need for a fresh notion of politics to resist it. This suggests putting democratic socialism on the agenda for change.

The struggle for democratic socialism is an important goal, especially in light of the reign of terror of the existing neoliberal mode of governance. It is crucial to remember that as a firm defender of the harsh politics and values of neoliberalism, Trump preyed on the atomization and loneliness many people felt in a neoliberal social order that derides dependency, solidarity, community, and any viable notion of the commons. He encouraged both the fantasy of a rugged individualism and the toxic discourse of a hyper-masculine notion of nativism, while at the same time offering his followers the swindle of a community rooted in an embrace of white supremacy, a white public sphere, and a hatred of those deemed irrevocably other. The ideology and public pedagogy of neoliberalism at the root of Trump's embrace of a new authoritarianism must be challenged and dismantled ideologically and politically.

Yet, the task of challenging the new authoritarianism will only succeed if progressives embrace an expansive understanding of politics. This means, among other things, refusing to view elections as the ultimate litmus test of democratic participation and rejecting the assumption that capitalism and democracy are synonymous. The demise of democracy must be challenged at all levels of public participation and must serve as a rallying cry to call into question the power and control of all institutions that bear down on everyday life. Moreover, any progressive struggle must move beyond the fragmentation that has undermined the left for decades. This suggests moving beyond single-issue movements in order to develop and emphasize the connections between diverse social formations. At stake here is the struggle for building a broad alliance that brings together different political movements and, as Cornell and Seely observe, a political formation willing to promote an ethical revolution whose goal "is not only socialism as an economic form of organization but a new way of being together with others that could begin to provide a collectively shared horizon of meaning."[12]

Central to *The Public in Peril* is a refusal of the mainstream politics of disconnect. In its place is a plea for expansive social movements and a more comprehensive understanding of politics in order to connect the dots between, for instance, police brutality and mass incarceration, on the one hand, and the diverse crises producing massive poverty, the destruction of the welfare state, and the assaults on the environment, workers, young people, and women on the other. As Peter Bohmer observes, the call for a meaningful living wage and full employment cannot be separated from demands "for access to quality education, affordable and quality housing and medical care, for quality child care, for reproductive rights and for clean air, drinkable water," and the pillaging of the environment by the ultra-rich and mega corporations.[13] He rightly argues:

> Connecting issues and social movements and organizations to each other has the potential to build a powerful movement of movements that is stronger than any of its individual parts. This means educating ourselves and in our groups about these issues and their causes and their interconnection.[14]

One approach to such a task would be to develop an expansive understanding of politics that necessarily links the calls for a living wage and environmental justice to demands for accessible quality health care and the elimination of conditions that enable the state to wage assaults against Black people, immigrants, workers, and women. Such relational analyses also suggest the merging of labor unions and social movements. In addition, progressives must address the crucial challenge of producing cultural apparatuses such as alternative media, think tanks, and social services in order to provide models of education that enhance the ability of individuals to make informed judgments and discriminate between evidence-based arguments and opinions, and to provide theoretical and political frameworks for rethinking the relationship between the self and others based on notions of compassion, justice, and solidarity.

Crucial to rethinking the space and meaning of the political imagination is the need to reach across specific identities and to move beyond single-issue movements and their specific agendas. This is not a matter of dismissing such movements, but creating new alliances that allow them to become stronger in the fight to succeed both in advancing their specific concerns and in enlarging the possibility of developing a radical democracy that benefits not just specific but general interests. As the Fifteenth Street Manifesto group expressed in its 2008 piece, "Left Turn: An Open Letter to U.S. Radicals," many groups on the left would grow stronger if they were to "perceive and refocus their struggles as part of a larger movement for social transformation."[15] Any feasible political agenda must merge the pedagogical and the political by employing a language and mode of analysis that resonates with people's needs while making social change a crucial element of the political and public imagination. At the same time, any politics that is going to take real change seriously must be highly critical of any reformist politics that does not include both a change of consciousness and structural change.

If progressives are to join in the fight against authoritarianism in the United States, they will need to create powerful political alliances and produce long-term organizations that can provide a view of the future that does not simply mimic the present. This is where matters of translation become crucial in developing wider ideological struggles and in fashioning a more comprehensive notion of politics. Movements require time to mature and come into fruition and depend on an educated public that is able to address both the structural conditions of oppression and how they are legitimated through their ideological impact on individual and collective attitudes and modes of experiencing the world. In this way radical ideas can be connected to action once workers and others recognize the need to take control of the conditions of their labor, communities, resources, and lives.

Struggles that take place in particular contexts must also be associated to similar efforts at home and abroad. For instance, the ongoing privatization of public goods such as schools can be analyzed within increasing attempts on the part of billionaires to eliminate the social state and gain control over commanding economic and cultural institutions in the U.S. At the same time, the modeling of schools after prisons can be connected to the ongoing criminalization of a wide range of everyday behaviors and the rise of the punishing state.

Moreover, oppressive economic, political, and cultural practices in the U.S. can be connected to other authoritarian societies that are following a comparable script of widespread repression. For instance, it is crucial to think about what racialized police violence in the United States has in common with violence waged by authoritarian states such as Egypt against Muslim protesters. This allows us to understand various social problems globally so as to make it easier to develop political formations that link such diverse social justice struggles across national borders. It also helps us to understand, name, and make visible the diverse authoritarian policies and pedagogical practices that point to the parameters of a totalitarian society.

In this instance, making the political more pedagogical becomes central to any viable notion of politics. That is, if the ideals and practices of democratic governance are not to be lost, there is a need for progressives to address and accelerate the production of critical public spheres that promote dialogue, debate, and, what James Baldwin once called, a "certain daring, a certain independence of mind" capable of teaching "some people to think and in order to teach some people to think, you have to teach them to think about everything."[16] Thinking is dangerous, especially under the cloud of an impending neo-fascism, because it is a crucial requirement for constructing new political institutions that can both fight against the impending authoritarianism and imagine a society in which democracy is viewed no longer as a remnant of the past but rather as an ideal that is worthy of continuous struggle. This merging of education, critical thinking, and politics is necessary for creating informed agents willing to fight the systemic violence and domestic forms of repression that mark the authoritarian policies and repressive practices of the Trump administration. Under the Trump presidency, the worst dimensions of a neoliberal order will be accelerated and will include: deregulating restrictions on corporate power, cutting taxes for the rich, expanding the military, privatizing public education, suppressing civil liberties, waging a war against dissent, treating Black communities as war zones, and dismantling all public goods. Such actions make it all the more imperative for progressives to challenge a market-driven society that erodes the symbolic and affective bonds and loyalties that give meaning to social existence. Appealing to the economic interests of the public is important, but it is not enough. Hope has to be fed by the lessons of history, the recognition for collective action, and the willingness to "feel one's way imaginatively into the situation of others."[17]

Developing a comprehensive view of politics must take on the crucial challenge of producing a critical formative culture along with corresponding institutions that promote a form of permanent criticism against all elements of oppression and unaccountable power. One important task of emancipation is to encourage educators, artists, workers, young people, and others to use their skills in the service of a politics in which public values, trust, and compassion can be used to chip away at neoliberalism's celebration of self-interest, the ruthless accumulation of capital, the survival-of-the-fittest ethos, and the financialization and market-driven corruption of the political system. Political responsibility is more than a challenge—it is the projection of a possibility in which new identification, affectations, and loyalties can be produced to enable and sustain new forms of civic action, political organizations, and transnational anti-capitalist movements. A radical democracy based on the best principles of a democratic socialism must be written back into the script of everyday life, and doing so demands overcoming the current crisis of memory, agency, and politics by collectively struggling for a society in which matters of justice, equity, and inclusion define what is possible.

Neo-fascism thrives on the disparagement of others, nativism, ultra-nationalism, an appeal to violence, an unchecked individualism, and the legitimation of an alleged preferred people to dominate others. These are the elements of a cultural formation rooted in nihilism, cynicism, economic insecurity, unrestrained anger, a paralyzing fear, and the collapse of public values and the ethical grammar that gives a democracy meaning. At work here is the undeniable fact of how education is at the center of politics and can be used for either oppressive or emancipatory ends. This suggests strategies aimed at the development of alternative, progressive educational apparatuses, grounded in the pedagogical necessity to make knowledge and ideas meaningful in order to make them critical and transformative. This means appropriating and using the symbolic and intellectual tools of persuasion, identification, and belief as crucial political strategies. I am not talking about a facile appeal to a notion of consciousness raising. Rather, I am emphasizing the necessity for progressives to work in conjunction with labor unions, educational unions, and other social movements to develop the institutions necessary to change the consciousness, desires, identities, and values necessary for providing a sense of agency for those individuals who lack the tools of civic literacy and critical frames of reference necessary for understanding the conditions that produce misery, exploitation, exclusion, and mass resentment, while paving the way for right-wing populist movements.

Under the reign of casino capitalism, democratic public spheres along with the public they support are disappearing. One consequence is a warfare state built not only on the militarization of the economy but also on what my colleague Brad Evans calls "armed ignorance." Such ignorance represents more than a paucity of ethical and social responsibility; it is also symptomatic of an educational and spiritual crisis in the United States. A culture of fear, hate, and bigotry has transformed American politics into a pathology. Fear cripples reason and makes it easier for authoritarian figures to engage in what might be called terror management. Trump's pre-election rally speeches mobilized millions with the drug-inducing appeal of uncertainty, fear, and hatred. David Dillard-Wright's insightful commentary on Trump's use of fear makes clear how he used it as both a political and pedagogical tool. He writes:

> The Trump rally speeches go through a litany of perceived threats to the American worker: the immigrants taking "our" jobs, the terrorists who want to kill "us," the media who want to silence "us." Trump is no social psychologist, but he has an instinctive sense for crowds: the purpose of this rhetoric is to tear down the listener to a point of malleability, at which point, he "alone" supplies the answer (as in his "I alone can fix it" speech at the Republican National Convention in the summer). He drowns the listener in fear and then reaches out a helping hand from the threat that he, himself, has conjured. This verbal waterboarding breaks down the Trump fan into a panicked rage and then channels that fear and anger into the pretend solution of a giant wall or jailing Hillary Clinton, which not incidentally, also places Trump at the center

of power and control over his fans' lives. Fear actually short-circuits rational thought and gets the rally-goer to accept the strongman as the only way to avoid the perceived threat.[18]

The appeal to mass-produced fear legitimates a politics that tramples the rights of minorities, young people, and dissidents. Moreover, it reinforces a violent and corrupt lawlessness that extends from the highest reaches of government and big corporations to the paramilitarization of our schools and police forces. Domestic terrorism becomes normalized as unarmed Blacks are killed by the police almost weekly, while more and more members of the population are considered excess, disposable, redundant, and subject to the bigotry of escalating right-wing groups, corrupt politicians, and policies that benefit the financial elite. And with the election of Donald Trump to the presidency, a fog of authoritarianism will all but diminish any vestige of democracy and civic literacy. Such a prophecy is not simply the stuff of science fiction. As David Remnick predicts, the upcoming Trump administration will usher in both a withering of public values and a democratic sensibility leading to a dystopian social order immersed in misery, violence, and cruelty:

> There are, inevitably, miseries to come: an increasingly reactionary Supreme Court; an emboldened right-wing Congress; a President whose disdain for women and minorities, civil liberties and scientific fact, to say nothing of simple decency, has been repeatedly demonstrated. Trump is vulgarity unbounded, a knowledge-free national leader who will not only set markets tumbling but will strike fear into the hearts of the vulnerable, the weak, and, above all, the many varieties of Other whom he has so deeply insulted. The African-American Other. The Hispanic Other. The female Other. The Jewish and Muslim Other. The most hopeful way to look at this grievous event—and it's a stretch—is that this election and the years to follow will be a test of the strength, or the fragility, of American institutions. It will be a test of our seriousness and resolve.[19]

The world is on the brink of nuclear war, ecological extinction, an accelerating refugee crisis, and a growing culture saturated in violence; yet, the public is persuaded that the burning issues of the day focus on the break-up of Brad Pitt and Angelina Jolie, Kim Kardashian's loss of $11 million in jewelry to thieves, or the endless focus on the banality of reality TV and celebrity culture. In addition, violence is now treated as a theatrical performance, paving the way each day for the next news cycle operating primarily as spectacle and entertainment. Moral and political hysteria is in fashion and has undermined the public spheres that promote self-reflection, dialogue, and informed judgment. Informed exchanges and arguments that rely on evidence have been displaced by a culture of shouting, emotion, lying, and thuggery. War comes in many forms and is as powerful as a form of ideology and identification as it is in the service of multiple forms of violence. Once we recognize the metrics of war as crises of both politics and education, we can mobilize against its ideological and material relations of power. But time is running out.

The American public needs a new discourse to resuscitate historical memories and develop new methods of opposition in order to address the connections between the escalating destabilization of the Earth's biosphere, impoverishment, inequality, police violence, mass incarceration, corporate crime, and the lead poisoning of low-income communities. Once again, not only are social movements from below needed, there is also a need to merge diverse single-issue movements that range from calls for racial justice to calls for economic fairness. Of course, there are significant examples of this in the Black Lives Matter and Moral Monday movements and the ongoing strikes by workers for a living wage.[20] But these are only the beginning of what is needed to contest state violence, institutionalized racism, and the savage machinery of neoliberal capitalism.

There has never been a more pressing time to rethink the meaning of politics, justice, struggle, collective action, and the development of new political parties and social movements. The ongoing violence against Black youth, the impending ecological crisis, the use of prisons to warehouse people who represent social problems, the lead poisoning of children due to neoliberal fiscal policies, and the ongoing war on women's reproductive rights, among other crises, demand a new language for developing modes of creative long-term struggle, a wider understanding of politics, and a new urgency to create modes of collective struggles rooted in more enduring and unified political formations.

Such struggles demand an increasingly focused commitment to a new kind of activism. As Robin D. G. Kelley has noted, there is a need for more pedagogical, cultural, and social spaces that allow us to think and act together, to take risks and to get to the roots of the conditions that are submerging the United States in a new form of authoritarianism wrapped in the flag, the dollar sign, and the cross.[21] Kelley is right in calling for a politics that places justice at its core, one that takes seriously what it means to be an individual and social agent while engaging in collective struggles. We don't need tepid calls for repairing the system; instead, we need to invent a new system from the ashes of one that is terminally broken. We don't need calls for moral uplift or personal responsibility. We need calls for economic, political, gender, and racial justice. Such a politics must be rooted in particular demands, be open to direct action, and take seriously strategies designed to both educate a wider public and mobilize them to take back democratic institutions.

Trump's willingness to rely upon openly fascist elements prefigures the emergence of an American-style mode of authoritarianism that threatens to further foreclose venues for social justice and civil rights. The need for resistance has become urgent. The struggle is not simply over specific institutions such as higher education or so-called democratic procedures such as the validity of elections, but over what it means to get to the root of the problems facing the United States. At the heart of such a movement is the need to draw more people into subversive actions modeled after the militancy of the labor strikes of the 1930s, the civil rights movements of the 1950s, and the struggle for participatory democracy by the New Left in the 1960s, while building upon the strategies and successes of the more recent movements for economic, social, gender, and environmental justice such as Black Lives Matter, Our Revolution, and gay and lesbian rights movements. At the same time, there is a need to reclaim the social imagination and to infuse it with a spirited battle for an independent politics that regards a radical democracy as part of a never-ending struggle.

None of this can happen unless progressives understand education as a political and moral practice crucial to creating new forms of agency, mobilizing a desire for change, and providing a language that underwrites the capacity to think, speak, and act so as to challenge the sexist, racist, economic, and political grammars of suffering produced by the new authoritarianism. The left needs a language of critique that enables people to ask questions that appear unspeakable within the existing vocabularies of oppression. We also need a language of hope that is firmly aware of the ideological and structural obstacles that are undermining democracy. We need a language in which the oppressed can recognize themselves. This should be a discourse that reframes our activist politics as a creative act that responds to the promises and possibilities of a radical democracy.

Wider social movements cannot materialize overnight. They require educated agents who are able to connect structural conditions of oppression to the oppressive cultural apparatuses that legitimate, persuade, and shape individual and collective attitudes in the service of oppressive ideas and values. No wide-ranging social movement can develop without educating a public about the diverse economic, political, cultural, and pedagogical conditions that provide a discourse of critique and inquiry on the one hand and a vocabulary of action and hope on the other. Under such conditions, radical ideas can be connected to action once diverse groups recognize the need to take control of the political, economic, and cultural conditions which shape their world views, exploit their labor, control their communities, appropriate their resources, and undermine their dignity and lives. Raising consciousness alone will not change authoritarian societies, although it does provide the foundation for making oppression visible and for developing from below what Etienne Balibar calls "practices of resistance and solidarity."[22] We need more than radical critique of capitalism, racism, and other forms of oppression. Any viable struggle for justice and a radical democracy also needs to nourish a critical formative culture and politics that inspires, energizes, and provides a radical education project in the service of a broad-based movement for democratic socialism.

The Public in Peril represents an attempt to develop a political discourse and call to action by addressing not only the impending crisis of authoritarianism evident in the rise of Donald Trump and other extremists in the United States, including the misery and culture of cruelty endemic to casino capitalism, but also to analyze the various ways in which the registers of authoritarianism are impacting on everyday life.

Part I deals with the emerging authoritarianism in the United States through the scourge of anti-politics, which I define as the emptying of politics of democratic values, public participation, and justice. In addition, this section provides a critique of the rise of white supremacy headed by Donald Trump, and the growth of armed ignorance as a function of manufactured illiteracy and the ideologies and structures that enforce it. This section also focuses on a notion of politics that highlights both the pedagogical and political dimensions of authoritarianism.

Part II focuses on the concept of domestic terrorism and the impact of authoritarianism on youth, especially Black youth, as the most vulnerable of populations to be assaulted by the warfare state. It examines the ways in which prison culture has seeped into public schools and how a police state has redefined young people within a culture of criminality. The section also examines a revealing expression of racism in popular culture, one that is symptomatic of the loss of public memory and the waning of the ethical imagination.

Part III examines the influence of neoliberalism on higher education while defending the role of teachers as crucial public servants in a democracy. It also examines the liminal notion of exile as a metaphor for a space of opposition and pedagogy as a work of art.

Part IV analyzes some distinctive and powerful registers of neoliberal culture, focusing specifically on its embrace of a war culture, precarity, and markets as a tool to govern all of social life rather than just the economy. At the same time, the chapter focuses on possible modes of struggle that connect a pedagogy of militant and courageous hope with a politics that needs to become more pedagogical in its resistance to neoliberal tyranny and the emerging forces of authoritarianism.

Notes

1   Robert Kuttner, "The Audacity of Hope," *American Prospect* (December 16, 2016). Online: http://prospect.org/article/audacity-hope

2   Drucilla Cornell and Stephen D. Seely, "Seven Theses on Trump," *Critical Legal Thinking* (November 28, 2016). Online: http://criticallegalthinking.com/2016/11/28/seven-theses-trump/

3   Ibid.

4   For a brilliant analysis of the anger and fears among those working-class individuals and groups written out of the American Dream, see Arlie Russell Hochschild, *Strangers in Their Own Land* (New York: New Press, 2016). See also, George Packer, *The Unwinding: An Inner History of the New America* (New York: Farrar, Straus and Giroux, 2014).

5   Alex Honneth, *Pathologies of Reason* (New York: Columbia University Press, 2009), p. 188.

6   TelSur, "In Aftermath of Trump's Win, We Are Witnessing More than 1,000 Hate Crimes in a Month," *AlterNet* (December 19, 2016). Online: www.alternet.org/human-rights/aftermath-trumps-win-we-are-witnessing-more-1000-hate-crimes-month

7   Kuttner, "The Audacity of Hope."

8   See, for instance, a number of insightful articles on police violence against people of color in Maya Schenwar, Joe Macare, and Alana Yu-lan Price, eds, *Who Do You Serve, Who Do You Protect?* (Chicago: Haymarket Books, 2016).

9   On the militarization of everyday life, see: Rosa Brooks, *How Everything Became War and the Military Became Everything: Tales from the Pentagon* (New York: Simon and Fraser, 2016); Radley Balko, *Rise of the Warrior Cop: The Militarization of America's Police Forces* (New York: Public Affairs, 2014); Nick Turse, *The Complex: How the Military Invades Our Everyday Lives* (New York: Metropolitan Books, 2008).

10 Guardian staff, "Tyre King, 13-Year-Old Boy Shot Dead by Columbus Police, Laid to Rest in Ohio," *Guardian* (September 24, 2016). Online: www.theguardian.com/us-news/2016/sep/24/tyre-king-shooting-funeral-columbus-police-officer-bryan-mason

11 Nicholas Powers, "Killing the Future: The Theft of Black Life." In Maya Schenwar, Joe Macare, and Alana Yu-lan Price, eds, *Who Do You Serve, Who Do You Protect?* (Chicago: Haymarket Books, 2016), p. 14.

12 Cornell and Seely, "Seven Theses on Trump."

13 Peter Bohmer, "Connecting $15 an Hour Movement to Other Social Movements," *CounterPunch* (September 28, 2015). Online: www.counterpunch.org/2015/09/28/connecting-15-an-hour-movement-to-other-social-movements/; see also, Charles Derber, *Welcome to the Revolution: Universalizing Resistance for Social Justice and Democracy in Perilous Times* (New York: Routledge, 2018)

14 Ibid.

15 Situations, *Left Turn: An Open Letter to U.S. Radicals* (New York: Fifteenth Street Manifesto Group, March 2008), p. 1.

16 James Baldwin, *James Baldwin: The Last Interview and Other Conversations* (Cambridge: Polity Press, 2016), p. 22.

17 Terry Eagleton, "Reappraisals: What Is the Worth of Social Democracy?" *Harper's Magazine* (October 2010), p. 79.

18 David Dillard-Wright, "Explaining the Cult of Trump," *AlterNet* (December 16, 2016). Online: www.alternet.org/election-2016/explaining-cult-trump?akid=15019.40823.vKP jTe&rd=1&src=newsletter1069107&t=2

19 David Remnick, "American Tragedy," *New Yorker* (November 9, 2016). Online: www.newyorker.com/news/news-desk/an-american-tragedy-2?mbid=nl_Daily%20Newsletter

%20091716%20(1)&CNDID=42733863&spMailingID=9846224&spUserID=MTM4
NzE1OTE4NjE5S0&spJobID=1040744742&spReportId=MTA0MDc0NDc0MgS2

20   Alicia Garza, "A Herstory of the #BlackLivesMatter Movement," *Feminist Wire*
(October 7, 2014). Online: www.thefeministwire.com/2014/10/blacklivesmatter-2/;
Keeanga-Yamahtta Taylor, "The Rise of the #BlackLivesMatter Movement," *Socialist
Worker.org* (January 13, 2015). Online: http://socialistworker.org/2015/01/13/the-
rise-of-blacklivesmatter; Elizabeth Day, "#BlackLivesMatter: The Birth of a New
Civil Rights Movement," *Guardian* (July 19, 2015). Online: www.theguardian.com/
world/2015/jul/19/blacklivesmatter-birth-civil-rights-movement. For a more extensive
analysis, see Keeanga-Yamahtta Taylor, *From #BlackLivesMatter to Black Liberation*
(Chicago: Haymarket, 2018); Christopher J. Lebron, *The Making of Black Lives Matter:
A Brief History of an Idea* (New York: Oxford University Press, 2018).

21   Robin D. G. Kelley, "Black Study, Black Struggle," *Boston Review* (March 7, 2016).
Online: https://bostonreview.net/forum/robin-d-g-kelley-black-study-black-struggle

22   Clement Petitjean, "Etienne Balibar: War, Racism and Nationalism," *Verso Book Blog*
(November 17, 2015). Online: www.versobooks.com/blogs/1559-etienne-balibar-war-
racism-and-nationalismmouse

PART I

RETHINKING POLITICS AND THE POST RACIAL

1

ANTI-POLITICS AND THE TORTURING OF DEMOCRACY

CO-AUTHORED WITH DEBADITYA BHATTACHARYA

> Ignorance, allied with power, is the most ferocious enemy justice can have.
>
> (James Baldwin)

Prior to the election of Donald Trump as President of the United States, the Greek chorus from both the left and right loudly proclaimed that Donald Trump was a fascist or neo-fascist. Pundits and journalists across the ideological spectrum compared Trump to Hitler and Mussolini or referred to him as an unbridled tyrant. For example, the liberal magazine *Slate*[1] found common ground with the conservative journal *National Review*[2] in denouncing Trump as a tyrant, while liberals such as former Secretary of Labor Robert Reich and the actor George Clooney joined hands with conservatives such as Andrew Sullivan and Robert Kagan in arguing that Trump represented a loud echo, if not a strong register of a fascist past,[3] updated to correlate with the age of reality TV and a fatuous celebrity culture.[4] While such condemnations contained more than a shred of truth, they only scratched the surface of the conditions that produced the existing political landscape. Such arguments too often ignored and continue to ignore the latent authoritarian and anti-democratic forces that have a long legacy in American politics and society.

The collective anger fueling the new populism may be misdirected but that was no excuse for the mainstream media, politicians, and liberal pundits to have ignored the conditions that drove Trump's politics of fear, bigotry, xenophobia, and loneliness. Entire communities have been devastated by neoliberal trade policies such as NAFTA. Under the regime of neoliberalism, increasing numbers of people live in poverty, young people cannot imagine a better future, social mobility has reached a dead end, and as inequality widens wages drop and prices go up. Mainstream politicians and the financial elite live in a political and ethical bubble indifferent to the problems they have created for millions of Americans. At the same time, a range of groups extending from poor youth to those who because of the housing crisis were treated as disposable were denied the right to be heard and represented in the alleged script of democracy. Rather than condemn Trump's presence on the political landscape as the rise of a populist demagogue and his followers as delusional bigots, it makes much more sense as Gary Younge points out to address the deep-rooted economic, political, and social conditions driving such misdirected anger, the collective embrace of Trump by millions of people, and the widespread condemnation of established politicians such as Hillary Clinton.[5]

Unfortunately, recognizing that the United States because of Trump's electoral victory is about to tip over the edge into the abyss of authoritarianism is not enough. There is a need to understand the context—historical, cultural, political, and economic—that has created this moment in American society in which authoritarianism becomes an endpoint. Trump is only symptomatic of the problem, and condemning him exclusively does nothing to contain it.[6] Moreover, such arguments often ignore the fact that Hillary Clinton was the underside of the new neoliberal oligarchy, which indulged some progressive issues but was indebted ideologically and politically to a criminogenic culture of finance, racism, and war.[7] Put differently, she represented a less obscene, less in-your-face form of authoritarianism—hardly a viable alternative to Trump.

Maybe this is all understandable in a corporate-controlled neoliberal society which uses new communication technologies to erase history by producing a notion of time wedded to a culture of immediacy, speed, simultaneity, and endless flows of fragmented knowledge. As Manuel Castells writes in *Communication Power*, we live in a space of "digital-time" in which everything that happens only takes place in the present, a time that "has no past and no future."[8] Time is accelerated in this new information-saturated culture, and it also flattens out everyday knowledge, experience, competency, and the capacity for informed judgment. Time has thus been transformed to provide the ideological support that neoliberal values and a fast-food, temp-worker economy require to survive. But the speeding up of time and the over-abundance of information is more a symptom than a cause of politics being emptied out, rejected, and serving as the backdrop to the rise of dangerous forms of populism and ultra-nationalism. Time is now mobilized to undermine reason, elevate the pleasure principle, embrace the simplicity of unchecked rage, and produce a crisis of civic literacy. Time has not only been sped up, serving to subvert the connection between contemplation and critique, it has also become a way of emptying politics of any substance by turning it into a theatrical performance, if not spectacle, that merges the idiocy of consumer culture with the intense focus on the personal and survival of the fittest ethic characteristic of reality TV.

A Culture of Forgetting and Lies

Language has also been transformed to produce and legitimate a culture of forgetting that relishes a flight from responsibility. Capitalism, racism, consumerism, and patriarchy feed off each other and are mobilized largely through a notion of common sense, which wraps itself in a vocabulary of certainty and eschews any notion of self-reflection, and shows little sign of losing its power as a pedagogical force. As a result, we are living through an ongoing crisis of democracy, a denuding of politics, in which both the agents and institutions necessary for such social order are being dismantled at an accelerating rate in the face of a massive assault by predatory capitalism, even while there is a growing resistance to the impending authoritarianism. It gets worse. We live in a moment of political change in which democratic public spheres are disappearing before our eyes, language is turned into a weapon, and ideology is transformed into an act of hate, fear, racism, and destruction—all of which is informed by a dark history of political intolerance and ethnic cleansing. The war on democracy has produced both widespread misery and suffering and finds its ideological counterpart in a culture of cruelty that has become normalized. And such forces will intensify under a Trump administration which is being populated at the highest levels of government with billionaires, Islamophobists, racists, religious fundamentalists, and warmongers.

Trump's appointment of a number of generals, including James Mattis as Secretary of Defense, John F. Kelly as Director of Homeland Security, and Lt. Gen. H. R. McMaster as National Security Advisor, "symbolize[s] the ongoing process of subversion of civilian control of the military and points to a future of more war and more violent military interventions against what these men see as the existential threat of radical Islam."[9] But Trump's cabinet selections suggest more than the emerging war culture and militarization that characterize the new authoritarianism. He has appointed a host of neoliberal fundamentalists to high-ranking positions whose aim is to destroy the very institutions they will head. The latter appointments represent a war on the welfare state, social contract, and the legacy of Franklin D. Roosevelt's New Deal and Lyndon Johnson's Great Society programs. The dark side of Trump's administration resides in the appointment of a host of racists, white supremacists, and ultra-nationalists that while once relegated to the margins of American politics have now moved to its center. For instance, Chief Strategist, Stephen Bannon, was the head of Breitbart News Network, a clearing house for a wide range of right-wing extremist groups including neo-Nazis, ultra-nationalists, and white supremacists. Mike Pompeo, who will head the CIA, and Secretary for Housing and Urban Development, Ben Carson are anti-Muslim extremists. Jeff Sessions, whose history of racist views and disdain for civil rights is well documented, has been appointed Attorney General.[10] The merging of militarism, racism, and an extreme version of casino capitalism finds a close ally in a deep-seated anti-intellectualism characteristic of a number of cabinet appointments, all of whom are climate change deniers and enemies of evidence and fact-based arguments. For example, Ben Carson, who has no experience in government and has been appointed as Secretary of Housing and Urban Development, is a believer in conspiracy theories and not only refutes that human activity promotes climate change, he also has argued that government regulations aimed at helping the poor are a form of totalitarian rule. Rick Perry, another climate change denier, in what appears to be a Halloween joke, has been appointed as Secretary of Energy. This is the same agency Perry once claimed that if elected president he would eliminate, though he forgot its name when asked what three government agencies he would get rid of. Betsy DeVos, who has been appointed as Secretary of Education, is a staunch opponent of public education and in her senate hearings refused to commit to funding public schools. She also supported allowing guns in schools. This level of incompetence is hard to make up, and is even now disparaged by mainstream politicians. Congressman Jared Hoffmann (Democrat, California), in his commentary on the political essence of these appointments, appears right on target:

> With only a few exceptions, the individuals that President-Elect Trump has appointed is the greatest collection of stooges and cronies and misfits we have ever seen in a presidential administration. Some of these folks' only qualifications for the jobs they are being appointed for is that they have attempted to dismantle and undermine and destroy the very agencies they are now hoping to run. Think about that. Think about the kind of person who actually wants the job of destroying an agency. Think about how craven that is.[11]

Those who will benefit from the Trump government will not be the angry working-class populists that gave Trump a victory, but the bankers, hedge-fund managers, financial elite, and CEOs who rule America's commanding institutions, most of whom have become the modern version of Mr. Kurtz in Conrad's *Heart of Darkness*. As Hannah Arendt describes them in *The Origins of Totalitarianism*, citing Conrad: "'these men were hollow to the core, reckless without hardihood, greedy without audacity and cruel without courage . . .' the only talent that could possibly burgeon in their hollow souls was the gift of fascination which makes a splendid leader of an extreme party."[12] In the age of savage neoliberalism, anticipation no longer imagines a better world but seems mired in a dystopian dread, mimicking the restlessness, chaos, and uncertainty that precedes a historical moment unable to deal with its horrors and on the verge of a terrible catastrophe.

Anti-democratic tendencies, extending from the militarization of everyday life to the takeover of the commanding institutions of society by the financial elite, work in tandem to neutralize dissent, eliminate antagonisms, and create spectacles to divert the masses from real social and political problems. In addition, empathy, as paralyzed by the mobilization of hate, and sympathy for the other, are replaced by a culture of cruelty and politics of vengeance. Under such circumstances, anger, indignation, and misery slip into a politics that has no aim outside of misdirected rage. Moreover, when focused on single issues anger is short-circuited of any political possibilities and is limited in its ability to connect with a more comprehensive understanding of the systemic conditions that produce an array of oppressive policies and practices. Single-issue movements often reach a point when they exhaust their potential for change because they become fortress-like in their unwillingness to understand the limits of the singular politics and their place in a larger totality of oppression that provides such isolated movements with a shared understanding of the forces at work in their reproduction. To make sense politically, single-issue movements need to take a detour through those ethical, political, and social models of analysis that connect individual issues to larger social problems in ways that fight, rather than justify, the transformation of grievances into a Trump-like version of American authoritarianism.

We live in a historical moment in which mainstream politics has shed its ideals and has fallen prey to choices that resemble the stacked deck of cards that mimic the values of casino capitalism and reinforce the slippage into an authoritarian society. Even a die-hard conservative such as *New York Times* op-ed columnist David Brooks argues that

"Politics is in retreat and authoritarianism is on the rise worldwide."[13] Unfortunately, for Brooks the enemy of politics is the ignorance of the masses and not the unchecked power and corruption wielded by a neoliberal order dominated by the ultra-rich and financial and corporate elites. While politics is being hollowed out and filled with acts of violent and legal lawlessness and misdirected rage, a loss of faith in electoral politics has given rise to a right-wing populism that is more than willing to dispense with democracy itself. The great tragedy in American politics, especially since the late 1970s, is that capitalism has come to represent the highest expression of democracy and as capitalism failed to address the most basic needs of most Americans, a growing number of people lost their faith not only in so-called free-market capitalism, but in democracy itself, making it all the easier to turn to the authoritarian politics of Donald Trump.

Many conservative and liberal politicians have returned to the dark age of 1975 when the financial elite of the Trilateral Commission argued that the United States suffered from an excess of democracy, which was allegedly caused by the students revolting and the rise of the free speech and civil rights movements of the 1960s. Noam Chomsky reminds us of the ideology that drove the commission's report, one that bears a striking resemblance to the present. He writes:

> What particularly troubled the Trilateral scholars was the "excess of democracy" during the time of troubles, the 1960s, when normally passive and apathetic parts of the population entered the political arena to advance their concerns: minorities, women, the young, the old, working people . . . in short, the population, sometimes called the "special interests." They are to be distinguished from those whom Adam Smith called the "masters of mankind," who are "the principal architects" of government policy and pursue their "vile maxim": "All for ourselves and nothing for other people." The role of the masters in the political arena is not deplored, or discussed, in the Trilateral volume, presumably because the masters represent "the national interest," like those who applauded themselves for leading the country to war "after the

utmost deliberation by the more thoughtful members of the community" had reached its "moral verdict." To overcome the excessive burden imposed on the state by the special interests, the Trilateralists called for more "moderation in democracy," a return to passivity on the part of the less deserving, perhaps even a return to the happy days when "Truman had been able to govern the country with the cooperation of a relatively small number of Wall Street lawyers and bankers," and democracy therefore flourished.[14]

Once again, the financial elite and intellectual pundits such as David Brooks are making a strong bid to do away with even the pretense of democracy.[15] In this instance, the masses are viewed as corrupt, incapable of assuming any viable social responsibility, and hence are considered a dispensable liability to be controlled by the financial and corporate elite, who are more enlightened than the rest of us. This is the rhetoric of an updated authoritarianism, covered over in the polite language of the Ivy League elites, being peddled as a cure for societies that are too democratic and weak in their willingness to hand power over to the uninformed masses and, of course, to the likes of a reality TV celebrity such as Donald Trump. Lost here is a refusal to name a new historical conjuncture in which the very nature of politics has changed—insofar that the traditional state has become a tool of economic sovereignty, power now floats globally and has no allegiance to the older social contract. Not only is the state and its identity in profound crisis, but the masses have been expelled from the practice of politics, reduced to cogs mobilized on occasions to participate in elections that are as corrupt as they are anti-democratic.[16] Not only does corruption get turned on its head in this type of discourse, but politics sheds any apology for becoming authoritarian and with a brutal realism reveals and celebrates its move towards an American-style neo-fascism.

Prior to the election, demands to support Hillary Clinton as a lesser evil compared to Trump refused to acknowledge that such mandates do not offer real choices and only serve to keep existing relations of power intact or suggest something even more ominous. Such actions represent more than a hollowing out of politics—they represent a refusal of the affirmative nature of political struggle. They also represent the surrender of any hope of moving beyond the enveloping fog of authoritarianism and a broken political system. Put bluntly, such choices sabotage any real hope for developing a new politics and a radical democracy. These limited choices also undermine the need to develop a capacious vision of struggle, a comprehensive politics, and the need to engage multiple publics in the quest to rethink the political terrain outside of a neoliberal notion of the future. At issue here is the moral blight that permeates America: a politics of the lowest expectations, one saturated in lies, deceptions, and acts of bad faith. At the same time, I do believe that many progressives who argued that Clinton was a greater evil than Trump committed a grave error, if not an act of bad faith, in not taking a principled stand against Trump and his band of radical extremists, or what Noam Chomsky has called "the most dangerous organization in the world."[17]

Voting against Trump was not an endorsement of Clinton, though her policy positions on almost every issue were better than Trump's, but a stand against a radical extremism that views the social contract and the ideal of American democracy with disdain if not as a pathology. What these progressives refused to recognize was that Trump's America is a script for the reactionary ideology of white identity, a public space defined by white supremacy, which during the election eliminated the distinction between the truth and falsehoods, informed judgments and reckless opinions. Trump's campaign was one that pitted winners against losers, a war against dispossessed and vulnerable populations. The 2016 presidential campaign was not simply a choice between two unpopular candidates but a campaign that as Adam Shatz observes tapped "into an ideological fantasy among voters who would like to return to a world in which borders counted for something, white men were the 'natural leaders,' and women and minorities knew their place."[18]

Historical memory brims with the lies of mainstream politicians. The list is too lengthy to develop but extends from the Gulf of Tonkin falsehoods that led to the Vietnam War to the lies that produced the wars in Iraq, Afghanistan, and Pakistan, which have left 1.3 million dead. As documented by Elizabeth Hinton in *From the War on Poverty to the War on Crime: The Making of Mass Incarceration in America*, the politics of lying by politicians and their intellectual collaborators fueled a regressive neoliberal war on poverty and crime that morphed into a racist war on the poor and helped produce the carceral state under Nixon, Reagan, Bush, and Clinton.[19] In addition, during the Obama administration, the politics of hope quickly became a politics without hope, functioning to legitimate and accelerate a flight from social responsibility that provided a blank check for Obama's refusal to prosecute government officials who engaged in egregious acts of torture, to conduct immoral drone attacks, to expand the nuclear arsenal, and to display a cold indifference to the criminal environment of Wall Street. All of this adds up to a notion of politics partly driven by a culture of ignorance and lying that has surpassed previous historical eras, marking an entry into what *Toronto Star* reporter Olivia Ward calls a "post-truth universe."[20] Trump has elevated the notion of post truth to new heights of legitimacy by championing his own manufactured realities, ignoring the distinction between facts and fiction, and producing an endless array of falsehoods that appear almost daily in his tweets. Not only has he undermined and abandoned traditional sources of information, evidence gathering, and facts themselves but he has also reinforced the increasingly accepted notion that in a world of competing claims universally acknowledged standards of truth are irrelevant. The age of Trump has become the age of disinformation. Jonathan Mahler sums it up well in his comments:

> somewhere along the way, the democratization of the flow of information became the democratization of the flow of disinformation. The distinction between fact and fiction was erased, creating a sprawling universe of competing claims . . . A universe of competing claims is the perfect environment for the rise to power of a politician who has made a career of championing his own truths and manufacturing his own realities . . . In the age of Trump, you don't need to act to create your own reality; you can just tweet, whether it's bogus crime and unemployment statistics or made-up accusations of widespread voter fraud. For that matter, you don't

even need to tweet; you can just retweet. In a world with no universally recognized standards for truth—a world in which journalists engaged in the study of discernible reality are dismissed as "dishonest" and "corrupt"—everything is fair game.[21]

In this instance, the politics of performance denigrates language and shamelessly indulges a culture in which the truth is sacrificed to shouting, dirty tricks, and spin doctors and paves the way for an updated form of American authoritarianism. But there is more at work here than simply the rhetorical breakdown of meaning, language, and judgment. With the rise of a corporate-controlled media, the emergence of a fatuous, infantilizing celebrity culture, a dominant culture of commodification, a suffocating culture of fear, and a growing anti-intellectualism, the American public has not only had its political horizons limited, but has been subjected to an endless barrage of what can be called rituals of depoliticization. The American Dream has been replaced by an avalanche of nightmares, and the nightmares have morphed into a political reality. A culture of lawlessness has emerged fed by an entertainment and culture industry that revels in extreme violence and the fog of stupidity and thoughtlessness. Hatred has replaced the ability to love with courage and a war fever has overtaken American society in which there are only friends and enemies, winners and losers, the select and the vanquished.

We are now approaching a moment in American history in which truth is either viewed as a liability or ignored; at the same time, lies become more plausible, because as Hannah Arendt argued in *Crises of the Republic*, "the liar has the great advantage of knowing beforehand what the audience wishes or expects to hear."[22] Lying is now the currency of mainstream politicians and finds its counterpart in the wild west of talk radio, cable television, and the mainstream media. Under such conditions, referentiality and truth disappear along with contexts, causes, evidence, and informed judgment. A manufactured ignorance and the terrifying power and infusion of money in politics and society have corrupted democratic principles and civic life. A combination of arrogance, power, and deceit among the financial elite is exemplified by Trump, who has repeatedly lied about his business transactions, his former misdeeds with the media, being totally against the war in Iraq, his claim that the birther movement was started by Hillary Clinton, the false claim that inner-city crime is at record levels, and the insistence that he personally hired instructors for Trump University.[23] As reported in the *New York Times*, Trump lied repeatedly and shamelessly in his presidential debates with Hillary Clinton.[24] Eugene Robinson, writing in the *Washington Post*, goes further and states that

> Donald Trump must be the biggest liar in the history of American politics, and that's saying something. Trump lies the way other people breathe. We're used to politicians who stretch the truth, who waffle or dissemble, who emphasize some facts while omitting others. But I can't think of any other political figure who so brazenly tells lie after lie, spraying audiences with such a fusillade of untruths that it is almost impossible to keep track.[25]

When actually confronted with his lies and misrepresentations of the truth, Trump either ignores such inquiries or responds with answers that have nothing to do with the questions asked. What is particularly disturbing is that once elected as president, he continued to lie using his Twitter account to falsely claim that he won the popular election by a landslide, when in fact he lost it by more than 2.8 million votes. He also falsely claimed that the election was marked by massive voter fraud, when there is no evidence to support the claim. Of course, he also denies that Russia did not try to influence the election in his favor by hacking into a number of accounts. There is more than a recklessness at work here. There seems to be an instability, immaturity, paranoia, and narcissistic impulsiveness that ordinarily would disqualify someone from holding any position of social and political responsibility.

Fortunes of Civil Society: From Politics to Anti-Politics

Desperation among many segments of the American public has become personal, furthering a generalized anger ripe for right-wing populism or worse. One consequence is that xenophobia and economic insecurity coupled with ignorance and collective rage breed the conditions for symbolic and real violence, as took place at many pre-election Trump rallies. When language is emptied of any substance and politics loses its ability to place limits on unchecked power, the stage is set for a "civil social" order that allows poor Black and Brown youth to continue to be objects of domestic terrorism, and provides a cover for corporate and political criminals to ravage the earth and loot the public treasury. In the age of Trump, truth becomes the enemy of governance and politics tips over into enthusiastic fantasies of a popular vigilantism while supporting state violence and repression. One cannot minimize the power of the presidency, nor should one underestimate the damage that can be done by someone as vindictive as Trump.

Robin D. G. Kelley highlights the racial and class violence that will potentially be unleashed under Trump's law and order regime. He writes:

> Pay attention: Trump's success means mass deportation; massive military spending; the continuation and escalation of global war; a conservative Supreme Court poised to roll back Roe v. Wade, marriage equality, and too many rights to name here; a justice department and FBI dedicated to growing the Bush/Obama-era surveillance state and waging COINTELPRO-style war on activists; fiscal policies that will accelerate income inequality; massive cuts in social spending; the weakening or elimination of the Affordable Care Act; and the partial dismantling and corporatization of government.[26]

What Alexis de Tocqueville had hailed in the early nineteenth century as the source of American democracy's vitalism and its potential for survival—the citizen's right to free civil association[27]—has returned as historical irony in the euphoria of the pre-election contest between Trump and Clinton. The structures of political decision making that served allegedly to construct *democratic agency* morphed into a choice between a politics of racial cleansing and economic imperialism, and were united in purpose and vision. Despite their polemical disavowal of one another in the manner of an electoral theater of rivalries, the Trump–Clinton binary actually struck at the roots of the democratic project piggybacking on a phantasm of the contemporary "civil society."

By making use of an ethic of disillusionment with/within structural politics, civil society has long been advertised as a potential tool for resisting the excesses of the state and enabling processes of democratization from below. The fabled role of the "civil society" in effecting the Velvet Revolution in Czechoslovakia sufficiently testifies to this reorganization of social forces of resistance within fields/forms of non-political alliance. The watchdog function of civil society vis-à-vis the state entails mobilizations of both the disenfranchised subject's sentiments of neglect and betrayal as much as the bourgeois elite's disdain for mass appeasement as symptomatic of the failure of political structures. In this context, the premise on which the "civil-social" contract is forged is a cognitive voiding of the *political* as an inadequate remedy to everyday problems and conditions of living. The effect of a structural negation of politics—cognitively, reframing opposition *as* pure "anti-politics"—is what brings civil society together. It becomes a politically neutralized space of rights-based self-determination and voluntarism. Ajay Gudavarthy discerningly contends in *Politics of Post-Civil Society* that civil society practices tend to inscribe a pure individual realm of freedom by "de-politicizing power relations in negotiating them outside their structural context."[28] Freedom has been privatized, reduced to the sphere of consumption and the intimate and singular pursuits of keeping up with changing lifestyles. As Zygmunt Bauman and Leonidas Donskis observe, freedom is no longer associated with visions, improving the common good, or justice. They write:

> Simply put, our freedom today becomes localized in the sphere of consumption and self-renewal but it has lost any connection with the most important thing: believing that you can change something in the world. This belief was shared by all the great prophets, theoreticians, ideologues and writers of modernity. Today all the great utopias have vanished. We are living in a period of dreary

novels of warning and dystopias, though even the latter quickly turn into objects of easy, uncomplicated consumption.[29]

Power relations now tip over into the dead-end language of individual responsibility, character, and shame. It is here that such practices run the risk of replicating those same structural exclusions and reproducing relations of power that the state is accused of, in their privileging of the "personal" over the failed promises of the "political." When the language of the social is used, it is reduced to a call to voluntary participation and active "passionate" citizenship, which translates into a form of political purity and moral vigilantism against the state as much as its own members.

The civil society, in displacing the potential for democratic trans-formation onto an autonomous space of the social, might experience solidarity in the very moments of its potential fracturing through erstwhile cognitive coalitions of the "majority." On the other hand, the *re*forming of the social in self-legitimating markers of "identity" makes way for a fantasy of immanence and an immunity to critique. The "mediatized" public sphere *trumps* up this nostalgia for essence (for example, the "great American past" endlessly represented in the slogan "make America great again") and comes to thrive on multiple specters of terroristic *otherness*, repeatedly manufactured as the obsessive sites of a "popular consensus." The imminent condition of possibility of the "civil" can be a permanent fear of the immigrant as toxic to the constitution of the social. To take a recent example from Europe, the result of the June 23 referendum in Britain—culminating in what has been termed "Brexit"—exactly marks the historical accretion of popular angst against a financialized state, expressed in diabolically racist terms. At a time when, as per United Nations High Commissioner for Refugees updates, one in every 113 of the world's population suffers from a condition of statelessness owing to forces of internal displacement or global immigration,[30] civil society's hunger for identity fetishism can only make rights and claims incumbent upon severe xenophobic anxieties and hence repeat varied forms of state violence. Right-wing populism, in the likes of a Donald Trump, makes possible this intimate future of civil society—parading from an apolitical consensus against the terrorizing state to the anti-political pledge of a genocide as integral to the cause of civility and civilization.

This is a politics that celebrates saviors, denigrates relations of power and policy, and provides a mode of escape in which heartfelt trauma and pain are used not to mobilize people into democratic movements but to blame others who are equally oppressed. This signals an anti-politics that kills both empathy and the imagination, a politics that uses pain to inflict further pain on others. Under neoliberal tyranny, the self is cut off from the social and privatization reduces people to narrating themselves at the expense of developing an ethical imagination that can understand and empathize with the pain of others. One consequence is that atomization on a global scale has become a new form of invisible violence because it shackles people to become prisoners of their own experiences, cut off from the larger systemic forces that both shape them and for which they bear little responsibility and over which they have no control.

Given such maniacal will to ethnocidal violence guaranteed by a reality TV version of public opinion, how might Hillary Clinton have become the other alternative foisted by contemporary global civil society? Not surprisingly, the decline of state welfarism and the consequent ushering of neoliberal policy reforms in America around the late 1970s and onwards found a fit partner in a proactive civil society. The insidious curtailing of state spending and weakening of controls over agendas of planned development reverberated with calls for an intensification of civil society to register violations of human rights or constitutional entitlements. Serving as an alibi for the state to withdraw from its constitutional responsibility to ensure social justice and economic empowerment of its citizenry, the civil society was promoted as a grievance-redressal institution pitted against both the incursions of the state and the market. In the process, the neoliberal dream of an open-market democracy could steer clear of state regulations or controls, as well as persuasively minimizing the latter's interventions in private multilateral trade investment through deliberative bargains with civil society forces. Such practices not only normalized and derecognized the widening extent of democratic deficit, they also made up for it by often projecting civil society as the sole arbitrational force negotiating between workers and multinational companies, displaced peoples and mining corporations or farmers and credit institutions. Furthermore, alternative infrastructures of aid and distress management were sought to be set up by non-governmental organizations, thus limiting and exonerating the role and responsibility of the state in ensuring delivery of basic public goods like education, housing, health care, rehabilitation, and employment.

By doubling up as corrective instrument for both dwindling state support and encroaching private institutions, the civil society produced a rationale for increasing the privatization and financialization of social sectors within the global economy. America's conjuring of fantasies of developmental governance through a benign collaboration of the market and civil society was soon sold out to developing nations as the only viable route to higher rates of economic growth as well as greater foreign aid to tide over debt crises. What John Williamson called the "Washington Consensus"[31] in 1989 went on to commission a strong civil society presence in debt-besieged countries as a structural requirement for loans from the World Bank and the International Monetary Fund.

In all of this, American civil society—working by force of example and as a precedent for ailing economies across the world—visibly performed a depoliticization of the idea of "development" as *entrepreneurial cooperation* among individual stakeholders. Neera Chandhoke rightly maintains in her book *The Conceits of Civil Society*: "[A]s part of a neoliberal agenda, civil society has been relentlessly and deliberately stripped of its ambiguities, its dark areas, and its oppressions, and presented to us as an area of solidarity, self-help and goodwill."[32] Ideologically speaking, this redefinition of the civil society as marking a logical move from the irreducible freedom of the individual to the freedom of the market is germane to its very conceptualization. In vouching for a liberal individualism of economic and social rights, the civil society was fated from the very beginning to act against collective interests of democratic consensus vested within the welfare state.

Its concurrent attempt to imagine development as the citizen's freedom to pursue economic goals, unencumbered by the constraints of the state, only serves to hide the political nature of the alliance between the state and corporate capital. In this, the American civil society's vindication of Hillary Clinton as a presidential candidate finally scales the distance between a politics of "developmental" common sense and the anti-politics of corporate World-Take-Over (at the behest of the World Trade Organization, as William K. Tabb ironically renames it).[33]

Faced with its own failures, it is incumbent that the civil society be unhinged of epiphanies of consent rooted in citizens' *disgruntlement*— and instead be organized into forms and practices of *disobedience*. Given the political impasse peddled by strategic illusions of electoral choice and change, the American public finds itself in a moment of dispassion and disaffection that now begs being chased out of the mere formality of franchise. Substantive claims on democracy can begin only by reclaiming a language of sociality that is losing its potential for imagining the unimaginable, confronting words, images, and power relations that are in the service of violence, hatred, and racism.

A New Language of Liberation

The present is a moment in which meaning slips into slogans, thought is emptied of substance, and ideas descend into platitudes and sound bites. This is an instance in which the only choices are between political narratives that represent the hard and soft versions of authoritarianism— narratives that embrace neo-fascism on the one side and a war-mongering neoliberal worldview on the other. This is the age of a savage capitalism, one that the film and television director Ken Loach insists produces a "conscious cruelty."[34] The evidence is everywhere—not only in the vulgar blustering of Donald Trump and Fox News, but also in the language of the corporate-controlled media apparatuses that demonize and prey on the vulnerable and proclaim the primacy of self-interest over the common good, reinforce a pathological individualism, enrich themselves in ratings rooted in a never-ending spectacle of violence, and legitimate a notion of freedom that collapses into the scourge of privatization and atomization.

The left and other progressives need a new language that will enable one to rethink politics, develop a militant sense of hope, embrace an empowering sense of solidarity, and engage a willingness to think outside of established political orthodoxies that serve the global financial elite. This new language, in looking beyond available models of political (re)cognition, has to bear the courage of a radical imagination. The power of the imagination, as Gayatri Chakravorty Spivak would say, is "the power to think the absent,"[35] the power to intuit the absolute *other* to cognition. Significantly, the new language of radical transformation must emerge from the concreteness of political struggles on the ground and non-violent expressions of disobedience in the everyday—not as lawlessness, but as a relentless questioning of what passes as the "norm." To mark the threshold between an alternative imagination of sociality and an anarchic dissolution is the task ahead of us, but one that binds every measure taken to a critical consciousness of its own conditions of emergence. It is only then that a movement-based language of solidarity can begin to take shape, in a willingness to subject its own forms and practices of articulation/mobilization to constant critical questioning. In it would lie the surest challenge to hegemonic sites of reproduction of power, whether in the state, the market, or civil society.

We need a new vocabulary that refuses to be commodified, declines to look away—a language that as the brilliant writer Maaza Mengiste argues "will take us from shock and stunned silence toward a coherent, visceral speech, one as strong as the force that is charging at us."[36] Progressives need a vocabulary that moves people, allows them to feel compassion for the other and gives them the courage to talk back. We need a vocabulary that enables us to confront a sense of responsibility in the face of the unspeakable, and to do so with a sense of dignity, self-reflection, and the courage to act in the service of a radical democracy. We need a vocabulary that allows us to recognize ourselves as agents, not victims, in the discourse of radical democratic politics. Of course, there is more at stake here than a struggle over meaning, there is also the struggle over power, over the need to create a formative culture that will produce new modes of critical agency and contribute to a broad social movement that will translate meaning into a fierce struggle for economic, political, and social justice. In part, this suggests protecting the most vulnerable by resisting any roll-backs of crucial social provisions such as Medicare and Medicaid; redoubling the fight against the fossil fuel industries; defending targeted communities such as poor Blacks; fighting the gun and defense lobbies; overturning the electoral college; creating powerful labor unions that can work with all-inclusive social movements; waging a fierce struggle against institutionalized racism and fascism; unifying single-issue movements while developing institutional power bases to sustain them for a long-term struggle; and creating thousands of alternative media outlets to wage pedagogical struggle against the rising fascism.[37] And these recommendations only touch the surface, but what is crucial to acknowledge is that the endpoint of such interventions has to be the elimination of capitalism and the building of a democratic socialist society.

What happens to language when it is reduced to a vehicle for violence? What does it take for a society to strip language of its emancipatory power and reduce it, as Mengiste states, "to a rhetoric of desperation and devastation molded into the incomprehensible, then vomited out in images and words that we cannot ignore though we have tried"?[38] What does it mean to define language as a tool—rather than a weapon of domination—in the service of economic and political justice? What institutions do we need to sustain and create to make sure that in the face of the unspeakable we can resist and change unaccountable power? Language is an archive of public memory, informed, in part, by "traces" that allow oppressed people to narrate themselves as part of a broad collective struggle. We see evidence of this among the Black Lives Matter movement, the Democracy Movement, the movements for a $15 an hour minimum wage and gay and lesbian rights, and other emerging social movements. Suppressed histories of violence become visible in such movements and their narratives for justice form part of a genealogy that puts current acts of oppression and domestic terrorism in perspective. For instance, capital punishment is framed within the historical context of slavery, lynchings, and the emerging violence of a police state.

Domination in the Age of Trump

The hate-filled, xenophobic, humiliating, and bigoted language, images, and stories produced in the age of Trump constitute one of the most pernicious forms of domination because it takes as its object subjectivity itself. This toxic mode of domination empties subjectivity of any sense of critical agency, turning people into spectators and consumers of a pernicious identity, on the one hand, and a collective medium for symbolic and real violence, on the other. Identities have become commodities, and agency a site of struggle for the advertising industries, corporate elite, and in the age of Trump for a brand of white ultra-nationalism. After 50 years of a neoliberal culture of taking, unbridled individualism, militaristic violence, and a self-righteous indifference to the common good, the demands of citizenship have not merely weakened, they have been practically obliterated. In their book *Babel*, Zygmunt Bauman and Ezio Mauro speak to the denigration of politics and citizen rights in an age of generalized rage and emerging right-wing populism. They write:

> The "culture of taking," divorced from all rights-duties of giving and of contributing positively, is not merely a reduction of citizenship relations to a bare minimum: it is actually perfectly instrumental to a populist and charismatic simplification of politics and leadership, or rather a post-modern interpretation of a right-wing tradition, in which the leader is the demiurge who can work out public issues by himself, freeing citizens from the burden of their general civic duties, and leaving them to the solitary sovereignty of their privacy, spurring them to participate not in national political events but in single outbursts of collective emotional reaction, triggered by the oversimplification of love and hate on which populism feeds.[39]

The fusion of culture, power, and politics has produced a society marked by a retreat from political and social responsibility. In an age in which five or six corporations dominate the media landscape and produce the stories that shape our lives, the democratic fabric of trust evaporates, public virtues give way to a predatory form of casino capitalism, and thought is limited to a culture of the immediate. Politics is now performance, a kind of anti-politics wedded to the spectacle.

As Mark Danner points out in the *New York Review of Books*, much of Trump's success and image stems from his highly successful role on *The Apprentice* as "the business magus, the grand vizier of capitalism, the wise man of the boardroom, a living confection whose every step and word bespoke gravitas and experience and power and authority and . . . money. Endless amounts of money."[40] Not only did *The Apprentice* at its height in 2004 have an audience of 20.7 million, catapulting Trump into a reality TV star, but Trump's fame played a large role in attracting 24 million to tune in and watch his initial presidential primary debate with a host of largely unheard of Republican politicians.

Corporate media love Donald Trump. He is the perfect embodiment of the spectacle that drives up their ratings. Danner observes that Trump is "a ratings extravaganza," capable of delivering "audiences as no other candidate ever has or could."[41] A point that is well taken, given as the *Financial Times* reported that the networks gave him $4.6 billion worth of airtime.[42] According to Danner, Trump's willingness to embrace ignorance over critical reasoning offers him an opportunity not to "let 'political correctness' prevent him [from] making sexist and bigoted remarks [while pandering to and reinforcing] his fans' euphoric enjoyment of their hero's reveling in the pleasures of free speech," and his addiction to lying becomes an established part of the anti-politics of performance and showmanship.[43]

Beyond a "Lesser of Two Evils" Political Framework

The American left and progressives have no future if they cannot imagine a new language that moves beyond the dead-end politics of the two-party system or its malleable constituencies of civil society resonance, and explores how to build an expansive social movement to challenge it. One fruitful beginning would be to confront the fact that our times are burdened not only by the violence of casino capitalism but also by the myth that capitalism and democracy are the same thing. Capitalism cannot rectify wage stagnation among large segments of the population, the growing destruction of the eco-system, the defunding of public and higher education, the decline in life expectancy among the poor and middle classes, police violence against Black youth, the rise of the punishing state, the role of money in corrupting politics, and the widening income gap between the very rich and everyone else. If the left and progressives are to shift the terms of the debate that shape American politics, they will also have to challenge much of what passes for neoliberal common sense. That means challenging the anti-government rhetoric of the civil society and the notion that citizens are simply consumers, that freedom is largely defined through self-interest, and that the market should govern all of social life. It means challenging the celebration of the possessive individual and atomized self, and debunking the claim that inequality is intrinsic to society, among others. And this is just a beginning. Theorizing a new understanding of politics under the reign of neoliberal globalization may be one of the most important challenges facing intellectuals, artists, journalists, and other cultural workers in the 21st century. This is especially important at a dystopian moment in which unfettered capitalism, as Tom Engelhardt observes, has put into place

> its version of 1% politics [and] has elevated to the pinnacle of power a bizarre billionaire and his "basket of deplorables" ... These include a series of generals ready to lead us into a new set of crusades and a crew of billionaires and multimillionaires prepared to make America theirs again.[44]

When the discourse of politics amounts to a choice between Donald Trump and Hillary Clinton, we enter a world in which the language of fundamental, radical, democratic, social, and economic change disappears. What liberals and others trapped in a lesser-of-two-evils politics forget is that elections no longer work on the popular imagination, because they are rigged and driven by the wealth of the financial elite. Elections bear no relationship to real change and offer instead the mirage or swindle of real choice. Moreover, changing governments results in very little real change when it comes to the concentration of power and the decimation of the commons and public good. At the same time, politicians in the age of reality TV embody Neil Postman's statement in *Amusing Ourselves to Death* that "cosmetics has replaced ideology" which hides behind the spectacle of glitzy performance, and has helped to usher in the age of authoritarianism.[45] Power hides in the dictates of common sense and wields destruction and misery through the "innocent criminals" who produce austerity policies and delight in a global social order dominated by precarity, fear, anxiety, and isolation.

What happens when politics turns into a form of entertainment that washes out all that matters? What happens to mainstream society when the dominant and more visible avenues of communication encourage and legitimate a mode of infantilism that becomes the modus operandi of newscasters, and trivia becomes the only acceptable mode of narration? What happens when compassion is treated as a pathology and the culture of cruelty becomes a source of humor and an object of veneration? What happens to a democracy when it loses all semblance of public memory, and the welfare state and social contract are abandoned in order to fill the coffers of bankers, hedge fund managers, and the corporate elite? What are the consequences of turning higher education into a "assets to debt swapping regime," one that will burden students with paying back loans in many cases until they are in their 40s and 50s?[46] What happens when disposable populations are brushed clean from our collective conscience, and become the object of unchecked humiliation and disdain by the financial elite? Bauman and Mauro are right to ask "How much capitalism can a democracy endure?"[47]

What language and public spheres do we need to make hope realistic and a new politics possible? What will it take for progressives to move beyond a deep sense of political disorientation? What does politics mean in the face of an impending authoritarianism when the conversation among many liberals and some conservatives was dominated by a call to avoid electing an upfront demagogue by voting instead for Hillary Clinton, a warmonger and neoliberal hawk who denounced political authoritarianism while supporting a regime of financial tyranny? What does resistance mean when it is reduced to a call to participate in rigged elections that reproduce a descent into an updated form of oligarchy and condemn millions to misery and no future, all the while emptying out politics of any substance? Instead of tying the fortunes of democracy to rigged elections and "apolitical" vote banks, we need non-violent, massive forms of civil disobedience. We need to read Howard Zinn, among others, once again to remind ourselves where change comes from, making clear that it does not come from the top but from the organized social formations and collective struggles. It emerges out of an outrage that is structured, collective, fierce, embattled, and willing to fight for a society that is never just enough. The established financial elites who control both parties have been exposed and the biggest problem Americans face is that the crisis of ideas needs to be matched by an informed politics that refuses the old orthodoxies, thinks outside of the box, and learns to act individually and collectively in ways that address the unthinkable, the improbable, the impossible—a new future.

As politics is reduced to a carnival of unbridled narcissism, deception, spectacle, and overloaded sensation, an anti-politics emerges that unburdens people of any responsibility to challenge the fundamental precepts of a society drenched in corruption, inequality, racism, and violence. This anti-politics also removes many individuals from the most relevant social, moral, and political bonds. This is especially tragic at a historical moment marked by an endless chain of horrors and a kind of rootlessness that undermines all foundations and creates an uncertainty of unprecedented scale. Fear, insecurity, and precarity now govern our lives, rendering even more widespread feelings of loneliness, powerlessness, and existential dread.

Conclusion

I have argued that progressive politics needs a new language of radical transformation that can defeat the violent implosions of meaning within agendas of hate and greed. But, will this language of justice be adequate to the fascist paradox of (non)sense, where hate needs no reference worthy of a proper name and may effectively be activated by the absence of an object? The task of radical politics is precisely in confronting the infinite *possibility of the anti-political* as post-referential *jouissance*,[48] parading inconsequentially as an endless form of entertainment and a revenue-building enterprise of mainstream media. As Juan and Eva Perón, Mussolini, and Hitler made clear, fascism is entertaining and in elevating the spectacle to the center of everyday life can effectively both hide the contradictions of oppressive regimes and turn the worst forms of bigotry, repression, and hate into a normalized performance that drives mainstream media and screen culture.

Under these circumstances, established politics offers nothing but scorn, if not an immense disregard for the destruction of all viable bonds of solidarity and the misery that accompanies such devastation. Zygmunt Bauman and Ezio Mauro, in their book *Babel*, are right in arguing that we live at a time in which feeling no responsibility means rejecting any sense of critical agency and refusing to recognize the bonds we have with others.[49] Time is running out and more progressives and people on the left need to wake up to the discourse of refusal, and join those who are advocating for radical social and structural transformation. This is not merely an empty abstraction, because it means thinking politics anew with young people, diverse social movements, unions, educators, environmentalists, and others concerned about the fate of humanity. It is crucial to acknowledge that we live in a historical conjuncture in which the present obliterates the past and can only think about the future in dystopian terms. It is time to unpack the ideological and structural mechanisms that keep the war machine of capitalism functioning. It is also time to recognize that there are no shortcuts to addressing the anti-democratic forces now wreaking havoc on American (or, for that matter, every other) society. The ideologies, grammar, and structures of domination can only be addressed as part of a long-term collective struggle.

The good news is that the contradictions and brutality of casino capitalism are no longer invisible, a new language about inequality is being popularized, poor Black and Brown youth are battling against state violence, people are waking up to the danger of ecological devastation, and the increased potential for a nuclear apocalypse is gaining momentum. What is needed is a new democratic vision, a radical imaginary, short-term and long-term strategies, and a comprehensive social movement to act on such a vision. Such a vision is already being articulated in a variety of ways: Michael Lerner's call for a new Marshall Plan; Stanley Aronowitz's call for reviving a radical labor movement; my own call for making education central to politics and the development of an expansive social movement; Angela Davis' cry for abolishing capital punishment and the mass incarceration system; Nancy Fraser's and Wendy Brown's important work on dismantling neoliberalism, the ongoing work of Alicia Garza, Patrisse Cullors, and Opal Tometi of the Black Lives Matter movement to develop a comprehensive politics that connects police violence with other forms of state violence; Gene Sharp's strategies for civil disobedience against authoritarian states; and the progressive agendas for a radical democracy developed by Salvatore Babones are just a few of the theoretical and practical resources available to galvanize a new understanding of politics and collective resistance. In light of the terror looming on the political horizon, let's hope that radical thought and action will live up to their potential and not be reduced to a regressive and pale debate over electoral politics. Hope means living without illusions and being fully aware of the practical difficulties and risks involved in meaningful struggles for real change, while at the same time being radically optimistic.

Notes

1   Jamelle Bouie, "Donald Trump Is a Fascist," *Slate* (November 25, 2015). Online: www.slate.com/articles/news_and_politics/politics/2015/11/donald_trump_is_a_fascist_it_is_the_political_label_that_best_describes.html

2   Andrew McCarthy, "Donald Trump: Thin-Skinned Tyrant," *National Review* (January 28, 2016). Online: www.nationalreview.com/article/430393/donald-trump-thin-skinned-tyrant

3   Robert Reich, "The American Fascist," *RobertReich.org* (March 8, 2016). Online: http://robertreich.org/post/140705539195; Andrew Pulver, "George Clooney Interview: 'Donald Trump Is a Xenophobic Fascist,'" *Guardian* (March 3, 2016). Online: www.theguardian.com/film/2016/mar/03/george-clooney-donald-trump-is-a-xenophobic-fascist; Andrew Sullivan, "Democracies End When They Are Too Democratic," *New York* (May 1, 2016). Online: http://nymag.com/daily/intelligencer/2016/04/america-tyranny-donald-trump.html; Robert Kagan, "Trump Is the GOP's Frankenstein Monster. Now He's Strong Enough to Destroy the Party," *Washington Post* (February

25, 2016). Online: www.washingtonpost.com/opinions/trump-is-the-gops-franken stein-monster-now-hes-strong-enough-to-destroy-the-party/2016/02/25/3e443f28-dbc1-11e5-925f-1d10062cc82d_story.html

4   Mark Danner, "The Magic of Donald Trump," *New York Review of Books* (May 26, 2016). Online: www.nybooks.com/articles/2016/05/26/the-magic-of-donald-trump/

5   Gary Younge, "You've Put Trump Behind You—Take It from a Brit, Right-Wing Populism Will Thrive until You Deal with It Genuinely," *Nation* (October 31, 2016). Online: www.thenation.com/article/note-to-america-dont-be-so-sure-youve-put-trump-behind-you/

6   For an excellent work on Trump's background and business dealings, see David Cay Johnston, *The Making of Donald Trump* (New York: Melville House, 2016).

7   Thomas Frank, "Why Hillary Clinton's 90s Nostalgia Is so Dangerous," *Guardian* (May 20, 2016). Online: www.theguardian.com/commentisfree/2016/may/20/hillary-clinton-90s-bill-clinton-economy-thomas-frank

8   Manuel Castells, *Communication Power* (New York: Oxford University Press, 2013), p. 55.

9   William J. Astore, "Trump's Cabinet Is a Coup Waiting to Happen," *Nation* (December 20, 2016). Online: www.thenation.com/article/trumps-cabinet-is-a-coup-waiting-to-happen/

10   Ellen Nakashima and Sari Horwitz, "Trump's Pick for Attorney General Is Shadowed by Race and History," *Washington Post* (December 24, 2016). Online: www.washing tonpost.com/world/national-security/trumps-pick-for-attorney-general-is-shadowed-by-race-and-history/2016/12/24/1432cffa-b650-11e6-959c-172c82123976_story.html?utm_term=.20edd890bbdb&wpisrc=nl_evening&wpmm=1

11   Jason Easley, "Liberal House Democrats Blast Trump for Filling His Cabinet with Misfits and Stooges," *Politicus USA* (December 8, 2016). Online: www.politicusa.com/2016/12/08/liberal-house-democrats-blast-trump-filling-cabinet-misfits-stooges.html

12   Hannah Arendt, *The Origins of Totalitarianism* (New York: Harcourt Brace Jovanovich, 1973), p. 189.

13   David Brooks, "The Governing Cancer of Our Times," *New York Times* (February 26, 2016). Online: www.nytimes.com/2016/02/26/opinion/the-governing-cancer-of-our-time.html?_r=0

14   Noam Chomsky, "The Responsibility of Intellectuals, Redux," *Boston Review* (September/October 2011). Online: www.bostonreview.net/BR36.5/noam_chomsky_responsibility_of_intellectuals_redux.php

15   See, for instance, the analysis by Matt Taibbi, "In Response to Trump, Another Dangerous Movement Appears," *Rolling Stone* (June 30, 2016). Online: www.rolling stone.com/politics/news/in-response-to-trump-another-dangerous-movement-appears-20160630

16   Zygmunt Bauman and Ezio Mauro, *Babel* (Cambridge: Polity Press, 2016).

17   Deirdre Fulton, "Those Who Failed to Recognize Trump as 'Greater Evil' Made a 'Bad Mistake': Chomsky," *CommonDreams* (November 25, 2016). Online: www.commondreams.org/news/2016/11/25/those-who-failed-recognize-trump-greater-evil-made-bad-mistake-chomsky

18   Adam Shatz, "The Nightmare Begins," *London Review of Books* (November 2016). Online: www.lrb.co.uk/blog/2016/11/10/adam-shatz/the-nightmare-begins/

19   Elizabeth Hinton, *From the War on Poverty to the War on Crime: The Making of Mass Incarceration in America* (Cambridge, MA: Harvard University Press, 2016).

20 Olivia Ward, "Have Donald Trump's Lies Pushed U.S. into a 'Post-Truth' Universe?" *Toronto Star* (May 24, 2016). Online: www.thestar.com/news/world/2016/05/24/have-donald-trumps-lies-pushed-us-into-a-post-truth-universe.html

21 Jonathan Mahler, "The Problem with 'Self-Investigation' in a Post-Truth Era," *New York Times Magazine* (January 1, 2017). Online: www.nytimes.com/2016/12/27/maga zine/the-problem-with-self-investigation-in-a-post-truth-era.html

22 Hannah Arendt, "Lying in Politics." In *Crisis of the Republic* (New York: Harvest/HBJ Books, 1969), p. 6.

23 For a list of the many lies propagated by Trump, see Hank Berrien, "Lyin' Donald: 101 of Trump's Greatest Lies," *Daily Wire* (April 11, 2016). Online: www.dailywire.com/news/4834/trumps-101-lies-hank-berrien

24 David Leonhardt, "The Lies Trump Told," *New York Times* (September 27, 2016). Online: www.nytimes.com/2016/09/27/opinion/campaign-stops/the-lies-trump-told.html

25 Eugene Robinson, "The Challenges in Covering Trump's Relentless Assault on the Truth," *Washington Post* (June 16, 2016). Online: www.washingtonpost.com/opinions/the-challenges-in-covering-trumps-relentless-assault-on-the-truth/2016/06/16/076b367a-33fd-11e6-8ff7-7b6c1998b7a0_story.html?utm_term=.8b0439f098ff

26 Robin D. G. Kelley, "After Trump," *Boston Review* (November 15, 2016). Online: http://bostonreview.net/forum/after-trump/robin-d-g-kelley-trump-says-go-back-we-say-fight-back

27 Alexis De Tocqueville, "Political Associations in the United States." In *Democracy in America*, Volume I (New York: Harper Classics, 2000 [1835]), p. 332.

28 Ajay Gudavarthy, "Why beyond Civil Society?" In *Politics of Post-Civil Society* (New Delhi: SAGE Publications, 2013), p. 19.

29 Zygmunt Bauman and Leonidas Donskis, *Liquid Evil* (London: Polity, 2016), p. 8.

30 United Nations High Commissioner for Refugees, "With 1 Human in Every 113 Affected, Forced Displacement Hits Record High," press release (June 20, 2016). Online: www.unhcr.org/news/press/2016/6/5763ace54/1-human-113-affected-forced-displacement-hits-record-high.html

31 John Williamson, *Latin American Adjustment: How Much Has Happened?* (Washington, DC: Institute for International Economics, 1990).

32 Neera Chandhoke, "Introduction." In *The Conceits of Civil Society* (New Delhi: Oxford University Press, 2003), pp. 9–10.

33 William K. Tabb, "The World Trade Organization? Stop World Take Over," *Monthly Review* Vol. 51 No. 10 (March 2000), pp. 1–18.

34 AFP, "Loach Film on Shame of Poverty in Britain Moves Cannes to Tears," *News Republic* (May 13, 2016). Online: http://nr.news-republic.com/Web/ArticleWeb.aspx?regionid=4&articleid=64344845

35 Gayatri Chakravorty Spivak, "Foreword." In *Other Asias* (Malden: Blackwell, 2008), p. 4.

36 Maaza Mengiste, "Unheard-of Things," *Massachusetts Review* Vol. 57 No. 1 (2016), p. 89.

37 I have taken many of these recommendations from Kelley, "After Trump."

38 Mengiste, "Unheard-of Things," pp. 88–9.

39 Bauman and Mauro, *Babel*, p. 37.

40 Danner, "The Magic of Donald Trump."

41 Ibid.

42 Theodore Bunker, "FT: Media Gave Trump $4.6 Billion in Free Coverage," *NewsMax.com* (November 11, 2016). Online: www.newsmax.com/Politics/media-trump-free-coverage-billions/2016/11/11/id/758445/

43   Danner, "The Magic of Donald Trump."
44   Tom Engelhardt, "Will Trump Make 1984 Look Like a Nursery Tale?" *TomDispatch* (December 22, 2016). Online: www.tomdispatch.com/blog/176225/tomgram%3A_engelhardt,_will_trump_make_1984_look_like_a_nursery_tale/
45   Neil Postman, *Amusing Ourselves to Death* (New York: Penguin Books, 1985), p. 4.
46   Irvine Welsh, "How the Banks Stole Higher Education," *Vice* (April 24, 2016). Online: www.vice.com/en_ca/read/irvine-welsh-how-the-banks-stole-higher-education
47   Bauman and Mauro, *Babel*, p. 53.
48   The word *jouissance*, used in a Lacanian sense here, implies the "satisfaction of a drive"— a drive that propels us towards the fullness of "meaning" in reference, comparable to sexual desire. This issue is taken up throughout Jacques Lacan, Jacques Alain-Miller, Ed., and Dennis Porter, trans., *The Seminar of Jacques Lacan: The Ethics of Psychoanalysis*, Vol. VII (New York: W.W. Norton, 1997).
49   Bauman and Mauro, *Babel*, p. 83.

2

WHITE SUPREMACY AND RACIAL CLEANSING UNDER THE REGIME OF DONALD TRUMP

> The question that really obsesses me today is not whether or not
> I like violence, or whether or not you like it—unless the situation
> is ameliorated, and very, very quickly, there will be violence.
>
> (James Baldwin)

Peter Thiel, the silicon billionaire and one of the six ultra-rich financial elite to speak at the Republican National Convention, once wrote that he did not "believe that freedom and democracy were compatible."[1] This blatant anti-democratic mindset has emerged once again, without apology, as a major organizing principle of the Republican Party under Donald Trump. In addition to expressing a hatred of Muslims, Mexicans, women, journalists, dissidents, and others whom he views as outside the pale of what constitutes a true American, Trump appears to harbor a core disdain for democracy, bringing back Theodor Adorno's warning that "the true danger [of fascism] lay in the traces of the fascist mentality within the democratic political system."[2] What has become clear is that the current political crisis represents a return to ideologies, values, and policies based upon a poisonous mix of white supremacy and ultra-nationalism, opening up a politics that "could lead back to political totalitarianism."[3] Of course, Trump's presence on the American political landscape is symptomatic of much darker forces that have been developing in the United States in the last few decades, raising the question of how in following him so many Americans could have abandoned their humanity.

Throughout the 2016 Republican National Convention the hateful discourse of red-faced anger and unbridled fear mongering added up to more than an appeal to protect America and make it safe again. Such weakly coded invocations also echoed the days of Jim Crow, the undoing of civil rights, forced expulsions, and forms of state terrorism sanctioned in the strident calls for safety and law and order. Invoking law and order, the Republicans hawked back to the shameful legacies of Nixon's southern strategy, Reagan's war on drugs, and Clinton's racist crime bills. Law and order, in this context, reiterated the notion that the Black community is defined by lawlessness, criminal behavior, and could only be controlled by unleashing the legal and violent tools of the state on Black people. These historical legacies of terror represent wounded topographies of the past that have been erased in a culture in which historical memory no longer counts for much.

Commenting on Trump's convention speech, columnist Eugene Robinson argued that his talk added up to what few journalists were willing to acknowledge—"a notorious white supremacist account."[4] What is shocking is the refusal in many mainstream media circles to examine in detail the role that white supremacy has played in creating the conditions for Trump to emerge as the head of the Republican Party. This structured silence is completely at odds with Trump's longstanding legacy of discrimination, including his recent and relentless derogatory remarks concerning President Obama's birthplace, his race-based attacks on U.S. District Judge Gonzalo Curiel (who tried a case against Trump University), in which Trump claimed he could not be fair because of his Mexican heritage, his denunciation of all Muslims as terrorists, and his attempt to paint Mexican immigrants as criminals, drug dealers, and rapists.[5] Far from a recent ideological and racist turn in order to win over white voters, Trump has a long history of racial discrimination, especially in his developing housing empire. For instance, as Jonathan Mahler and Steve Eder pointed out in the *New York Times*,

> As Donald J. Trump assumed an increasingly prominent role in the business, the company's practice of turning away potential black tenants was painstakingly documented by activists and organizations that viewed equal housing as the next frontier in the civil rights struggle. The Justice Department undertook its own investigation and, in 1973, sued Trump Management for discriminating against blacks.[6]

Trump's racism was not only on full display in the 1970s when he engaged in housing battles against the civil rights movement; it also gained public attention in the late 1980s during the Central Park jogger case in which five teenagers were charged (and later exonerated) for raping a white woman. Trump responded to the event by fanning the flames of racial hatred by taking out a full-page $100,000 ad condemning the Central Park Five and calling for the death penalty for the five young Black boys, while also urging tougher police practices. Implied in the ad was the notion that these five young boys fit neatly into the then popular category of superpredators—code for Black youth echoing the usual white supremacist response to alleged Black on white crime. Commenting on Trump's ads in the *Daily News*, Amy Davidson writes:

> Perhaps he thought it gave him gravitas, that spring, to weigh in on the character of the teenagers in the park: "How can our great society tolerate the continued brutalization of its citizens by crazed misfits? Criminals must be told that their civil liberties end when an attack on our safety begins!" And his headline suggested what ought to be done with them: "BRING BACK THE DEATH PENALTY. BRING BACK OUR POLICE!"[7]

Trump was also upset when the five men, accused as teenagers of the crime, were given a settlement in 2014. It gets worse. Paul Krugman observed that in October 2016, Trump *continued to insist* "that the

Central Park Five, who were exonerated by DNA evidence, were guilty and should have been executed."[8] Krugman goes on to say that these comments were much worse than revelations about Trump's comments in which he boasted about being able to sexually assault women because of his celebrity status.

On a number of other occasions Trump has strongly implied that the culture of criminality is equated with the culture of blackness. For instance, he has argued that the Black community is exclusively defined by a culture of drugs, murders, crime, and "bad hombres."[9] Far from being an assertion of truth, Trump's claim is a transparent form of racial stereotyping that supports the increasing criminalization of Black behavior while painting Black communities in derogatory racist stereotypes. Trump's implication that the culture of criminality is symptomatic of Black culture in general is also echoed in his repeated claims that he is the law and order candidate who will be tough on crime. He bolsters this assertion with the call to reinstitute racial profiling on a national level. Racial profiling has been challenged by the courts as unconstitutional and racist.[10]

Revealing another instance of Trump's racism, Nicholas Kristof quotes Kip Brown, a former Trump casino worker, who stated that "When Donald and Ivana came to the casino, the bosses would order all the black people off the floor . . . They put us all in the back."[11] He also cites another casino worker who stated that Trump made the following remarks about one of his Black accountants:

> Black guys counting my money! I hate it. The only kind of people I want counting my money are short guys that wear yarmulkes every day . . . I think that the guy is lazy. And it's probably not his fault, because laziness is a trait in blacks. It really is, I believe that. It's not anything they can control.[12]

Trump eventually got the accountant fired.

The visibility of such racist accounts and the deep investments in the ongoing mobilization of fear by political extremists in the United States surely have their roots in a number of factors, including dire economic conditions that have left millions suffering and proliferated zones of social abandonment. These economic conditions have resulted in an exponential increase in the individuals and groups condemned to live under machineries of inscription, punishment, and disposability. The current mobilization of fear also has its roots, rarely mentioned by those critical of Trump, in a legacy of white supremacy that is used to divert anger over dire economic and political conditions into the diversionary cesspool of racial hatred. Racial amnesia was one consequence of the heralding of what David Theo Goldberg has called in his book, *Are We All Postracial Yet?*, a "post-racial" era in American history after the first Black president was elected to office in 2008. This collective racial amnesia coded as post racialism was momentarily dispelled with the execution of Troy Davis, the shooting of Jordan Davis and Trayvon Martin, and the rise of the Black Lives Matter movement. Yet, even today, in spite of the cell-phone videos that have made visible an endless array of Black men being killed by police, much of the American public (and particularly, the white American public) seems immune to the ongoing revelations revealing the reach, depth, and scope of institutional racism in America. As Nathaniel Rich observes:

> Today, like sixty years ago, much of the public rhetoric about race is devoted to explaining to an incurious white public, in rudimentary terms, the contours of institutional racism. It must be spelled out, as if for the first time, that police killings of unarmed black children, indifference to providing clean drinking water to a majority-black city, or efforts to curtail the voting rights of minority citizens are not freak incidents but outbreaks of a chronic national disease. Nebulous bureaucratic terms like "white privilege" have been substituted for "white supremacy," or "micro-aggressions" for "casual racism."[13]

Across the globe, fascism and white supremacy in their diverse forms are on the rise. In Greece, France, Poland, Austria, and Germany, among other nations, right-wing extremists have used the hateful discourse of racism, xenophobia, and white nationalism to demonize immigrants and undermine democratic modes of rule and policies. As Chris Hedges observes, much of the right-wing, racist rhetoric coming out of these countries mimics what Trump and his followers are saying in the United States.[14] One consequence is that the public spheres that produce a critically engaged citizenry and make a democracy possible are under siege and in rapid retreat. Economic stagnation, massive inequality, the rise of religious fundamentalism, and growing forms of ultra-nationalism now aim to put democratic nations to rest. Echoes of the right-wing movements in Europe have come home with a vengeance. Demagogues wrapped in xenophobia, white supremacy, and the false appeal to a lost past echo a brutally familiar fascism, with slogans similar to Donald Trump's call to "Make America Great Again" and "Make America Safe Again"—all euphemisms for Making America White Again.

Trump's insistence on racial profiling echoes increasing calls among European right-wing extremists to legitimate a police state where refugees and others are viewed as a threat, unwanted, and disposable. How else to explain Trump's insistence on reintroducing nationwide "stop and frisk policies" after the demonstrations in Charlottesville, North Carolina over the police killing of an African American, Keith Lamont Scott, in September 2016? Trump willingly reproduces similar right-wing ideologies such as those condemning and demonizing Syrian and other immigrants trying to reach Europe. He does so by producing moral panics, the aim of which is to generate mass anxiety and legitimate policies that mimic forms of ethnic and social cleansing.[15] Trump joins a growing global movement of racial exclusion, one that is on the march spewing hatred, embracing forms of anti-Semitism, white supremacy, and a deep-seated disdain for any form of justice on the side of democracy. As Peter Foster points out in the UK's the *Telegraph*, "The toxic combination of the most prolonged period of economic stagnation and the worst refugee crisis since the end of the Second World War has seen the far-Right surging across the continent, from Athens to Amsterdam and many points in between."[16]

State-manufactured lawlessness has become normalized and extends from the ongoing and often brutalizing and murderous police violence against Black people and other vulnerable groups to a criminogenic market-based system run by a financial elite that strips everyone but the upper 1 percent of a future not only by stealing their possessions but also by condemning them to a life in which the only available option is to fall back on one's individual resources in order to barely survive. In addition, as Kathy Kelly points out, at the national level, lawlessness now drives a militarized foreign policy intent on assassinating alleged enemies rather than using traditional forms of interrogation, arrest, and conviction.[17] The killing of people abroad based on race is paralleled by (and connected with) the killing of Black people at home. Kelly correctly notes that the whole world has become a battlefield driven by racial profiling, where lethal violence replaces the protocols of serve and protect.[18]

Fear is the reigning ideology and war its operative mode of action, pitting different groups against each other, shutting down the possibilities of shared responsibility, and legitimating the growth of a paramilitary police force that kills Black people with impunity. State-manufactured fear offers up new forms of domestic terrorism embodied in the rise of a surveillance state while providing a powerful platform for militarizing many aspects of society. One consequence is that, as Charles Derber argues, America has become a warrior society whose "culture and institutions . . . program civilians for violence at home as well as abroad."[19] And, as Zygmunt Bauman argues in his book *Liquid Fear*, in a society saturated in violence and hate, "human relations are a source of anxiety" and everyone is viewed with mistrust.[20] Compassion gives way to suspicion and a celebration of fear and revulsion accorded to those others who allegedly have the potential to become monsters, criminals, or, even worse, murderous terrorists. In such cases, the bonds of trust dissolve, while hating the other becomes normalized and lawlessness is elevated to a matter of common sense.

Politics is now a form of warfare creating and producing an expanding geography of combat zones that hold entire cities, such as Ferguson, Missouri, hostage to forms of extortion, violence, lock downs, and domestic terrorism—something I have demonstrated in detail in my book *America at War with Itself*.[21] These are cities where most of those targeted are Black. Within these zones of racial violence, Black people are often terrified by the presence of the police and subject to endless forms of domestic terrorism. Hannah Arendt once wrote that terror was the essence of totalitarianism.[22] She was right and we are witnessing the dystopian visions of the new authoritarians who now trade in terror, fear, hatred, demonization, violence, and racism. Trump and his neo-Nazi bulldogs are no longer on the fringe of political life and they have no interest in instilling values that will make America great. On the contrary, they are deeply concerned with creating expanding constellations of force and fear, while inculcating convictions that will destroy the ability to form critical capacities and modes of civic courage that offer a glimmer of resistance and justice.

Nicholas Confessore rightly argues that Trump's "anti-other language" and denigration of Mexican immigrants as "criminal rapists, murderers and drug dealers" has "electrified the world of white nationalists," who up until the Trump campaign had been relegated to the fringe of American politics.[23] No longer. All manner of white nationalist media such as the *Daily Stormer* and individuals such as Jared Tayler, a "self-described race realist," and David Duke, a racist and anti-Semitic Louisiana lawmaker and talk show host, have embraced Trump as a presidential candidate. And in a less than subtle way, Trump has embraced them. He has repeatedly tweeted messages that first appeared on racist or ultra-nationalist neo-Nazi Twitter accounts. Adele M. Stan pointed out in *Fortune* magazine that in March 2016 it was "reported that, since the start of his campaign, Trump had retweeted posts from white supremacist accounts some 75 times, including the famous meme featuring a photo of Democratic opponent Hillary Clinton against a background of cash, next to a Star of David."[24] As if to remove any doubt about his sympathy for white supremacists, Trump hired Stephen K. Bannon, former chairman of Breitbart News Media, to lead his campaign just before the November elections. Sarah Posner rightly argues that

> Under Bannon's leadership, the site has plunged into the fever swamps of conservatism, cheering white nationalist groups as an

"eclectic mix of renegades," accusing President Barack Obama of importing "more hating Muslims" and waging an incessant war against the purveyors of political correctness.[25]

Hillary Clinton stated in her first presidential debate with Trump that Bannon's website served as a racist billboard for white supremacists, anti-Semites, and racists. She signaled convincingly to one of Breitbart's particularly ugly posts, which read "Hoist it high and Proud: The Confederate Flag Proclaims a Glorious Heritage," which as she noted "came shortly after the Charleston massacre" in which a white supremacist murdered nine Black churchgoers.[26] Unfortunately, a number of newspapers ignored the substance of Clinton's accusations regarding Trump's long history of racism and reduced the issue to her going for the low hanging fruit by deciding to exchange racial barbs with Trump. For instance, the *Washington Post* lost all semblance of journalistic integrity by headlining the story with "Clinton, Trump exchange racially charged accusations" as if there is no difference between using racist discourse and criticizing it.[27] Chuck Todd, moderator of *Meet the Press*, appearing on the *Today Show* went even further stating that the presidential race reached a low point with Hillary Clinton and Donald Trump "hurling epithets at each other."[28]

Surely, such a cravenly and evasive statement which conceals Trump's racism and indicts Clinton for revealing it says something about the complicity of mainstream media with such racism. What is disturbing about Todd's comments is that he is referring to the same debate in which Trump made clear that his call for law and order was a central plank of his platform, which was aimed at African Americans whom he derided as living in neighborhoods filled with crime, drugs, poverty, and ignorance. This is a familiar stereotype that strongly suggests that Black culture is synonymous with a culture of crime—one that Trump believes can only be addressed through the heavy hand of the police and criminal justice system. Trump endorses this racist position in spite of the horrifying fact that "in the U.S., [young Black men] apparently serve as target practice for the white police, who kill them for no other reason than their race, and do so with nearly complete impunity."[29] Trump's insistence on Black culture as a culture of depravity is a severe distortion that leaves out the vibrant and crucial work of Black churches, civil rights leaders, young people fighting against police brutality, the integrity of Black politicians, or the inventive initiatives of Black-owned businesses; it is another embodiment of racism and white supremacy parading as common sense and objectivity.

Throughout his primary and presidential campaign, Trump invoked a language of racist violence that could only be understood in the historical context of the state repression unleashed in the fifties, sixties, and seventies in Mississippi, Alabama, Georgia, Arkansas, and other states where expressions of white supremacy, domestic terrorism, and police violence exploded in full view of the American people and larger world. On numerous occasions Trump told his backers:

> to knock the crap out of them [Black Lives Matter protesters], seriously, get them out of here. In the good old days this doesn't happen because they used to treat them very rough and when they protested once they would not do it again so easily. I'd like to punch them in the face, I'll tell you. I love the good old days. You know what they used to do to guys like that in a place like this? They would be carried out on a stretcher, folks.[30]

The backdrop of this discourse reaches back into a time of racist terror and was captured in images of the young Black protesters being beaten by police and white patrons when they tried to integrate lunch counters in cities such as Nashville, Tennessee, and Greenville, North Carolina. It was also on full display when Black protesters were attacked by police dogs in Detroit, hosed down by high-power water cannons in Alabama, and when nine young African American students were taunted and shoved as they attempted to enter the all-white Central High School in Little Rock, Arkansas. The latter are "the good old days" that Trump celebrates in his speeches—when protesters were "ripped out of their seat," "punched in the face," and "would be carried out on a stretcher."[31] These "good old days" also gave us the lynchings of Black people, the murder of Emmett Till, and the church bombing in Birmingham, Alabama that killed four young Black girls. The "good old days" in this context serve as a legitimation not only for a ruthless return to racist terror and the suppression of dissent, but the celebration of a type of lawlessness endemic to fascism and updated for the new authoritarianism.

What is being suggested here is that this American form of neo-fascism is largely about social and racial cleansing and its endpoint is the construction of prisons, detention centers, enclosures, walls, and all the other varieties of murderous apparatuses that accompany the discourse of national greatness and racial purity. Americans have lived through 40 years of the dismantling of the welfare state, the elimination of democratic public spheres such as schools and libraries, and the attack on public goods and social provisions. In their place, we have the rise of the punishing state, with its support for a range of criminogenic institutions extending from banks and hedge funds to state governments and militarized police departments that depend on extortion to meet their budgets.

What is clear is that Trump's racism is only one register of his ideology of hatred, bigotry, and cruelty. Recent displays of Trump's misogyny and acts of violence towards women were on full display given revelations regarding his vulgar, crude, sexist exchanges with Howard Stern and Billy Bush. According to a report and transcript prepared by the *New York Times*, Trump made remarks in 2005 picked up by a hot-mic while riding on a bus with television personality Billy Bush of "Access Hollywood." The transcript and video reveals Trump boasting how he not only was attracted to beautiful women like a magnet but would also proceed to grope them. In Trump's own words, "You know, I'm automatically attracted to beautiful—I just start kissing them. It's like a magnet. Just kiss. I don't even wait. And when you're a star, they let you do it. You can do anything." Apparently, even grab women by their genitals. Trump boasted about "moving on" a married woman he referred to as a "bitch."[32] Surely, such comments coming from a presidential candidate are abhorrent and unprecedented. Yet, what is truly shocking about the disclosures of Trump's misogyny, sexual violence, and rape charges is that they should provoke any type of surprise among the press or American public.[33] These reactionary sentiments aimed at Blacks, women, immigrants, and others are part of a script that the Republican Party has been developing for years. Trump has simply been upfront about such sentiments and his willingness to use them to mobilize his followers. As Adele M. Stan observes:

> This is the Republican Party that seeks to revoke public funding for poor women to get basic health screenings for breast cancer, cervical cancer and sexually transmitted diseases (and whose vice presidential nominee has already done so in his own state) and which uses deceptively edited "sting" videos to smear the organization, Planned Parenthood, which provides those services, as well as birth control, to women throughout the nation. Essentially, this is the Republican Party that has made contempt for and control of women part of its brand ever since the Supreme Court afforded women a modicum of agency over their own bodies with its 1972 decision in Roe v. Wade. The truth is, for at least the last 36 years, the Republican Party has been the grab-em-by-the-pussy party. Donald Trump simply made it plain.[34]

Where are the institutions that do not support a rabid individualism, a culture of cruelty, and a society based on social combat—that refuse to militarize social problems, and reject the white supremacist discourses, laws, and practices spreading throughout the United States? What happens when a society is shaped by a poisonous neoliberalism that separates economic activities from social costs, when privatization becomes the only sanctioned orbit for agency, and when the measure of social relations is entirely reduced to exchange values?

How do we talk about the way in which language is transformed into a tool of violence, as happened at the 2016 Republican National Convention and in Trump's debates with Hillary Clinton? Moreover, how does language act in the service of violence less through an overt discourse of hate and bigotry than through its complicity with all manner of symbolic and real violence? What happens to a society when moral witnessing is hollowed out by a shameless entertainment industry that is willing to produce and distribute spectacles of extreme violence on a massive scale? What happens to a society when music is used as a method of torture (as it was at Guantanamo) and when a fascist politics of torture and disappearance are endorsed by the President of the United States and many of his supporters? What happens to the truth, evidence, and justice when language is weaponized so as to inflict pain or empty racist discourse of any meaning? Instead of addressing these questions—as well as the state-sanctioned torture and lynchings that form the backdrop for this violence—we have been hearing a lot of talk about violence waged against police. This is not to suggest that the recent isolated acts of violence against police are justified—of course they are not—but the real question is why we don't see much more of such violence, given how rampant police violence has long been in the service of white supremacy. As Ta-Nehisi Coates observes, the killing of police officers cannot be addressed outside the historical legacy of discrimination, harassment, and violence against Black people. He writes:

> When the law shoots down 12-year-old children, or beats down old women on traffic islands, or chokes people to death over cigarettes; when the law shoots people over compact discs, traffic stops, drivers' licenses, loud conversation, or car trouble; when the law auctions off its monopoly on lethal violence to bemused civilians, when these civilians then kill, and when their victims are mocked in their death throes; when people stand up to defend police as officers of the state, and when these defenders are killed by these very same officers; when much of this is recorded, uploaded, live-streamed, tweeted, and broadcast; and when government seems powerless, or unwilling, to stop any of it, then it ceases, in the eyes of citizens, to be any sort of respectable law at all. It simply becomes "force."[35]

As Patrick Healy and Jonathan Martin argue, the call for law and order is in actuality a call to sanction more state violence while telling white people that "their country is spiralling out of control and that they yearn for a leader who will take aggressive, even extreme, actions to protect them."[36] Trump extended his discourse of fear, threats, and potential violence in his final debate with Hillary Clinton by arguing without any substantive evidence that the election process is rigged and that if he loses it will be because of a corrupt political system.[37] In fact, Trump refused in the debate to agree that he would accept election results if Clinton won and in doing so implied that a smooth transition politically to a new administration would not be accepted by either him or his supporters. He later claimed he would only accept the results if he won.

Some interpret this as a not so subtle suggestion that his followers would have his approval to engage in violence in protesting the results of a Clinton presidency. What this claim makes clear is that Trump is not only shrill and unapologetic about his neo-fascist beliefs and policies, but he also consistently hints that if he does not get his way, he supports the potential for civic strife, if not mass violence. By claiming the possibility of electoral fraud, Trump draws from a playbook that "echoes that of dictators who seize power by force and firebrand populists who weaken democracy for personal gain."[38] Steven Levitsky, a Harvard University professor of political science, observes that Trump's emphasis on the illegitimacy of the election and his refusal to concede a loss makes it possible "to provoke a fair amount of violence" from extremists at the fringes of American politics.[39]

A peaceful transition to power is central to any viable democracy and yet Trump refused to acknowledge this central tenet of democratic rule. Trump's appeal to aggression, hatred, and violence coupled with the overt sexism and racism supported by large numbers of his followers does not augur well for the future of American politics. Of course, Trump is partly right in claiming that elections are rigged because they have been emptied of any substance in a neoliberal society in which money drives politics. But that is not his argument. He is claiming that they are rigged by Clinton and other liberals so that he will lose.

Most disturbing is that the potential consequences of the rhetoric of violence and hate in the year leading up to Trump's presidential election were marked or covered over in the mainstream media and larger public with well-intentioned but misguided calls for love and empathy. These are empty calls when they do not address the root causes of violence, and when they ignore a ruthless climate of cruelty that calls poor people moochers. This is a culture that is increasingly militarized by day, criminalizes marginalized people while blaming them for wider social problems, and perpetuates a discourse of hate that is normalized by the Republican Party and covered up by the Democratic Party.

What cannot be ignored is that Hillary Clinton has supported a war machine that has resulted in the death of millions, while also supporting a neoliberal economy that has produced massive amounts of suffering and created a mass incarceration state. Yet all of that is forgotten as the mainstream press focuses on stories about Clinton's emails and the details of her electoral run for the presidency. At the same time, it is crucial to note that she hides her crimes in the discourse of freedom and appeals to democracy while Trump overtly disdains such a discourse. In the end, state and domestic violence saturate American society and the only time this fact gets noticed is when the beatings and murders of Black men are caught on camera and spread through social media. And the videos revealing such needless police violence seem to appear with accelerated frequency, with some of the most publicized depicting the deaths of Eric Garner and Freddie Gray, and the fatal police shooting of Philando Castile and Alton Sterling. In addition, there was the shocking fatal shooting of Terrence Crutcher in Tulsa, Oklahoma by white officer Betty Shelby. The video of the incident makes clear that the 40-year-old African American was unarmed and shot while his hands were in the air.

Where are the mainstream public outcries for the millions of Black and Brown people incarcerated in America's carceral state? When the mainstream media can write and air allegedly objective stories about a fascist candidate who delights white nationalists and neo-Nazis, without highlighting that he advocates for policies that are racist and constitute war crimes, it makes visible how America has forgotten what it should be ashamed of: the fact that we've built a society in which collective morality and the ethical imagination no longer matter. Comparisons to the 1930s have a bearing but what counts even more is that they have been forgotten or are held in disdain.[40] Much of the American public appears to have forgotten that totalitarian and white supremacist societies are too often legitimated by a supplicant mainstream media, cowardly politicians, right-wing and liberal pundits, academics, and other cultural workers who either overlook or support the hateful bigotry of demagogues such as Trump. What is also forgotten by many is the racist legacy of policies implemented by the Democratic Party that have resulted in a punitive culture of criminalization, incarceration, and shooting of untold numbers of Black people.[41] Moreover, rather than engage in the masochistic practice of supporting Trump's nativism, ignorance, and bigotry along with his warlike fantasies of what it will take to make America great again, white workers who have been driven to despair by the ravaging policies of the financial elite and their shameless political and corporate allies should be in the streets protesting not only against what is called establishment politics, but also the rise of an unvarnished neo-Nazi demagogue.

Evidence of such complicity comes in many forms, some of which are wrapped in the discourse of a supine liberalism that bows down in the face of an authoritarianism largely driven by the ethos of white supremacy. One example can be found in an article that appeared in the *New York Times* written by Sam Tanenhaus and titled "How Trump can save the G.O.P." This stuff is hard to make up. In the article, Tanenhaus compares Trump to former presidents Eisenhower and Lyndon Johnson and then uses this comparison to praise Trump for the pragmatism of some of his economic policies—as if the spirit behind Trump's policies had any relationship to the spirit that animated Eisenhower's resistance to the military-industrial complex or to Johnson's deep concern for eliminating poverty and dismantling racism in American society. Does it matter to Tanenhaus that Trump is a bigot, potential war criminal, and unapologetic about his neo-Nazi followers, wants to expel 11 million Mexicans, hates Muslims, and speaks glowingly about instituting torture if elected as president of the United States? How is it possible to forget that, overall, Trump is a demagogue, misogynist, racist, and bigot who is unequivocally dangerous to the promises and ideals of a democracy? Apparently, it is possible. Yes, the fascists and Nazis were also efficient, particularly in the end when it came to building a war machine and committing acts of genocide. So much for pragmatism without a conscience.

As the elected president of the United States, Trump is a real danger to the species, country, and world in general. His views on war and climate change—along with the promise of violence against his enemies and his unapologetic racism, bigotry, and hatred of constitutional rights—pose some of the greatest dangers to democracy and freedom the U.S. has ever faced.

As Adam Gopnik argues in the *New Yorker*, democracies do not simply commit suicide; they are killed by murderers, by people like Trump.[42] Most expressions of support for Trump vastly underestimate the immediate danger Trump poses to the world and minorities of class, race, and ethnicity. In contrast, while Hillary Clinton is a warmonger, a cheerleader for neoliberalism, and a high-ranking member of the Democratic Party establishment, she did not threaten to take an immediate set of actions that would threaten the lives and livelihood of people of color, immigrants, and the working class. Instead, she should have been viewed as part of a corrupt financial and political system that should be overthrown. While posing danger on a number of economic, political, and foreign fronts, Clinton if elected could have been criticized by exposing through her actions and policies the mythological nature of the idea that democracy and capitalism are the same thing. Hopefully, all those young people who followed the dead-end of the Bernie Sanders movement—and the false suggestion that a political revolution can be achieved by reforming the Democratic Party—would object to this contradiction. Sanders revitalized the discourse of inequality, injustice, and the need to break down the financial monopolies, but he failed in choosing a political avenue in which such real and systemic change can come about. As a result, he was abandoned by the Democratic Party once it was clear that Hillary Clinton had the presidential nomination. Jill Stein's campaign offered the left a moral referent for not voting for either Trump or Clinton, but not a crucial instrumental reason for voting against Trump.

With Trump's victory, there is a great danger that his toxic views will be normalized. Evidence of such a politics was on display within two weeks after his election. In front of an audience of millions, CBS News correspondent Jericka Duncan asked Richard Spencer, an American white supremacist, "if he was 'an advocate for an all-white United States of America,' and allowed Spencer to respond 'No, I don't think that is going to happen,' without offering a follow-up question or pressing him on his past racist comments."[43] Forgetting that he is a white supremacist and that is exactly what they advocate, the reporter shockingly referred to him not as a racist and white supremacist but as "an advocate for white America." The category "an advocate for white America" is more than a sweetening of the racist poison and toxic ideology this monster supports, it also provides a hint of how outright racist individuals and organizations will now be labeled, as advocates for extremism—which I am assuming will become legitimate rhetorical fare for the news media to view as acceptable! How else to explain NPR both hosting and asking Spencer in an interview to describe his vision of a white America. This marks the beginning of the normalization of the nightmare that has already begun with the Trump administration. Mr. Spencer, when asked about whether he supported an all-white America, stated while looking right into the camera that he just wanted to raise consciousness and further insisted that he wanted to help implement policies for his hero Donald Trump. We got a hint of what these policies would look like when Megyn Kelly on Fox News queried Carl Higbie, a spokesperson for the pro-Trump Great America PAC, about his defense of the United States' use of internment camps for Japanese Americans during World War II as a "precedent" for creating what Trump called a "Muslim registry." Higbie justified his ethically and politically horrendous suggestion by stating that "the president needs to protect America first."[44] If this is not a measure of the neo-fascism to come, what is?

The mainstream media's normalization of neo-fascist principles should surprise no one. According to *MarketWatch*, Donald Trump received from the mainstream media billions of dollars in free advertising during his presidential campaign.[45] Mainstream cultural apparatuses have become the ideological pipeline for a neo-fascist culture. We live in a time in which people are presented with a politics that celebrates saviors, denigrates democratic relations of power and policy, and provides a mode of escape in which heartfelt trauma and pain are used to mobilize people not into democratic movements but into venting their anger by blaming others who are equally oppressed. This is a politics that kills both empathy and the imagination, a politics that uses pain to inflict further pain on others. Atomization on a global scale is a new form of invisible violence because it shackles people to their own experiences, cutting them off from a shared awareness of the larger systemic forces that shape their lives. Anger, indignation, and misery need to take a detour through the ethical, political, and social models of analysis that connect individual issues to larger social problems. Only then can we resist the transformation of grievances into a Trump-like version of American fascism.[46]

Americans need to continue to develop comprehensive movements that reject the established political parties and rethink the social formations necessary to bring about a radical democracy. We see this in the Black Lives Matter movement as well as in a range of other movements that are resisting corporate money in politics, the widespread destruction of the environment, nuclear war, and the mass incarceration state. Hopefully, these important social movements will continue to break new ground in experimenting with new ways to come together and form coalitions between fragmented sub-groups.

In the end, it's vital to foster anti-fascist, pro-radical democracy movements that understand short-term and long-term strategies. Short-term strategies include participating in an electoral process to make sure a fascist or religious fundamentalist does not control a school board or gain leadership roles regarding public governance. Such practices do not represent a sell-out but a strategic effort to make immediate progressive gains on the way to tearing down the entire system. Strategies built on the divide of being in or out of the system are too simplistic. Progressives must forge policies that function as part of a larger movement for creating a radical democracy. Such actions are not the same as giving into a capitalist world view, especially when the long-term plan is to overthrow such a system. There seems to be a certain kind of theoretical infantilism that dominates some segments of the left on this issue, a form of political purity stuck in an either/or mindset. Such ideological fundamentalism (which might assert, for example, that those who vote are "giving in" or "selling out") is not helpful for successful short-term planning or for long-term strategies for developing the institutions, cultural apparatuses, and social movements necessary for radical change in the U.S. and elsewhere.

If we are to fight for a democratic future that matters, progressives and the left need to ask how we would go forward if the looming authoritarian nightmare succeeds in descending upon the United States. What can we learn about the costs of allowing our society to become lawless in its modes of governance and to lose its historical understanding of the legacy of slavery, lynching, and bigotry that have given rise to mass incarceration and the punishing state? What does it mean when money rules and corrupts politics, disavows economic actions from social costs, and wages war against public trust, values, and goods? These are just some of the questions that need to be addressed in order to break free from a neoliberal system that sounds the death knell for democracy.

With the election of Donald Trump to the presidency, America is in a new historical moment in which the old is dying and the new is waiting to emerge. What must be made clear is that what is distinctive in this historical moment is that American democracy, however fragile, is slipping away into the dark shadows of authoritarianism. Yet, all societies contain sites of resistance and progressives need desperately to join with those who have been written out of the script of democracy to rethink politics, find a new beginning, and develop a vision that is on the side of justice and democracy. Hope in the abstract is not enough. It has to become the foundation for action or what might be called hope in action, a new force of collective resistance and a vehicle for anger transformed into collective struggle, a principle for making despair unconvincing and struggle possible. While we may be entering a period of counter-revolutionary change, it must be remembered that such periods of radical change are as hopeful as they are dangerous. Hope at the moment resides in those young people and others intent on turning despair into hope, struggling to reclaim the radical imagination, and working to build an expansive collective movement for real symbolic and structural change in the pursuit of political and economic justice. We need to accelerate such movements before it is too late.

Notes

1   Peter Thiel, "The Education of a Libertarian," *Cato Unbound* (April 13, 2009). Online: www.cato-unbound.org/2009/04/13/peter-thiel/education-libertarian; this issue came to my attention in Bill Moyers and Michael Winship, "Donald Trump's Dark and Scary Night," *Moyers and Company* (July 22, 2016). Online: http://billmoyers.com/story/donald-trumps-dark-scary-convention-night/
2   Adorno cited in Peter Uwe Hohendahl, "Education after the Holocaust." In *Prismatic Thought: Theodor Adorno* (Lincoln: University of Nebraska Press, 1995), p. 56.
3   Hohendahl, "Education after the Holocaust," p. 60.
4   Media Matters Staff, "MSNBC's Eugene Robinson: Trump's RNC Speech Was 'a Message . . . to White America: Be Afraid. I Will Protect You,'" *Media Matters for America* (July 22, 2016). Online: https://mediamatters.org/video/2016/07/22/msnbc-eugene-robinson-trumps-rnc-speech-was-message-white-america-be-afraid-i-will-protect-you/211816
5   Nicholas Kristof, "Donald Trump Is a Racist," *New York Times* (July 24, 2016). Online: www.nytimes.com/2016/07/24/opinion/sunday/is-donald-trump-a-racist.html?action=click&pgtype=Homepage&region=CColumn&module=MostViewed&version=Full&src=mv&WT.nav=MostViewed
6   Jonathan Mahler and Steve Eder, "'No Vacancies' for Blacks: How Donald Trump Got His Start, and Was First Accused of Bias," *New York Times* (August 27, 2016). Online: www.nytimes.com/2016/08/28/us/politics/donald-trump-housing-race.html
7   Amy Davidson, "Donald Trump and the Central Park Five," *New Yorker* (June 23, 2014). Online: www.newyorker.com/news/amy-davidson/donald-trump-and-the-central-park-five
8   Paul Krugman, "Predators in Arms," *New York Times* (October 10, 2016). Online: www.nytimes.com/2016/10/10/opinion/predators-in-arms.html?action=click&pgtype=Homepage&clickSource=story-heading&module=opinion-c-col-left-region&region=opinion-c-col-left-region&WT.nav=opinion-c-col-left-region
9   David Martosko, "Trump Catches Flak for Telling White Audience that Black Neighborhoods Are Less Safe than Afghanistan—While Riots Turn Parts of Charlotte into War Zone," *MailOnline* (September 21, 2016). Online: www.dailymail.co.uk/news/article-3800248/Trump-catches-flak-telling-white-audience-black-neighborhoods-safe-Afghanistan-riots-turn-parts-Charlotte-war-zone.html#ixzz4Nqa3JQFc
10 Alan Yuhas, "Trump Proposes Racial Profiling as a Tactic 'to Start Thinking About,'" *Guardian* (June 19, 2016). Online: www.theguardian.com/us-news/2016/jun/19/donald-trump-proposes-racial-profiling-gun-control-nra
11 Nicholas Kristof, "Is Donald Trump a Racist?" *New York Times* (July 23, 2016). Online: www.nytimes.com/2016/07/24/opinion/sunday/is-donald-trump-a-racist.html?_r=0
12 Ibid.
13 Nathaniel Rich, "James Baldwin and the Fear of a Nation," *NY Books* (May 12, 2016). Online: www.nybooks.com/articles/2016/05/12/james-baldwin-fear-of-a-nation/
14 Chris Hedges, "The New European Fascists," *Truthdig* (July 24, 2016). Online: www.truthdig.com/report/item/the_new_european_fascists_20160724
15 For a brilliant commentary on the refugee crisis and the reactionary political response to it, see Zygmunt Bauman, *Strangers at the Door* (London: Polity, 2016).
16 Peter Foster, "The Rise of the Far-Right in Europe Is Not a False Alarm," *Telegraph* (May 19, 2016). Online: www.telegraph.co.uk/news/2016/05/19/the-rise-of-the-far-right-in-europe-is-not-a-false-alarm/; see also, Ryan Harvey, "Donald Trump and the Rise of the Far Right on Both Sides of the Atlantic," *Truthout* (June 22, 2016). Online:

www.truth-out.org/news/item/36523-donald-trump-and-the-rise-of-the-far-right-on-both-sides-of-the-atlantic

17   Kathy Kelly, "Of Lethal Drones and Police Shootings," *Truthout* (July 8, 2016). Online: www.truth-out.org/opinion/item/36747-of-lethal-drones-and-police-shootings

18   Ibid.

19   Charles Derber and Yale Magrass, "When Wars Come Home," *Truthout* (February 19, 2013). Online: www.truth-out.org/opinion/item/14539-when-wars-come-home

20   Zygmunt Bauman, *Liquid Fear* (London: Polity, 2006), pp. 69–70.

21   I take this up in detail in Henry A. Giroux, *America at War with Itself* (San Francisco: City Lights Books, 2016).

22   Hannah Arendt, "Ideology and Terror: A Novel Form of Government." In *The Origins of Totalitarianism* (New York: Houghton Mifflin Harcourt, 2001), p. 464.

23   Nicholas Confessore, "For Whites Sensing Decline, Donald Trump Unleashes Words of Resistance," *New York Times* (July 13, 2016). Online: www.nytimes.com/2016/07/14/us/politics/donald-trump-white-identity.html?_r=0

24   Adele M. Stan, "The Trump Campaign Is Now Fully Aligned with White Supremacists," *AlterNet* (August 22, 2016). Online: www.alternet.org/election-2016/trump-campaign-chief-bannon-cements-white-nationalist-ideology

25   Sarah Posner, "How Donald Trump's New Campaign Chief Created an Online Haven for White Nationalists," *Mother Jones* (August 22, 2016). Online: www.motherjones.com/politics/2016/08/stephen-bannon-donald-trump-alt-right-breitbart-news. See also Jim Naurecklas, "A Guided Tour of the Racist 'Alt-Right' by the Trump Campaign Chief's Website," *AlterNet* (August 30, 2016). Online: www.alternet.org/election-2016/guided-tour-racist-alt-right-trump-campaign-chiefs-website

26   Julie Craven, "Hillary Clinton Made History by Calling Donald Trump 'Racist' during the Debate," *Huffington Post* (September 28, 2016). Online: www.huffingtonpost.com/entry/clinton-calls-trump-racist_us_57eaceb4e4b024a52d2b30b6

27   John Wagner and Jenna Johnson, "Clinton, Trump Exchange Racially Charged Accusations," *Washington Post* (August 25, 2016). Online: www.washingtonpost.com/politics/ahead-of-speech-targeting-trump-clinton-accuses-him-of-peddling-hate/2016/08/25/fc3f1ade-6a78-11e6-8225-fbb8a6fc65bc_story.html

28   Todd's statement can be seen at www.today.com/video/donald-trump-hillary-clinton-in-a-race-to-the-bottom-chuck-todd-says-751666243772

29   Robert Fantina, "You Can't Have a War without Racism," *CounterPunch* (September 29, 2016). Online: www.counterpunch.org/2016/09/29/you-cant-have-war-without-racism/

30   These quotes have been compiled along with historical context that gives them meaning in Ava DuVernay's brilliant film, *13th*, which is available on *Netflix*.

31   Ibid.

32   See Editors, "Transcript: Donald Trump's Taped Comments about Women," *New York Times* (October 8, 2016). Online: www.nytimes.com/2016/10/08/us./donald-trump-tape-transcript.html?_r=0

33   For a summary and analysis of Trump's sexual transgressions and attacks on women, see John Wilson, "Trump's Record: Decades of Sexual Attacks and Blaming the Victims," *Truthout* (October 19, 2016). Online: www.truth-out.org/news/item/38047-trump-s-record-decades-of-sexual-attacks-and-blaming-the-victims

34   Adele M. Stan, "Why Paul Ryan's Refusal to Defend Donald Trump Is Not Enough—Especially Following Brutal Debate," *AlterNet* (October 8, 2016). Online: www.alternet.org/election-2016/republican-party-must-apologize-america-trump?akid=14751.40823.u8hvVM&rd=1&src=newsletter1065140&t=4

35   Ta-Nehisi Coates, "The Near Certainty of Anti-Police Violence," *Atlantic* (July 12, 2016). Online: www.theatlantic.com/politics/archive/2016/07/the-near-certainty-of-anti-police-violence/490541/

36   Patrick Healy and Jonathan Martin, "His Tone Dark, Donald Trump Takes G.O.P. Mantle," *New York Times* (July 21, 2016). Online: www.nytimes.com/2016/07/22/us/politics/donald-trump-rnc-speech.html

37   Ari Berman, "Fair Elections under Attack, Just Not in the Way Donald Trump Wants You to Believe," *Real News* (October 19, 2016). Online: http://therealnews.com/t2/index.php?option=com_content&task=view&id=31&Itemid=74&jumival=17464#news letter1

38   Max Fisher, "Donald Trump's Threat to Reject Election Results Alarms Scholars," *New York Times* (October 23, 2016). Online: www.nytimes.com/2016/10/23/world/americas/donald-trump-rigged-election.html?em_pos=medium&emc=edit_cn_20161024&nl=first-draft&nl_art=7&nlid=51563793&ref=headline&te=1&_r=0

39   Ibid.

40   Charles Derber, "Facing Down Trump's Demagoguery: Lessons from Weimar Germany," *Truthout* (July 22, 2016). Online: www.truth-out.org/opinion/item/36938-facing-down-trump-s-demagoguery-lessons-from-weimar-germany

41   Elizabeth Hinton, *From the War on Poverty to the War on Crime: The Making of Mass Incarceration in America* (Cambridge, MA: Harvard University Press, 2016).

42   Adam Gopnik, "The Dangerous Acceptance of Donald Trump," *New Yorker* (May 20, 2016). Online: www.newyorker.com/news/daily-comment/the-dangerous-acceptance-of-donald-trump

43   See, Media Matters Staff, "CBS Evening News Provides Platform for White Nationalist to Spin, without Pressing Him on Racist Views," *Media Matters* (November 17, 2016). Online: http://mediamatters.org/blog/2016/11/17/cbs-evening-news-provides-platform-white-nationalist-spin-without-pressing-him-racist-views/214535

44   Josh Feldman, "Megyn Kelly Scolds Trump Supporter: 'You Can't Be Citing Japanese Internment Camps as Precedent!'" *Mediaite* (November 16, 2016). Online: www.mediaite.com/tv/megyn-kelly-scolds-trump-supporter-you-cant-be-citing-japanese-internment-camps-as-precedent/

45   Robert Schroeder, "Trump Has Gotten Nearly $3 Billion in 'Free' Advertising," *MarketWatch* (May 6, 2016). Online: www.marketwatch.com/story/trump-has-gotten-nearly-3-billion-in-free-advertising-2016–05–06

46   For a damning critique of the threat that Trump poses to the world, see Editorial Board, "Donald Trump Is a Unique Threat to American Democracy," *Washington Post* (July 22, 2016). Online: www.washingtonpost.com/opinions/donald-trump-is-a-unique-threat-to-american-democracy/2016/07/22/a6d823cc-4f4f-11e6-aa14-e0c1087f7583_story.html

3
AUTHORITARIANISM IN THE AGE OF MANUFACTURED ILLITERACY

What I have seen . . . is language forced into the service of violence. A rhetoric of desperation and devastation molded into the incomprehensible, then vomited out in images and words that we cannot ignore though we have tried.

(Maaza Mengiste)

The dark times that haunt the current age no longer appear as an impending threat. They have materialized with the election of Donald Trump to the presidency. Trump and his administration of extremists epitomize the monsters that have come to rule America and who now dominate the major political parties and other commanding political and economic institutions. Trump's nightmarish reign of misery, violence, and disposability will become increasingly evident in the dominance of a repressive cultural apparatus that will continue to produce a vast machinery of manufactured stupidity, consumerist blight, inane game show culture, a spectacle of violence, and manufactured ignorance. This is a social formation that extends from the mainstream broadcast media and internet to a print culture, too many of which embrace the spectacle of violence, legitimize opinions over facts, and revel in a politics of ignorance and theatrics. Trump's ascent to the highest office in America is already being normalized by numerous pundits and politicians who are asking the American public to give Trump a chance or suggesting that the power and demands of the presidency will place some restraints on his unrestrained impetuousness and often unpredictable behavior.

Any talk of working with a president who has surrounded himself with militarists, racists, neo-fascists, anti-intellectuals, and neoliberal fundamentalists should be resisted at all cost. Normalization is simply a retreat from any sense of moral and political responsibility. Normalization and any reference supporting it should be seen as an act of political complicity with authoritarianism and condemned outright. What such arguments appear to overlook is that America is at war with its most basic democratic ideals and institutions and it is time to prepare for a battle in which all of humanity is at stake. The rhetoric of neo-fascism has become normalized in many parts of the world and the United States is no exception. Such a danger is all the more ominous given the current collapse of civic literacy and the public's inability to deal with complex issues, on one hand, and on the other, the attempt by those who maintain power to ruthlessly promote a crisis discourse of lies, simplicity, and fear of the other. The disaster of politics is now part of a crisis of agency exacerbated by a notion of common sense in which literacy is now regarded with disdain, words are reduced to data, and science is confused with pseudo-science. As such, historical and public memory have no place in the culture of fear and produce a moral vacuity tied directly to the extreme violence that now saturates American society.

Thinking is now regarded as an act of stupidity, and ignorance is deemed a virtue. All traces of critical thought appear only at the margins of the culture as civic illiteracy becomes one of the primary organizing principles of American society. One can go further and argue that ignorance has become weaponized posturing as a refusal to know and a type of armed knowledge that produces violence in the name of common sense. How else to explain the existence in 2016 of a president and a Republican Party in control of the United States government that denies climate change and argues for including creationism in school textbooks? Under Trump's presidential campaign, ignorance was weaponized. Not only did he run on a platform of bigotry, racism, and blatant misogyny, he also threatened immigrants with forced expulsion and Muslims with a ban on entering the country. Trump has also appointed as chief White House strategist Stephen Bannon, a declared white nationalist celebrated by the American Nazi Party and the Ku Klux Klan. Most of Trump's appointments to high government offices are both extremely reactionary and dangerous. Jeff Sessions, Trump's Attorney General, was once deemed so openly racist and exhibited such a deep hatred of civil rights legislation that Senate Republicans in 1986 killed his nomination by Ronald Reagan to become a federal judge. Vice President Mike Pence is a religious fundamentalist who has called for criminally punishing doctors who perform late-term abortions and has argued that "the only true safe sex . . . is no sex."[1]

The threads of such religious and educational fundamentalism run deep in American society. For instance, more than half of Americans cannot name more than one of the five freedoms guaranteed by the First Amendment, while 20 percent of Americans believe the sun revolves around the earth. Close to 20 percent cannot name the country from which the United States gained its independence, 80 percent did not know how many senators there were in Congress, and only 30 percent could identify the Holocaust.[2] Trump's presence on the political scene proved that the culture of lying, ignorance, and misinformation appears to be deeply embedded in American society. Trump repeatedly lied about his views on the Iraq War, pushed conspiracy theories regarding President Obama's birth, denied climate change was the result of human activity, claimed no one loved women more than him, in spite of his repeated insults aimed at women, and so it goes. In a country in which emotion and opinions appear for millions to have more credibility than reasoned arguments and scientific evidence, the culture of lying and ignorance thrives, just as public life withers. Unsurprisingly, education in the larger culture has become a disimagination machine, a tool for legitimating ignorance, and it is central to the formation of an authoritarian politics that has gutted any vestige of democracy from the ideology, policies, and institutions that now control American society.

I am not talking simply about the kind of anti-intellectualism that theorists such as Richard Hofstadter, Ed Herman, and Noam Chomsky, and more recently Susan Jacoby have documented, however insightful their analyses might be. I am pointing to a more lethal form of illiteracy that is often ignored. Illiteracy is now a scourge and a political tool designed primarily to make war on language, meaning, thinking, and the capacity for critical thought. Chris Hedges is right in stating that "the emptiness of language is a gift to demagogues and the corporations that saturate the landscape with manipulated images and the idiom of mass culture."[3] Words such as love, trust, freedom, responsibility, and choice have been deformed by a market logic that narrows their meaning to either a relationship to a commodity or a reductive notion of self-interest. Rather than love each other, Americans are commercially carpet bombed to love their new car, dishwasher, home, and a range of other goods. Instead of loving with courage, compassion, and desiring a more just society, we love a society saturated in commodities. Freedom now means removing one's self from any sense of social responsibility so one can retreat into privatized orbits of self-indulgence. George Monbiot points to the way in which freedom has been transformed under neoliberalism. He writes:

> The freedom that neoliberalism offers, which sounds so beguiling when expressed in general terms, turns out to mean freedom for the pike, not for the minnows. Freedom from trade unions and collective bargaining means the freedom to suppress wages. Freedom from regulation means the freedom to poison rivers, endanger workers, and charge iniquitous rates of interest and design exotic financial instruments. Freedom from tax means freedom from the distribution of wealth that lifts people out of poverty.[4]

The new form of illiteracy does not simply constitute an absence of learning, ideas, or knowledge. Nor can it be solely attributed to what has been called the "smartphone society."[5] On the contrary, it is a willful practice and goal used to actively depoliticize people and make them complicit with the forces that impose misery and suffering upon their lives. Trump's followers bought this script with enough gusto to ignore his repeated pre-election lies and stupidity to elect him to the highest office in the land.

Gore Vidal once called America the United States of Amnesia. The title should be extended to the United States of Amnesia and Willful Illiteracy. Illiteracy no longer simply marks populations immersed in poverty with little access to quality education; nor does it only suggest the lack of proficient skills enabling people to read and write with a degree of understanding and fluency. More profoundly, illiteracy is also about what it means not to be able to act from a position of thoughtfulness, informed judgment, and critical agency. Illiteracy has become a form of political repression that discourages a culture of questioning, renders agency as an act of intervention inoperable, and restages power as a mode of domination. Illiteracy serves to depoliticize people because it becomes difficult for individuals to develop informed judgments, analyze complex relationships, and draw upon a range of sources to understand how power works and how they might be able to shape the forces that shape their lives. Illiteracy provides the foundation for being governed, not how to govern.

It is precisely this mode of illiteracy that now constitutes the modus operandi of a society that privatizes, depoliticizes, and kills the imagination by poisoning it with falsehoods, consumer fantasies, data loops, and the need for instant gratification. This is a mode of manufactured illiteracy and education that has no language for relating the self to public life, social responsibility, or the demands of citizenship. It is important to recognize that the rise of this new mode of illiteracy is not simply about the failure of public and higher education to create critical and active citizens; it is about a society that eliminates those public spheres that make thinking possible while imposing a culture of fear in which there is the looming threat that anyone who holds power accountable will be punished. At stake here is not only the crisis of a democratic society, but a crisis of memory, ethics, and agency.

Evidence of such a repressive policy is visible in the growth of the surveillance state, the suppression of dissent, especially among Black youth, the elimination of tenure in states such as Wisconsin, the rise of the punishing state, and the militarization of the police. It is also evident in the demonization and assaults waged by the Obama administration on whistleblowers such as Edward Snowden, Chelsea Manning, and Jeffrey Sterling, among others. Under the Trump administration, the punishing of whistleblowers and those protesting globalization, deregulation, institutionalized racism, police violence, widespread poverty, and a wide variety of other social and economic injustices will be intensified. In that there is an absence of effective resistance by progressives, the repressive policies of a state that has been captured by right-wing extremists will certainly turn violent and in some cases deadly.

If Obama created a kill list supported by a growing fleet of drones functioning as robotic assassins, Trump has seized upon social media to use Twitter as a way to weaponize knowledge and arouse his followers to harass, insult, and humiliate anyone he puts in his 144 character crosshairs. As Tom Engelhardt points out,

> So when it comes to assassinations, we were already on dark terrain before Donald Trump ever thought about running for president. But give the man his due. Little noticed by anyone, he may already be developing the potential for a new style of presidential assassination—not in distant lands but right here at home. Start with his remarkable tweeting skills and the staggering 17.2 million followers of whatever he tweets, including numerous members of what's politely referred to as the alt-right. And believe me, that's one hell of an audience to stir up, something The Donald has shown that he can do with alacrity.[6]

Trump has already used his Twitter power to critique arms maker Lockheed-Martin, resulting in a $4 billion loss in its stock, berate a union leader, and engage in a shameful attack on a female talk show host. Not surprisingly, those targeted by Trump's insulting tweets are often subjected to a flood of threatening calls and abusive emails. When Trump used his Twitter account to go after Megyn Kelly, the Fox News host, she received death threats, her mother was harassed, and she was subjected to threats to beat her up and rape her. She said her life went "into lockdown."[7] It is quite probable, given Trump's vindictive temperament, that he will use his weaponized Tweets to go after prominent dissenters and social movements. Certainly, his white nationalist advisors will wage a relentless assault on Black resistance movements. In response, it is also quite reasonable to assume that any number of his deranged followers reared on fake news and living in a world in which dissent is viewed as unpatriotic will spring into action and conduct massive harassment campaigns against his critics, if not something even worse.

Robert Reich has argued that Trump will do everything he can to undermine a free press and control the media.[8] As Reich observes, not only will Trump endlessly berate the media on his Twitter account and in his public speeches for either misrepresenting his views or criticizing them, he will also blacklist certain news organizations, as he has done with the *Washington Post*. In doing so, he will prevent critical news outlets from gaining any access to him or to members of his administration. If that does not work, Trump has threatened to change libel laws "so that he can have an easier time suing news organizations."[9] Or, as Trump puts it, "One of the things I'm going to do if I win . . . I am going to open up our libel laws so when they write purposely negative and horrible and false articles, we can sue them and win lots of money."[10]

At the same time, Trump will continue to condemn the popular media such as *Saturday Night Live* for making him the object of satire. In addition, he will appeal directly to the public through his Twitter account in order to bypass the media and to discredit critical journalists as "liars" while reinforcing the notion that there is no place for serious reporting or dissent in American society. Trump will do everything possible to erode any sense of shared citizenship and will reinforce the culture of fear, greed, and selfishness that contributed to his election. Under Trump the aesthetics of vulgarity, falsehoods, and sensationalism will blur the lines between entertainment and politics, making it all the more possible to erase the legitimate distinction between fact and fiction, truth and opinion, justice and injustice.

The potential for such repression is palpable and too great to ignore. Targeted communities such as Black Lives Matter, Dream Defenders, labor unions, academics, Dakota Pipeline protesters, critical journalists, and others must stand together making clear that each group must join with each other and create links between their varied interests so as to transform single-issue movements into a powerful broad-based alliance. We see indications of this type of alliance in the Democracy Initiative of 2013 which created "a coalition of labor, environmental, racial justice and election-reform groups" and has brought together "almost 60 organizations" and "boasts 30 million members."[11] Most importantly, progressives cannot build such a movement without rethinking the limitation of struggles trapped in single-issue silos and those that only connect modes of domination with structural issues, whether talking about state repression or economic structures. As I have said elsewhere, there is a central need for the left and others to wage "an anti-fascist struggle that is not simply about remaking economic structures, but also about refashioning identities, values, and social relations as part of a democratic project that reconfigures what it means to desire a better and more democratic world."[12]

Any viable attempt at developing a radical politics must begin to address the role of education and civic literacy and what I have termed public pedagogy as central not only to politics itself but also to the creation of subjects capable of becoming individual and social agents willing to struggle against injustices and fight to reclaim and develop those institutions crucial to the functioning and promises of a substantive democracy. One way to begin to think through such a project is by addressing the meaning and role of pedagogy as part of the larger struggle for and practice of freedom.

The reach of pedagogy extends from schools to diverse cultural apparatuses such as the mainstream media, alternative screen cultures, and the expanding digital screen culture. Far more than a teaching method, pedagogy is a moral and political practice actively involved not only in the production of knowledge, skills, and values but also in the construction of identities, modes of identification, and forms of individual and social agency. Accordingly, pedagogy is at the heart of any understanding of politics and the ideological scaffolding of those framing mechanisms that mediate our everyday lives. Across the globe, the forces of free-market fundamentalism are using the educational force of the wider culture and the takeover of public and higher education both to reproduce the market-driven culture of a savage neoliberalism and to wage an assault on the historically guaranteed social provisions and civil rights provided by the welfare state, public schools, unions, women's reproductive rights, and civil liberties, among others, all the while undercutting public faith in the defining institutions of democracy.

As market mentalities and moralities tighten their grip on all aspects of society, democratic institutions and public spheres are being down-sized, if not altogether disappearing. As these institutions vanish—from public schools and alternative media to health-care centers—there is also a serious erosion of the discourses of community, justice, equality, and the common good. What is "new" about the long decline of public values in American society is not that they are again under attack but how they have become irrelevant to the existing contemporary neoliberal order, which saps the foundation of social solidarity, weakens the bonds of social obligation, and insists on the ability of markets to solve all social and individual problems.[13] This crisis of politics and agency speaks to more than a failed state, it also registers the failure of civic courage and a withdrawal from political life. As neoliberal societies accelerate their reliance on the self-interests of their subjects, the affective, symbolic, and social dimensions of everyday life are both subverted and wane under the force of a pedagogy of unchecked individualism and privatization. The crisis of politics and agency is also part of a politics that strips the social of any democratic ideals and undermines any understanding of education as a public good and pedagogy as an *empowering* practice, a practice which examines how knowledge, identities, desires, and values either subvert or expand the promise of a substantive democracy.

One of the challenges facing the current generation of educators, students, progressives, and other cultural workers is the need to address the role they might play in educating students to be critically engaged agents, attentive to addressing important social issues and being alert to the responsibility of deepening and expanding the meaning and practices of a vibrant democracy. At the heart of such a challenge is the question of what education should accomplish not simply in a democracy but at a historical moment when the United States is about to slip into the dark night of authoritarianism. What work do educators have to do to create the economic, political, and ethical conditions necessary to endow young people and the general public with the capacities to think, question, doubt, imagine the unimaginable, and defend education as essential for inspiring and energizing the citizens necessary for the existence of a robust democracy? In a world in which there is an increasing abandonment of egalitarian and democratic impulses, what will it take to provide young people and the broader polity with the knowledge and skills necessary to challenge authority and oppressive power relations?

What role might education and critical pedagogy have in a society in which the social has been individualized, emotional life collapses into the therapeutic, and education is reduced to either a private affair or a kind of algorithmic mode of regulation in which everything is reduced to a desired outcome? What role can education play to challenge the deadly neoliberal claim that all problems are individual, regardless of whether the roots of such problems lie in larger systemic forces? In a culture drowning in an updated love affair with instrumental rationality, it is not surprising that values that are not measurable—compassion, vision, the imagination, trust, solidarity, care for the other, and a passion for justice—wither.

Given the crisis of education, agency, and memory that haunts the current historical conjuncture, progressives need a new language for addressing the changing contexts and issues facing a world in which there is an unprecedented convergence of resources—financial, cultural, political, economic, scientific, military, and technological—increasingly used to exercise powerful and diverse forms of control and domination. Such a language needs to be political without being dogmatic and needs to recognize that pedagogy is always political because it is connected to the acquisition of agency. In this instance, making the pedagogical political means being vigilant about "that very moment in which identities are being produced and groups are being constituted, or objects are being created."[14] At the same time it means progressives need to be attentive to those practices in which critical modes of agency and particular identities are being denied. It also means developing a comprehensive understanding of politics, one that should begin with the call to reroute single-issue politics into a mass social movement under the banner of a defense of the public good, the commons, and a global democracy.

In part, this suggests developing pedagogical practices that not only inspire and energize people but are also capable of challenging the growing number of anti-democratic practices and policies under the global tyranny of casino capitalism. Such a vision suggests resurrecting a radical democratic project that provides the basis for imagining a life beyond a social order immersed in massive inequality, and endless assaults on the environment, and elevates war and militarization to the highest and most sanctified national ideals. One consequence is that education is reduced to an obsession with accountability schemes, an audit culture, market values, and an unreflective immersion in the crude empiricism of a data-obsessed market-driven society. In addition, it rejects the notion that all levels of schooling can be reduced to sites for training students for the workforce and that the culture of public and higher education is synonymous with the culture of business.

Any viable notion of radical politics must recognize that education is not a subset of politics but is central to its meaning, social relations, and effects. Not only is education a site of struggle in schools but also in the wider culture. Both sites are crucial to creating the public spaces necessary to both challenge the various threats being mobilized against the ideas of justice and democracy and create critical agents who can fight for those institutions, ideals, values, and policies that offer alternative modes of identity, thinking, social relations, and politics. This suggests forms of critical education that not only inform individuals about history, the legacy of great ideas, and intellectual treasures, but also inspire and energize them to connect what they learn to the obligations of being a critical citizen, one that is both ethically responsible and civically engaged. As a mode of politics, education takes place in multiple cultural landscapes and apparatuses that extend from schools and video games to the mainstream media and Hollywood films, all of which are teaching machines and not simply sources of information and entertainment. Any struggle for a radical democracy has to address the challenge of removing such pedagogical sites from the control of the financial elite and corporations who use them as propaganda and disimagination machines.

What might it mean to theorize pedagogy as a basic element of politics? Progressives might begin by recognizing that central to any viable notion of what makes pedagogy critical is, in part, the recognition that it is a moral and political practice that is always implicated in power relations because it narrates particular versions and visions of agency, civic life, community, the future, and how we might construct representations of ourselves, others, and our physical and social environment. It is in this respect that any discussion of pedagogy must be attentive to how pedagogical practices work in a variety of sites to produce particular structures in which identity, place, worth, and above all value are organized in the service of the practice of freedom and justice.[15] As a practice of freedom, pedagogy emphasizes critical reflection, bridging the gap between learning and everyday life, understanding the connection between power and difficult knowledge, and extending democratic rights and identities by using the resources of history and theory. At the core of analyzing and engaging culture as a pedagogical practice is the question of addressing what it means to engage common sense as a way to shape and influence popular opinion, and how diverse educational practices in multiple sites can be used to challenge the vocabularies, practices, and values of the oppressive forces at work under anti-democratic regimes of power.

There is an urgent political need for the American public to understand what it means for an authoritarian society to both weaponize and trivialize the discourse, vocabularies, images, and diverse means of communication in a society. How is language used to relegate citizenship to the singular pursuit of craven self-interests, legitimate shopping as the ultimate expression of one's identity, portray essential public services as reinforcing and weakening any viable sense of individual responsibility, and, among other instances, using the language of war and militarization to describe a vast array of problems we face as a nation? War has become an addiction, the war on terror a Pavlovian stimulant for control, and shared fears one of the few discourses available for defining any vestige of solidarity.

Falsehoods, lies, misrepresentations, and willful fabrications are now part of the reigning neoliberal ideology proving once again that pedagogy is central to politics itself because it is about changing the way people see things, recognizing that politics is educative and that domination resides not simply in repressive economic structures but also in the realm of ideas, beliefs, and modes of persuasion. Just as I would argue that pedagogy has to be able to speak to people in a way that is meaningful, offering them an opportunity to see a relationship between knowledge and their everyday lives, I think it is fair to argue that there is no politics without a pedagogy of identification; that is, people have to invest something of themselves in how they are addressed or recognize that any mode of education, argument, idea, or pedagogy has to speak to their condition and provide a moment of recognition.

Lacking this understanding, pedagogy all too easily becomes a form of symbolic and intellectual violence, one that assaults rather than educates. Another example of such violence can be seen in the forms of high-stakes testing and empirically driven teaching that dominate public schooling in the United States, which amounts to pedagogies of repression which serve primarily to numb the mind and produce what might be called dead zones of the imagination. These are pedagogies that are largely disciplinary and have little regard for contexts, history, making knowledge meaningful, or expanding what it means for students to be critically engaged agents. Of course, the ongoing corporatization of the university is driven by an audit culture and modes of assessment that undercut faculty autonomy, treat knowledge as a commodity, students as customers, and impose brutalizing structures of governance on higher education. One consequence is that pedagogy becomes a tool of control, stripping away any notion of friction, critique, and the power of the imagination from teaching, in an age in which politics dissolves into the therapeutic language of safe spaces, trauma, and comfort zones. Robert Guadino, a former professor at Williams College, got it right in arguing for forms of pedagogy that spoke to modes of learning that were "uncomfortable," while encouraging his students to engage learning as part of a process that had the "creative potential to unsettle and disturb."[16] Unsettling common sense as well as any idea, world view, and ideology that is taken for granted or appears to exist beyond critical inquiry should be central to any critical pedagogical practice.

The fundamental challenge facing educators within the current age of neoliberalism, militarism, and religious fundamentalism is to provide the conditions for students to address how knowledge is related to the power of both self-definition and social agency. In part, this suggests providing students with the skills, ideas, values, and authority necessary for them to nourish a substantive democracy, recognize anti-democratic forms of power, and to fight deeply rooted injustices in a society and world founded on systemic economic, racial, and gendered inequalities. As Hannah Arendt once argued in "The Crisis of Education," the centrality of education to politics is also manifest in the responsibility for the world that cultural workers have to assume when they engage in pedagogical practices to challenge forms of domination.

Such a project suggests developing a transformative pedagogy—rooted in what might be called a project of resurgent and insurrectional democracy—that relentlessly questions the kinds of labor, practices, and forms of production that are enacted in schools and other sites of education. The project in this sense speaks to the recognition that any pedagogical practice presupposes some notion of the future, prioritizes some forms of identification over others, upholds selective modes of social relations, and values some modes of knowing over others (think about how business schools are held in high esteem while schools of education are disdained and even the object in some cases of contempt). Moreover, such a pedagogy does not offer guarantees as much as it recognizes that its own position is grounded in particular modes of authority, values, and ethical principles that must be constantly debated for the ways in which they both open up and close down democratic relations, values, and identities. These are precisely the questions being asked by the Chicago Teachers' Union in their brave fight to regain some control over both the conditions of their work and their efforts to redefine the meaning of schooling as a democratic public sphere and learning in the interest of economic justice and progressive social change.

Such a project should be principled, relational, contextual, as well as self-reflective and theoretically rigorous. By relational, I mean that the

current crisis of schooling must be understood in relation to the comprehensive assault that is being waged against all aspects of democratic
public life. At the same time, any critical comprehension of those wider
forces that shape public and higher education must also be supplemented
by an attentiveness to the historical and conditional nature of pedagogy
itself. This suggests that pedagogy can never be treated as a fixed set of
principles and practices that can be applied indiscriminately across a
variety of pedagogical sites. Pedagogy is not some recipe or method-
ological fix that can be imposed on all classrooms. On the contrary, it
must always be contextually defined, allowing it to respond specifically
to the conditions, formations, and problems that arise in various sites
in which education takes place. Such a project suggests recasting
pedagogy as a practice that is indeterminate, open to constant revision,
and constantly in dialogue with its own assumptions.

The notion of a neutral, objective education is an oxymoron.
Education and pedagogy do not exist outside of relations of power,
values, and politics. Ethics on the pedagogical front demands an
openness to the other, a willingness to continually engage in a "politics
of possibility" through a continual critical engagement with texts, images,
events, and other registers of meaning as they are transformed into
pedagogical practices both within and outside of the classroom.
Pedagogy is never innocent and if it is to be understood and problem-
atized as a form of academic labor, cultural workers must have the
opportunity not only to critically question and register their own
subjective involvement in how and what they teach in and out of schools,
but also to resist all calls to depoliticize pedagogy through appeals to
either scientific objectivity or ideological dogmatism. This suggests the
need for educators to rethink the cultural and ideological baggage they
bring to each educational encounter; it also highlights the necessity of
making educators ethically and politically accountable and self-reflective
for the stories they produce, the claims they make upon public memory,
and the images of the future they deem legitimate. Understood as a form
of militant hope, pedagogy in this sense is not an antidote to politics,
a nostalgic yearning for a better time, or for some "inconceivably
alternative future." Instead, it is an "attempt to find a bridge between

the present and future in those forces within the present which are potentially able to transform it."[17]

At the dawn of the 21st century, the notions of the social and the public are not being erased as much as they are being reconstructed under circumstances in which public forums for serious debate, including public education, are being eroded. Reduced either to a crude instrumentalism, business culture, or defined as a purely private right rather than a public good, our major educational apparatuses are removed from the discourse of democracy and civic culture. Under the influence of powerful financial interests, we have witnessed the takeover of public and increasingly higher education and diverse media sites by a corporate logic that numbs both the mind and the soul, emphasizing repressive modes of ideology that promote winning at all costs, learning how not to question authority, and undermining the hard work of learning how to be thoughtful, critical, and attentive to the power relations that shape everyday life and the larger world. As learning is privatized, depoliticized, and reduced to teaching students how to be good consumers, any viable notions of the social, public values, citizenship, and democracy wither and die.

As a central element of an expansive cultural politics, critical pedagogy, in its various forms, when linked to the ongoing project of democratization can provide opportunities for educators and other cultural workers to redefine and transform the connections among language, desire, meaning, everyday life, and material relations of power as part of an expansive political movement to reclaim the promise and possibilities of a democratic public life. Critical pedagogy is dangerous to many people because it provides the conditions for students and the wider public to exercise their intellectual capacities, embrace the ethical imagination, question authority, and adopt a sense of social responsibility.

One of the most serious challenges facing teachers, artists, journalists, writers, and other cultural workers is the task of developing a discourse of both critique and possibility. This means developing discourses and pedagogical practices that connect reading the word with reading the world, and doing so in ways that enhance the capacities of young people as critical agents and engaged citizens. In taking up this project, educators and others should attempt to create the conditions that give students the opportunity to become critical and engaged citizens who have the knowledge, skils, and courage to participate in collective struggles in order to make desolation and cynicism unconvincing and hope practical. But raising consciousness is not enough. Students need to be stimulated and challenged to address important social issues, learning to translate their individual troubles into public issues, and to engage in forms of resistance that are both local and shared, while connecting such struggles to more global issues.

Democracy begins to fail and political life becomes impoverished in the absence of those vital public spheres such as public and higher education in which civic values, public scholarship, and social engagement allow for a more imaginative grasp of a future that takes seriously the demands of justice, equity, and civic courage. Democracy should be a way of thinking about education, one that thrives on connecting equity to excellence, learning to ethics, and agency to the imperatives of social responsibility and the public good. The question regarding what role education should play in democracy becomes all the more urgent at a time when the dark forces of authoritarianism are on the march in the United States. As public values, trust, solidarities, and modes of education are under siege, the discourses of hate, racism, rabid self-interest, and greed have exercised a poisonous influence in American society, most evident in the discourse of the right-wing extremists that competed with Trump in the Republican presidential primary. Civic illiteracy mistakes opinion for informed arguments, erases collective memory, and becomes complicit with the militarization of both individual and public spaces, and society itself.

In spite of Trump winning the presidency, all across the country there are and will be continued signs of hope. Young people have protested against student debt; environmentalists have aggressively fought corporate interests; the Chicago Teachers Union waged a brave fight against oppressive neoliberal modes of governance; Black youth continue to bravely resist and expose state violence in all of its forms; prison abolitionists have made their voices heard; and once again the threat of a nuclear winter is being widely discussed. In the age of financial and political monsters, neoliberalism has lost its ability to legitimate itself in a warped discourse of freedom, choice, deregulation, and privatization.

The discourse and representations of violence perpetuated in the daily spectacles exhibited by the mainstream media are becoming more visible in the relations of everyday life, making it more difficult for many Americans to believe that they are real and active participants in a democracy. What is truly baffling is that Trump won the presidency, though it was clear to many Americans, including his followers, that violence was woven into his language and used at his rallies to vilify protesters, women, Blacks, Muslims, and illegal immigrants. One can accept certain elements of Trump's policies, but there is no excuse for using that as a way to overlook his offensive racism, misogyny, denial of climate change, and blatant disregard for the constitution. While many bought or ignored his flagrant lies, there are millions of young people and others who exposed his falsehoods and recognized that the economic and political crises ushering in a new version of American authoritarianism are increasingly being matched by a crisis of ideas. If this momentum of growing critique and collective resistance continues, the support we saw for Bernie Sanders among young people will be matched by an increase in the growth of other oppositional groups. Groups organized around single issues such as building an insurgent labor movement, saving the environment, raising the minimum wage, eliminating police violence, reclaiming public education as a public good, and other emerging movements will hopefully come together, refusing to operate within the parameters of established power while working to create an integrated and wide-ranging social formation and political party. In the merging of power and culture, the creation of new public spheres and technologies, and the emergence of Black social movements, there is a hint of a new collective political sensibility emerging, one that offers a new mode of collective resistance and the possibility of taking democracy off life support. This is not a struggle over who will be elected the next president or ruling party of the United States, but a struggle over those who are willing to fight for a radical democracy and those who refuse. We are seeing a great deal of theorizing on this issue from insightful intellectuals such as Michael Lerner, Robin D. G. Kelley, Stanley Aronowitz, Angela Davis, Salvatore Babones, and John Asimakopoulos.[18] Social movements such as Black Lives Matter, Dream Defenders, Black Youth Project 110, and the Justice League NYC, among others, have also made impressive, significant connections between state violence and systemic oppression.[19] The strong winds of resistance are in the air, rattling established interests, forcing liberals to recognize their complicity with the established powers, and giving new life to what it means to fight for a democratic social order in which equity and justice triumph for everyone.

Notes

1   Jeremy Scahill, "Mike Pence Will Be the Most Powerful Christian Supremacist in U.S. History," *Intercept* (November 15, 2016). Online: https://theintercept.com/2016/11/15/mike-pence-will-be-the-most-powerful-christian-supremacist-in-us-history/

2   Nico Lang, "14 Surprising Things Americans Don't Know, According to Poll Numbers," *Thought Catolog* (October 13, 2014). Online: http://thoughtcatalog.com/nico-lang/2013/10/14-surprising-things-americans-dont-know-according-to-poll-numbers/

3   Chris Hedges, "The War on Language," *TruthDig* (September 28, 2009). Online: www.truthdig.com/report/item/20090928_the_war_on_language/

4   George Monbiot, "Neoliberalism: The Ideology at the Root of All Our Problems," *Truthout* (April 19, 2016). Online: www.truth-out.org/opinion/item/35692-neoliberalism-the-ideology-at-the-root-of-all-our-problems

5   Nicole Aschoff, "The Smartphone Society," *Jacobin Magazine*, No. 17 (Spring 2015). Online: www.jacobinmag.com/2015/03/smartphone-usage-technology-aschoff/

6   Tom Engelhardt, "Will Trump Make 1984 Look Like a Nursery Tale?" *TomDispatch* (December 22, 2016). Online: www.tomdispatch.com/blog/176225/tomgram%3A_engelhardt%2C_will_trump_make_1984_look_like_a_nursery_tale

7   Cited in Chris Hedges, "Demagogue-in-Chief," *Truth Dig* (December 11, 2016). Online: www.commondreams.org/views/2016/12/12/demagogue-chief

8   Robert Reich, "Donald Trump's 7 Techniques to Control the Media," *Salon* (December 4, 2016). Online: www.salon.com/2016/12/04/robert-reich-donald-trumps-7-techniques-to-control-the-media_partner/

9   Ibid.

10   Hadas Gold, "Donald Trump: We're Going to 'Open Up' Libel Laws," *Politico* (February 26, 2016). Online: www.politico.com/blogs/on-media/2016/02/donald-trump-libel-laws-219866

11   Frances Moore Lappé and Adam Eichen, "Dare for Democracy: Three Essential Steps," *Moyers and Company* (December 13, 2016). Online: http://billmoyers.com/story/dare-democracy-three-essential-steps/

12 Henry A. Giroux, *America at War With Itself* (San Francisco: City Lights Books, 2017), p. xiv.
13 A partial list of excellent sources on neoliberalism includes: Pierre Bourdieu, *Acts of Resistance: Against the Tyranny of the Market* (New York: New Press, 1998); Pierre Bourdieu, "The Essence of Neoliberalism," *Le Monde Diplomatique* (December 1998). Online: www.en.monde-diplomatique.fr/1998/12/08bourdieu; Zygmunt Bauman, *Work, Consumerism and the New Poor* (London: Polity, 1998); Noam Chomsky, *Profit over People: Neoliberalism and the Global Order* (New York: Seven Stories, 1999); Jean Comaroff and John L. Comaroff, *Millennial Capitalism and the Culture of Neoliberalism* (Durham, NC: Duke University Press, 2000); Anatole Anton, Milton Fisk, and Nancy Holmstrom, eds, *Not for Sale: In Defense of Public Goods* (Boulder, CO: Westview Press, 2000); Alain Touraine, *Beyond Neoliberalism* (London: Polity, 2001); Colin Leys, *Market Driven Politics* (London: Verso, 2001); Randy Martin, *Financialization of Daily Life* (Philadelphia: Temple University Press, 2002); Ulrich Beck, *Individualization* (London: Sage, 2002); Doug Henwood, *After the New Economy* (New York: New Press, 2003); Pierre Bourdieu, *Firing Back: Against the Tyranny of the Market 2*, trans. Loic Wacquant (New York: New Press, 2003); David Harvey, *The New Imperialism* (New York: Oxford University Press, 2003); David Harvey, *A Brief History of Neoliberalism* (New York: Oxford University Press, 2005); Henry A. Giroux, *Against the Terror of Neoliberalism* (Boulder, CO: Paradigm, 2008); Jodi Dean, *Democracy and Other Neoliberal Fantasies* (Durham, NC: Duke University Press, 2009); and Juliet B. Schor, *Plenitude: The New Economics of True Wealth* (New York: Penguin, 2010); Jeffrey R. Di Leo and Uppinder Mehan, eds, *Capital at the Brink: Overcoming the Destructive Legacies of Neoliberalism* (London: Open Humanities Press, 2014); Wendy Brown, *Undoing the Demos: Neoliberalism's Stealth Revolution* (New York: Zone Books, 2015); Sanford F. Schram, *The Return of Ordinary Capitalism: Neoliberalism, Precarity, Occupy* (New York: Oxford, 2015); Mathew Desmond, *Evicted: Poverty and Profit in the American Society* (New York: Crown Publishers, 2016).
14 Gary Olson and Lynn Worsham, "Staging the Politics of Difference: Homi Bhabha's Critical Literacy," *Journal of Advanced Composition* (1999), pp. 3–35.
15 Henry A. Giroux, *Education and the Crisis of Public Values*, 2nd edition (New York: Peter Lang, 2015).
16 I have taken this reference and quote from Roger Berkowitz's introductory talk at Bard College on October 20, 2016. See Robert Berkowitz, "Green Shoots," *Medium.com* (October 23, 2016). Online: https://medium.com/amor-mundi/green-shoots-c181b7e73927#.r9uflfekq
17 Terry Eagleton, *The Idea of Culture* (Malden, MA: Basil Blackwell, 2000), p. 22.
18 Michael Lerner, "Beyond the 2016 Ballot Box: Why We Need a National Organization on the Left—and How to Build It," *Tikkun* (January 26, 2016); Robin D. G. Kelley, "Black Study, Black Struggle," *Boston Review* (March 7, 2016). Online: https://bostonreview.net/forum/robin-d-g-kelley-black-study-black-struggle; Angela Davis, *Freedom Is a Constant Struggle* (Chicago: Haymarket, 2016); Stanley Aronowitz, "What Kind of Left Does America Need?" *Tikkun* (April 14, 2014). Online: www.tikkun.org/nextgen/what-kind-of-left-does-america-need; Salvatore Babones, *Sixteen for '16: A Progressive Agenda for a Better America* (Chicago: Policy Press, 2015); John Asimakopoulos, *Social Structures of Direct Democracy: On the Political Economy of Equality* (New York: Studies in Critical Science, 2016).
19 Richard W. Behan, "Black Lives Don't Matter, Black Votes Do: The Racial Hypocrisy of Hillary," *CounterPunch* (April 15, 2016). Online: www.counterpunch.org/2016/04/15/black-lives-dont-matter-black-votes-do-the-racial-hypocrisy-of-hillary-and-bill-

clinton/; Alicia Garza, "A Herstory of the #BlackLivesMatter Movement," *Feminist Wire* (October 7, 2014). Online: www.thefeministwire.com/2014/10/blacklivesmatter-2/; Keeanga-Yamahtta Taylor, "The Rise of the #BlackLivesMatter Movement," *Socialist Worker.org* (January 13, 2015). Online: http://socialistworker.org/2015/01/13/the-rise-of-blacklivesmatter; Elizabeth Day, "#BlackLivesMatter: The Birth of a New Civil Rights Movement," *Guardian* (July 19, 2015). Online: www.theguardian.com/world/2015/jul/19/blacklivesmatter-birth-civil-rights-movement

PART II

YOUTH, CRISIS, AND THE POLITICS OF DOMESTIC TERRORISM

4

TERRORIZING SCHOOL CHILDREN IN THE AMERICAN POLICE STATE

> Life of the younger generation is lived nowadays in the state of perpetual emergency.
>
> (Zygmunt Bauman)

Introduction: The Plague of Racist Violence

The problem of violence has become the problem of the 21st century. This claim is indebted to W. E. B. Du Bois' much quoted notion that "the problem of the Twentieth Century is the problem of color line."[1] For Du Bois, racism was one of the most pressing problems of the time and could not be understood outside of the gross inequities of wealth, power, opportunity, and access. What he did not anticipate was the degree to which the violent character of racism would come to define the 21st century on a national and global level. What he described as a ruthless ideology and attitude of racist hostility would later mutate in the new millennium into a raw display of police brutality and state terrorism, camouflaged under the guise of an alleged post-racial society.[2]

As brutalism comes to shape every public encounter, democratic values and the ethical imagination wither under the weight of neoliberal capitalism and post-racial racism. Giving way to the poisonous logics of self-interest, privatization, and the unfettered drive for wealth, American society reneges on the social contract and assumes the role of a punishing state, especially for minorities of color and class.[3] Under the regime of a predatory neoliberalism, compassion and respect for the other are viewed increasingly with contempt while the spectacle of violence titillates the multitudes and moves markets. As public space is privatized and a culture of immediacy and sensationalism becomes a major force in structuring social relations, there is not only a retreat from civic literacy but an abandonment of any allegiance to the common good. A free-market mentality now drives and corrupts politics, destroys social protections, celebrates a hyper-competitiveness, and deregulates economic activity. All human activities, practices, and institutions are now subject to market principles and the only relations that matter are defined in commercial terms. Public goods such as toll roads, libraries, and schools are privatized as the very idea of the common good becomes an object of disdain.[4] As Wendy Brown observes,

> Far more than a challenge to government spending and regulation, then, neoliberal rationality challenges the very idea of a public good—from libraries to pensions, preserved wilderness to public pools, clean transportation to a healthy educated public. Neoliberal rationality also displaces democracy and equality as governing principles in provisioning goods like education; instead of advancing these principles, education becomes an individual means to an individual end, something individuals may or may not choose to invest in.[5]

Consequently, under such circumstances equality, justice, and fairness as governing principles begin to disappear from the discourse of politics. Civic culture has been eroded and public service is viewed with disdain. As civic culture is replaced by a culture of greed and selfishness, shared citizenship gives way to shared fears. As politics is emptied of any sense of social responsibility, the apostles of casino capitalism preach that allegedly amoral economic activity exacts no social costs, and in doing so they accelerate the expanding wasteland of disposable goods and people.[6] One consequence is a vast and growing landscape of human suffering, amplified by a mass-mediated metaphysics of retribution and violence that creeps into every commanding institution of American society, now serving myriad functions such as sport, spectacle, entertainment, and punishment.

The neoliberal machinery of dispossession, accumulation, and social death more and more extends its reach across American society, dissolving the bonds of sociality and undermining social obligations. One outcome is the proliferation of neglect, exploitation, and suffering among diverse populations including poor and uneducated middle-aged whites, who are dying prematurely and unnecessarily in an epidemic of substance abuse, suicide, and poor health.[7] Neoliberalism's unbridled social Darwinism, elimination of social provisions, and culture of cruelty force people out of Medicaid, push millions into poverty, and eliminate social protections.[8] Alain Badiou rightly calls those who run our current political system a "regime of gangsters."[9] These so-called gangsters produce a unique form of social violence. According to Badiou, they:

> Privatize everything. Abolish help for the weak, the solitary, the sick and the unemployed. Abolish all aid for everyone except the banks. Don't look after the poor; let the elderly die. Reduce the wages of the poor, but reduce the taxes on the rich. Make everyone work until they are ninety. Only teach mathematics to traders, reading to big property-owners and history to on-duty ideologues. And the execution of these commands will in fact ruin the lives of millions of people.[10]

Increasingly, our major economic, cultural, and social institutions as well as schools, prisons, and detention centers are being organized around the production of violence. Rather than promote democratic values and a respect for others, they often function largely to humiliate, punish, and demonize certain populations while undermining any vestige of social responsibility. Violence permeates and drives foreign policy, dominates popular culture, and more and more is used to criminalize a wide range of social behaviors, especially among African Americans.[11] In part, the totality of violence in American society can be understood in terms of its doubling function. At one level, violence produces its own legitimating aesthetic as part of a wider spectacle of entertainment, offering consumers the pleasure of instant gratification, particularly in the visibility and celebration of extreme violence. This is evident in television series such as *Game of Thrones*, *Hannibal*, and *The Walking Dead* and also in endless Hollywood films such as *Mad Max: Fury Road* (2015), *Neon Demon* (2016), *Jason Bourne* (2016), and *John Wick: Chapter Two* (2017) and video games such as *Grand Theft Auto 4* (2008), *Mortal Combat* (2011), *Battlefield Hardline* (2015), and *Dark Souls III* (2016).

On another level, violence functions as a brutalizing practice used by the state to squelch dissent, incarcerate poor people and people of color, terrorize immigrants, wage a war on minority youth, and menace individuals and groups considered disposable or a threat. Not only does such violence destroy the conditions and institutions necessary to develop a democratic polity, it also accelerates abusive forms of punitiveness and control that extend from the prisons to other institutions such as schools. In this instance, violence becomes the ultimate force propagating what might be called punishment creep—the increasing criminalization of everyday behaviors coupled with increased harassment of vulnerable individuals. Punishment creep has moved from prisons to other public spheres and has a firm grip on both schools and the daily rituals of everyday life. Margaret Kimberly captures one instance of the racist underside of punishment creep when she writes:

> Black people are punished for driving, for walking down the street, for having children, for putting their children in school, for acting the way children act, and even for having children who are killed by other people. We are punished, in short, because we still exist.[12]

Violence in America has always been defined partly by a poisonous mix of chauvinism, exceptionalism, and terrorism that runs through a history marked by genocidal assaults against Native Americans, the brutality of slavery, and a persistent racism that extends from the horror of lynchings and chain gangs to the current practice of mass incarceration, which subjects many Black youth to the shameful dynamics of the school-to-prison-pipeline and unprecedented levels of police abuse.[13] Violence is the premier signature of what Ta-Nehisi Coates calls "The Dreamers," those individuals and groups who have

> signed on, either actively or passively, to complicity in everything from police shootings to real estate redline, which crowds blacks into substandard housing in dangerous neighborhoods ... The Dream is about the totality of white supremacy in American history and its cumulative weight on African-Americans, and how one attempts to live with that.[14]

In part, violence whether produced by the state, corporations, or racist individuals is difficult to abstract from an expression of white supremacy, which functions as an index for demanding "the full privileges of the state."[15]

Police violence against Black people has become highly visible and thrust into the national spotlight as a result of individuals recording acts of police abuse with their cell phones and other new technologies.[16] In the last few years, there has been what seems like a torrent of video footage showing unarmed Black people being assaulted by the police. For instance, there is the shocking video of Eric Garner dying as a result of being put in a choke hold by a white policeman who accused him of illegally selling cigarettes; the tragic killing of Freddie Gray who after making eye contact with a police officer was put in a police van and purposely given a jarring ride that resulted in his death; and the horrific shootings of 12-year-old Tamir Rice for playing with a pellet gun in the snow in a park and a 13-year-old boy, Tyre King, after he brandished what was later determined to be a BB gun. King was shot multiple times and then was smeared in the mainstream press as a petty thief, as if petty thievery or for that matter walking and driving while Black warrant a death sentence. All of these deaths are morally indefensible and are symptomatic of the deep-seated racism and propensity for violence in many police forces in the United States.

Yet, as Jaeah Lee observes, while such crimes have attracted national attention, the

> use of force by cops in schools . . . has drawn far less attention [in spite of the fact that] over the past five years at least 28 students have been seriously injured, and in one case shot to death, by so-called school resource officers—sworn, uniformed police assigned to provide security on k-12 campuses.[17]

Increasingly as public schools hand over even routine disciplinary problems to the police, there is a proliferation of cops in schools. There are over 17,000 school resource officers in more than half of the schools in the United States.[18] In spite of the fact that violence in schools has dropped precipitously, school resource officers are the fastest growing segment of law enforcement.

The Militarization of Schools

In part, the militarizing of schools and the accompanying surge of police officers are driven by the fear of school shootings, particularly in the aftermath of the Columbine High School tragedy in 1999 and the massacre that took place at Sandy Hook Elementary School in 2013, both of which have been accentuated by the ever present wave of paranoia that followed the terrorist attacks of 9/11.[19] What advocates of putting police in the schools refuse to acknowledge is that the presence of the police in schools has done nothing to stop such mass shootings. While the fear of school shootings is overestimated, the fact remains that schools are still one of the safest places for children to be. Caught under the weight of a culture of fear and a rush to violence, many young people in schools are the most recent victims of a punishing state in a society that "remains in a state of permanent, endless war," a war that is waged through militarized policies at home and abroad.[20] Following Stanley Aronowitz, I think it is fair to argue that with "the breakdown of the mission of public schools . . . today's authorities no longer offer hope" to this generation of young people. One consequence is that "under the doctrine of control they threaten punishment, which includes, although it is not necessarily associated with, incarceration."[21] Violence against young people in schools is a troubling index of the loss of faith in young people and the transformation of school from a source of social and economic mobility to despotic testing institutions for most youth, and repressive holding centers, primarily for youth of color.[22]

What has become clear is that cops in schools have not made schools safer. Erik Eckholm, reporting for the *New York Times*, stated that judges, youth advocates, parents, and other concerned citizens "are raising alarm about what they have seen in the schools where officers are already stationed: a surge in criminal charges against children for misbehavior that many believe is better handled" by teachers and school administrators.[23] In Texas, police officers have written "more than 100,000 misdemeanor tickets each year" and many of these students "face hundreds of dollars in fines, community service, and in some cases, a lasting record that could affect applications for jobs or the military."[24] The transformation of disciplinary problems into criminal violations has often resulted in absurd if not tragic results. For instance, in 2009, in Richardson, Texas "a 14-year-old boy with Asperger's syndrome was given a $364 police citation for using an expletive in his classroom."[25] It gets even more ludicrous. "A 12-year-old student in Stuart, Florida, was arrested in November 2008 for 'disrupting a school function.' The 'disruption' was that the student had 'passed gas.'"[26]

Similarly, a number of civil rights groups have reported that the presence of police in schools often "means more suspensions, which disproportionately affect minority students," according to an article in *USA Today*.[27] As reported in the *New York Times*, "police-driven policies have not made schools more secure. But they do make children more likely to drop out and become entangled with the justice system. And they disproportionately affect minority and disabled children, who are more likely to be singled out for the harshest forms of discipline."[28] In one instance, an 8 year old and 9 year old in a public school in Kenton County, Kentucky, both with severe disabilities that made it difficult for them to follow classroom instructions, were handcuffed by a deputy sheriff for misbehaving. One child was writhing and crying in pain because of the handcuffs placed around his biceps since his wrists were too small.[29] Such acts are more than shameful, they also are symptomatic of a society that is waging war on many of its children.

What must be recognized is that schools in general have become combat zones where it is routine for many students to be subjected to metal detectors, surveillance cameras, uniformed security guards, weapons searches, and in some cases SWAT team raids and police dogs sniffing for drugs.[30] As such, the purpose of schooling appears to be to contain and punish young people, especially those marginalized by race, class, and disabilities rather than educate them. What is beyond doubt is that "Arrests and police interactions . . . disproportionately affect low-income schools with large African-American and Latino populations."[31] For the many disadvantaged students being funneled into the "school-to-prison pipeline," schools ensure that their futures look grim indeed, as their educational experiences acclimatize them to forms of carceral treatment.[32] There is more at work here than a flight from responsibility on the part of educators, parents, and politicians who support and maintain policies that fuel this expanding edifice of law enforcement against the young and disenfranchised. Underlying the repeated decisions to turn away from helping young people is the growing sentiment that youth, particularly youth of color, constitute a threat to adults and the only effective way to deal with them is to subject them to mind-crushing punishment. Students being miseducated, criminalized, and arrested through a form of penal pedagogy in prison-type schools provides a grave reminder of the degree to which the ethos of containment and punishment now creeps into spheres of everyday life that were largely immune in the past from this type of state and institutional violence. How else to explain as Judith Browne Dianis observes that:

> Across the country, young people are being arrested for behavior that used to be solved through a trip to the principal's office or the intervention of a counselor. In Florida, a 14-year-old was arrested and charged for throwing a pencil at another student and spent

21 days in jail. In New York, a 12-year-old was arrested for doodling, "I love Abby and Faith" on her desk. In Chicago, 25 children, some as young as 11, were arrested for engaging in a food fight.[33]

Schools are no longer reliable spaces of joy, critical teaching, and support as too many are now institutions of containment and control that produce pedagogies of conformity and oppression and kill the imagination by teaching to the test. Within such schools, the lesson that young people are learning about themselves is that they can't engage in critical thinking, be trusted, rely on the informed judgments of teachers and administrators, and that their behavior is constantly subject to procedures that amount to both an assault on their dignity and a violation of their civil liberties. Schools have become institutions in which creativity is viewed as a threat, harsh discipline a virtue, and punishment the reward for not conforming to what amounts to the dictates of a police state. How many more images of young school children in handcuffs do we have to witness before it becomes clear that the educational system is broken, reduced largely to a punishing factory defined by a culture of fear and an utter distrust of young people?

I don't believe it is improbable to insist that under the Trump administration public schools will be increasingly defunded given this administration's support for charter schools and the appointment of billionaire activist and Republican fundraiser Betsy DeVos to head the Department of Education. DeVos is a strong advocate of private, charter, and religious schools and will do everything possible to defund and privatize public education, destroy teacher unions, and transform public education into training centers for a corporate labor force. As *Mother Jones* reported,

> Education historian Diane Ravitch believes that—if confirmed by the Senate—DeVos will become the most radical, anti-public-school education secretary since the Office of Education was established in 1867. "Never has anyone been appointed to lead in the past 150 years who was [more] hostile to public education."[34]

As the public schools are drained of resources, poor Black and Brown children will suffer the most. Moreover, this upcoming massive attack on public education will result in the further militarization of public schools given Trump's belief that most Blacks live in a culture of violence and his notion that Black people are lazy. This is a president who has been antagonistic toward the Black Lives Matter movement while siding up to white nationalists and remaining silent in the face of the blatant racism exhibited by some of his supporters.[35]

The School-to-Prison Pipeline

According to the *Advancement Project*, schools have become increasingly intolerant of young people, imposing draconian zero tolerance policies on them by furthering a culture steeped in criminalizing often minor, if not trivial, student behaviors.[36] What is truly alarming is not only the ways in which young people are being ushered into the criminal justice system and treated less as students than as criminals, but the harsh violence to which they are often subjected by school resource officers. In a report published in *Mother Jones*, Jonathan Hardin, a Louisville Metro Police officer, in 2014

> was fired after his alleged use of force in two incidents at Olmsted Academy North Middle School: He was accused of punching a 13-year-old student in the face for cutting the cafeteria line, and a week later of putting another 13-year-old student in a chokehold, allegedly knocking the student unconscious and causing a brain injury.[37]

In the second incident that year,

> Cesar Suquet, then a 16-year-old high school student in Houston, was being escorted by an officer out of the principal's office after a discussion about Suquet's confiscated cell phone. Following a verbal exchange, police officer Michael Y'Barbo struck Suquet at least 18 times with a police baton, injuring him on his head, neck and elsewhere.[38]

Y'Barbo claimed that beating a student with a police baton was "reasonable and necessary" and "remains on regular assignment including patrol."[39] There have also been incidents where students have been shot, suffered brain injuries, or have been psychologically traumatized. Jaeah Lee cites a young Black high school student in Detroit who after a troubling interaction with a school police officer speaks for many young people about the dread and anxiety that many students experience when police occupy their schools. He states that "Many young people today have fear of the police in their communities and schools."[40]

If one important measure of a democracy is how a society treats its children, especially young children who are Black, Brown, or suffer from disabilities, there can be little doubt that American society is failing. As the United States increasingly models its schools after prisons, students are no longer viewed as a social investment in the future. A deadly mixture of racism and violence in the 21st century has become increasingly evident in the attacks being waged against young people in American schools. If students in general are now viewed as a potential threat, Black students are regarded increasingly as criminals. One result is that schools increasingly have come to resemble war zones; spaces marked by distrust, fear, and demonization. With more police in the schools than ever before, security has become more important than providing children with a critical education and supportive learning environment. As authority in many of the schools is often handed over to the police and security forces who are now asked to deal with all alleged disciplinary problems, however broadly defined, the power and autonomy of teachers and school administrators are weakened at the expense of the safety of the students. This loss of authority is clear in New York City where school administrators have no control over security forces who report directly to local police departments.

This is worth repeating. In most cases, the disciplinary problems that take place in schools involve trivial infractions such as scribbling on a desk or holding a 2-inch toy gun. The assault on children in the public schools suggests that children of color cannot view schools as supportive spaces where they can be given a quality education. Instead, schools have become sites of control, testing, and punishment all too eager to produce pedagogies of repression, and more than willing to erect, once again, what has been called the school-to-prison pipeline, especially for youth of color. Roxane Gay is right in observing that

> Black children are not allowed to be children. They are not allowed to be safe, not at home, not at pool parties, not driving or sitting in cars listening to music, not walking down the street, not in school. For black children, for black people, to exist is to be endangered. Our bodies receive no sanctity or safe harbor.[41]

Police Brutality in the Classroom

It is inconceivable that in an alleged democracy poor youth of color at all grade levels in the public schools are subjected both to pedagogies of repression and to shameful criminal practices such as being hand-cuffed and carted off to jail for minor incidents—and that such draconian practices could take place in a society that views itself as a democracy. In an age in which public schools have become punishing factories all too willing to turn disciplinary authority over to the police, a growing number of schools have abdicated on their authority and have become adjuncts of the criminal justice system. The results have been devastating for youth of color. As the Advancement Project points out:

> Across the United States many public schools have turned into feeder schools for the juvenile and criminal justice systems. Youths are finding themselves increasingly at risk of falling into the school-to-prison pipeline through push-outs (systematic exclusion through suspensions, expulsions, discouragement, and high-stakes testing). Yet, an even more direct schoolhouse-to-jailhouse track is trans-ferring a growing number of youths to the penal system. In the name of school safety, schools have implemented unforgiving, overly harsh zero tolerance discipline practices that turn kids into criminals for acts that rarely constitute a crime when committed by an adult. No one is safe from zero tolerance—age, grade, past

behavior, and disabilities are often irrelevant. And, although students of all races and genders are victims of this track, it is especially reserved for children of color—and males in particular. Schools have teamed up with law enforcement to make this happen by imposing a "double dose" of punishment: suspension or expulsion and a trip to the juvenile justice system.[42]

One recent example of a particularly disturbing incident of police brutality was captured in a series of videos recorded at Spring Valley High School in South Carolina. Prior to the incident being filmed, a young Black student named Shakara took out her cell phone in class. The teacher asked her for it, and when she refused to hand it over, she was asked to leave the class. The teacher called the vice principal. Rather than attempt to defuse the situation, the vice principal called for a school resource officer. At this point, Officer Ben Fields enters the classroom. One of Shakara's classmates, Niya Kenny, immediately asked her classmates to begin filming because as she put it "I told them to get the cameras out, because we know his reputation—well, I know his reputation."[43] In what follows, one of the cell phone videos records the following: Officer Ben Fields approaches the young woman, appears to give her no time to stand up and proceeds by grabbing her left arm while placing his right arm around her neck; he then lifts her desk, pulls her out of her seat, slams her to the ground, and drags her across the floor before handcuffing her. The video is difficult to watch given the disproportionate level of violence used against this young Black woman. She was arrested, as was Kenny, who both filmed the incident and loudly protested the treatment of Shakara. Fields was fired soon afterwards, but incredulously both students are being charged with "disturbing schools, a crime punishable by up to ninety days in jail or a thousand dollar fine."[44]

After the incident went viral, information emerged indicating that Fields had a previous reputation for being aggressive with students, and he was viewed as a threat by many students who nicknamed him "Officer Slam." Moreover, he had a previous record of violently assaulting people.[45] The question that should be asked as a result of this shocking act of police violence against a young Black student is not how Fields got a job in a school working with children, but what kind of society believes that police should be in schools in the first place. Whatever happened to teacher and administrator responsibility? Sadly, it was a school administrator who called in the police at Spring Valley High School because the student would not turn over her phone. Even worse, when Sheriff Leon Lott announced his decision to fire Fields, he pointed out that the classroom teacher and administrator supported the actions of the police officer and made it clear that "they also had no problems with the physical part."[46] Both the teacher and administrator should be fired as well. This incident was in all probability a simple disciplinary problem that should have been handled by responsible educators. Students should not be treated like criminals. It is one thing not to assume responsibility for students, but another to subject them to brutal assaults by the police.

Violent lawlessness runs deep in American society and has been normalized. Brutal attacks on defenseless children rarely get the attention they deserve and, when they do, the corporate media refuse to acknowledge that America has become a suicidal society willing even to sacrifice its own children to an expanding punishing state that protects the interests of the corporate and financial elite.[47] How else to explain the shameless defense of such a brutal assault against a young Black girl by pundits such as CNN's Harry Houck and Don Lemon, who implied that such violence was warranted because Shakara did not respect the officer, as if the beating of a Black child by a police officer, who happens also to be a body-builder who can lift 300 pounds, justifies such actions. This is a familiar script in which Black people are often told that whatever violence they were subject to was legitimate because they acted out of place, did not follow rules that in reality oppress them, or simply refused to fall in line.

Grassroots Resistance

The other side of this racist script finds expression in those who argue that any critique of the police endangers public safety. In this dangerous discourse, the police are the victims, a line of argument recently voiced in different ways both by former President Obama and by James Comey, former Director of the Federal Bureau of Investigation. The most vociferous and strident voices opposing any critique of police violence come from police unions. As William Boardman observes,

> Two of the biggest police unions in the country are now on record in opposition to free speech. They are on record against constitutionally protected free speech that opposes the epidemic of police violence across America (more than 900 killed by police so far in 2015).[48]

This was particularly evident when Quentin Tarantino gave a talk criticizing police violence in New York as part of Rise Up October, three days of protest against police terror. While addressing a number of families whose members were victims of police brutality, Tarantino stated that: "I'm here to say I'm on the side of the murdered."[49]

The backlash from major police unions was quick and severe, as the unions began calling for a nationwide boycott of his films. This repressive discourse not only refuses to recognize the growing visibility of police violence, it also shores up one of the foundations of the authoritarian state, suggesting that the violence propagated by the police should not be subject to public scrutiny. As an editorial in the *New York Times* pointed out, this

> formulation implies that for the police to do their jobs, they need to have free rein to be abusive. It also implies that the public would be safer if Americans with cellphones never started circulating videos of officers battering suspects in the first place . . . This trend is straight out of Orwell.[50]

Of course, not everybody is "on the side of the murdered," as Tarantino put it. For example, the right-wing Media Research Council in August 2016 hosted a black tie event honoring three of the cops who were responsible for taking Freddie Gray on a torture ride. Syndicated columnist and pundit Cal Thomas, who was attending the event, went so far as to state "Boy, things have changed. When I was a kid growing up in this town you were taught the police officer was your friend. My, my, now they're your enemies. Not for me, though. They're still my heroes."[51] Apparently, when cops kill young people including 12 and 13 year olds such murderous acts are viewed by some conservatives as acts of heroism. The cops-as-victims narrative only goes so far and becomes shameless when used as a blanket statement to justify even the most obvious illegal and immoral acts of police violence. Such apologies represent more than a police culture and public in flight from the ugly truths of an ongoing series of murderous assaults on African Americans, they also suggest a broken and racist system of policing in the United States.

Educators, young people, parents, and others concerned about violence in schools need to organize and demand that the police be removed from school environments. Not only is their presence a waste of taxpayers' money and an interference with children's education, they also pose a threat to student safety.[52] Instead of putting police in schools, money should be spent on more guidance counselors, social workers, teachers, community intervention workers, and other professionals who are trained to provide a secure and supportive environment for young people. It is particularly crucial to support those social services, classroom practices, and policies that work to keep students in schools. Everything possible should be done to dismantle the school-to-prison pipeline and the underlying forces that produce it. At the same time, more profound change must take place on a national level since the violence waged by the police is symptomatic of a society now ruled by a financial elite who trade in cruelty, punishment, and despair. American society is broken, and the violence to which it appears addicted will continue until the current configurations of power, politics, inequality, and injustice are eliminated.

With the appointment by Trump of Jeff Sessions as Attorney General, the call for law and order will not only increase the power of institutionalized racism and attacks on people of color, but it will embolden police departments to continue treating poor Black neighborhoods as war zones and Black people, especially youth, as enemy combatants. Mass incarceration will continue to expand and will be viewed as the default welfare institution for dealing with poor Blacks, immigrants, refugees, and others deemed excess and disposable.

The increasing visibility of police brutality in schools and in the streets speaks to a larger issue regarding the wilting of democracy in the United States and the growing mayhem that prevails in a society in which violence is one of the few resources left to address social problems. As the Black Lives Matter movement has made clear, the Spring Valley High School case and others are part of a larger trend that has turned too many schools across the country into detention centers and educators into hapless bystanders as classroom management is ceded to the police. What we see in this incident (and in many others that have escaped national attention because they are not caught on cell phones) are the rudiments of a growing police state. Violence is now a normalized and celebrated ideal for how America defines itself—an ideal that views democracy as an excess or, even worse, a pathology. This is something Americans must acknowledge, interrogate, and resist if they don't want to live under a system of total terror and escalating violence, one that appears more ominous now with the election of Trump to the presidency than in any other time in American history.

Notes

1   W. E. B. Du Bois, *The Souls of Black Folk* (New York: New American Library, 1903), p. 19.

2   For a brilliant book on the alleged post-racial society, see David Theo Goldberg, *Are We All Postracial Yet?* (London: Polity, 2015).

3   I have taken up this theme in *The Violence of Organized Forgetting* (San Francisco: City Lights Books, 2014).

4   Wendy Brown, "Neoliberalized Knowledge," *History of the Present: A Journal of Critical History*, Vol. 1, No. 1 (Summer 2011), pp. 118–19.

5   Ibid., p. 119.

6   Brad Evans and Henry A. Giroux, *Disposable Futures: The Seduction of Violence in the Age of the Spectacle* (San Francisco: City Lights Books, 2015).

7   Gina Kolata, "Death Rates Rising for Middle-Aged White Americans, Study Finds," *New York Times* (November 3, 2015). Online: www.nytimes.com/2015/11/03/health/death-rates-rising-for-middle-aged-white-americans-study-finds.html?_r=0

8   For a brilliant analysis of the merging of neoliberal politics and policies and the liberal press coverage of the rising death rates among poor middle-class whites, see Karen Garcia, "The Culling of the American Herd (Update)," *Sardonicky* (November 3, 2015). Online: http://kmgarcia2000.blogspot.ca/2015/11/the-culling-of-american-herd-update.html

9 Alain Badiou, *The Rebirth of History* (London: Verso, 2012), p. 12.

10 Ibid., 13.

11 Jody Sokolower, "Schools and the New Jim Crow: An Interview with Michelle Alexander," *Truthout* (June 4, 2013). Online: www.truth-out.org/news/item/16756-schools-and-the-new-jim-crow-an-interview-with-michelle-alexander

12 Margaret Kimberly, "Jail for Sending Their Kid to School? How America Treats Black Women and Children Like Criminals," *AlterNet* (May 9, 2012). Online: www.alternet.org/story/155330/jail_for_sending_their_kid_to_school_how_america_treats_black_women_and_children_like_criminals/

13 Henry A. Giroux, *Youth in a Suspect Society* (Boulder, CO: Paradigm, 2008).

14 Mary Ann Gwinn, "Author Ta-Nehisi Coates: 'In This Country, White Is Receiving the Full Privileges of the State,'" *Seattle Times* (October 14, 2015). Online: www.seattletimes.com/entertainment/books/qa-with-ta-nehisi-coates-author-of-between-the-world-and-me/

15 Ibid.

16 Rev. Daniel Buford, "Police Assaults on African American Women: Close Encounters of a Dangerous Kind," *Tikkun* (September 28, 2016). Online: www.tikkun.org/nextgen/police-assaults-on-african-american-women-close-encounters-of-a-dangerous-kind-by-rev-daniel-buford

17 Jaeah Lee, "Chokeholds, Brain Injuries, Beatings: When School Cops Go Bad," *Mother Jones* (July 14, 2015). Online: www.motherjones.com/politics/2015/05/police-school-resource-officers-k-12-misconduct-violence

18 Amy Goodman, "When School Cops Go Bad: South Carolina Incident Highlights Growing Police Presence in Classrooms," *Democracy Now!* (October 27, 2015). Online: www.democracynow.org/2015/10/28/when_school_cops_go_bad_south

19 Jessica Glenza, "'Good Guys' with Guns: How Police Officers Became Fixtures in US Schools," *Guardian* (October 28, 2015). Online: www.theguardian.com/us-news/2015/oct/28/sworn-police-officers-us-schools-guns

20 Glenn Greenwald, "Arrest of 14-Year-Old Student for Making a Clock: The Fruits of Sustained Fearmongering and Anti-Muslim Animus," *Intercept* (September 16, 2015). Online: https://theintercept.com/2015/09/16/arrest-14-year-old-student-making-clock-fruits-15-years-fear-mongering-anti-muslim-animus/

21 Stanley Aronowitz, *Against Schooling: For an Education that Matters* (Boulder, CO: Paradigm, 2008), p. 48.

22 Advancement Project, *Test, Punish, and Push Out: How "Zero Tolerance" and High-Stakes Testing Funnel Youth in the School-to-Prison Pipeline* (Washington, DC: Advancement Project, March 2010). Online: www.advancementproject.org/sites/default/files/publications/rev_fin.pdf

23 Erik Eckholm, "With Police in Schools, More Children in Court," *New York Times* (April 12, 2013). Online: www.nytimes.com/2013/04/12/education/with-police-in-schools-more-children-in-court.html

24 Ibid.

25 Advancement Project, *Test, Punish, and Push Out.*

26 Ibid.

27 Greg Toppo, "Civil Rights Groups: Cops in Schools Don't Make Students Safer," *USA Today* (October 28, 2015). Online: www.usatoday.com/story/news/2015/10/28/school-resource-officer-civil-rights/74751574/

28 Editorial, "Schoolkids in Handcuffs," *New York Times* (November 4, 2015). Online: www.nytimes.com/2015/11/04/opinion/schoolkids-in-handcuffs.html?_r=0

29 Ibid.

30   One truly absurd example of this kind of militarism can be found at John Vibes, "SWAT
      Team Shows Up to Elementary School to Promote Police State USA," *Free Thought
      Project* (March 8, 2015). Online: http://thefreethoughtproject.com/swat-team-shows-
      elementary-school-career-day/#UkM6m4fIOLeZzyJU.99
31   Smartypants, "A Failure of Imagination," *Smartypants Blog Spot* (March 3, 2010).
      Online: http://immasmartypants.blogspot.com/2010/03/failure-of-imagination.html
32   See Mark P. Fancher, *Reclaiming Michigan's Throwaway Kids: Students Trapped in the
      School-to-Prison Pipeline* (New York: ACLU, 2011). Online: www.njjn.org/uploads/
      digital_library/resource_1287.pdf; Advancement Project, *Test, Punish, and Push Out.*
33   Judith Browne Dianis, "Interrupting the School-to-Prison Pipeline," *America's Wire*
      (June 14, 2013). Online: http://americaswire.org/drupal7/?q=content/interrupting-
      school-prison-pipeline-0
34   Kristina Rizga, "Trump's Billionaire Education Secretary Has Been Trying to Gut Public
      Schools for Years," *MotherJones* (November 29, 2016). Online: www.motherjones.com/
      politics/2016/11/education-secretary-betsy-devos-vouchers-michigan-trump
35   Zeba Blay, "12 Reasons Donald Trump Would Not Be Great for 'the Blacks,'"
      Huffington Post (March 11, 2016). Online: www.huffingtonpost.com/entry/8-reasons-
      donald-trump-would-not-be-great-for-the-blacks_us_56e0729fe4b065e2e3d47e82
36   Advancement Project in partnership with Padres and Jovenes Unidos, Southwest Youth
      Collaborative, *Education on Lockdown: The Schoolhouse to Jailhouse Track* (New York:
      Children and Family Justice Center of Northwestern University School of Law, March
      24, 2005), pp. 5–58.
37   Lee, "Chokeholds, Brain Injuries, Beatings."
38   Ibid.
39   Ibid.
40   Ibid.
41   Roxane Gay, "Where Are Black Children Safe?" *New York Times* (October 27, 2015).
      Online: www.nytimes.com/2015/10/30/opinion/where-are-black-children-safe.html
42   Advancement Project in partnership with Padres and Jovenes Unidos, Southwest Youth
      Collaborative, *Education on Lockdown*, p. 11.
43   Cited in Amy Davidson, "What Niya Kenny Saw," *New Yorker* (October 30, 2015).
      Online: www.newyorker.com/news/amy-davidson/what-niya-kenny-saw?mbid=nl_151
      031_Daily&CNDID=14760251&spMailingID=8208167&spUserID=MjY0MzU4ND
      M2ODAS1&spJobID=783800743&spReportId=NzgzODAwNzQzS0
44   Arisha Rashad, Lyla Scott and the rest of the Color of Change Team, "Editorial," *Color
      of Change* (October 27, 2015). Email correspondence.
45   Andrew Emett, "Same Cop Who Attacked School Girl Also Caught Assaulting Army
      Vet in Similar Takedown," *Free Thought Project.com* (October 27, 2015). Online:
      http://thefreethoughtproject.com/cop-slammed-high-school-girl-ground-assaulted-
      army-vet-similar-takedown/; see also Goodman, "When School Cops Go Bad."
46   Davidson, "What Niya Kenny Saw."
47   Sonali Kolhatkar, "Police Are the Greatest Threat Facing Black Kids in Schools,"
      Truth Dig (October 27, 2015). Online: www.truthdig.com/report/item/police_are_the_
      greatest_threat_facing_black_kids_in_school_20151028
48   William Boardman, "Police Unions Sustain Police Violence Epidemic," *Reader Supported
      News* (October 31, 2015). Online: http://readersupportednews.org/opinion2/277-75/
      33238-focus-police-unions-sustain-police-violence-epidemic
49   Nigel M. Smith, "Quentin Tarantino: Film Maverick and Police Critic Delights in
      Controversy," *Guardian* (November 6, 2015). Online: www.theguardian.com/film/2015/
      nov/06/quentin-tarantino-film-maverick-police-critic-delights-in-controversy

50 Editorial, "Political Lies about Police Brutality," *New York Times* (October 27, 2015). Online: www.nytimes.com/2015/10/27/opinion/political-lies-about-police-brutality.html?_r=0

51 Andrew Kirell and Asawin Suebsaeng, "Right-Wing Gala Gave Freddie Gray Cops Standing Ovation," *Daily Beast* (September 26, 2016). Online: www.thedailybeast.com/articles/2016/09/26/right-wing-gala-gave-freddie-gray-cops-standing-ovation.html

52 See, for instance, Amanda Petteruti, "Education under Arrest: The Case against Police in Schools," *Just Policy Institute* (2011). Online: www.justicepolicy.org/uploads/justicepolicy/documents/educationunderarrest_fullreport.pdf

5

DOMESTIC TERRORISM, YOUTH, AND THE POLITICS OF DISPOSABILITY

> The danger is that a global, universally interrelated civilization may produce barbarians from its own midst by forcing millions of people into conditions which, despite all appearances, are the conditions of savages.
>
> (Hannah Arendt)

Following Hanna Arendt, a dark cloud of political and ethical ignorance has descended on the United States.[1] Thoughtlessness has become something that now occupies a privileged, if not celebrated, place in the political landscape and the mainstream cultural apparatuses. A new kind of infantilism now shapes daily life as adults gleefully take on the role of unthinking children and children are taught to be adults, stripped of their innocence and subject to a range of disciplinary pressures designed to cripple their ability to be imaginative.[2] Under such circumstances, agency devolves into a kind of anti-intellectual cretinism evident in the babble of banality produced by Fox News, a militarized culture, schools modeled after prisons, and politicians who support creationism, argue against climate change, and denounce almost any form of reason. The citizen is now urged to become a consumer, the politician's only option is to be reduced to a puppet whose strings are tied to corporate money and power, and the burgeoning army of anti-public intellectuals in the mainstream media mostly present themselves as unapologetic enemies of anything that suggests compassion, a respect for the commons, and democracy itself. Education is no longer viewed as a public good but a private right, just as critical thinking is devalued as a fundamental necessity for creating an engaged and socially responsible citizenship. Neoliberalism's disdain for the social is no longer a quote made famous by Margaret Thatcher. The public sphere is now replaced by private interests and unbridled individualism rails against any viable notion of solidarity that might inform the vibrancy of struggle, change, and an expansion of an enlightened and democratic body politic.

One outcome is that we live at a time in which institutions that were designed to limit human suffering and indignity and protect the public from the boom and bust cycles of capitalist markets have been either undermined or obliterated.[3] Free-market policies, values, and practices with their now unrestrained emphasis on the privatization of public wealth, the denigration of social protections, and the deregulation of economic activity influence practically every commanding political and economic institution in North America. Finance capitalism now drives politics, governance, and policy in unprecedented ways and is more than willing to sacrifice the future of young people for short-term political and economic gain, regardless of talk about the need to not burden future generations with heavy tuition debt and a future of low-wage jobs.

Under market fundamentalism, there is a separation of market values, behavior, and practices from ethical considerations and social costs giving rise to a growing culture of malice, abuse, and corruption. For example, Wells Fargo put a lot of pressure on its employees to open new deposit accounts, even going so far as to give them financial incentives to do so. The result was that 5,300 bank branch employees created millions of dollars "in fake deposit accounts for customers in order to hit sales quotas set by upper management."[4] As a result, the bank was fined $185 million. Far from being an isolated criminal act of robbery, the bank has also been fined $1.2 billion for falsely certifying mortgages, $4 million for student loan abuses, and $70 million for other violations.[5] John Stumpf, the CEO of Wells Fargo, appeared before congressional committees and seemed clueless regarding the criminal actions of the bank, responding to charges of misconduct by stating that he would not resign and wanted to exercise a new level of leadership. While Stumpf was eventually forced to resign, Wells Fargo rewarded his criminal behavior by allowing him "to take about $133.1 million into retirement."[6] Instead of being given a financial payoff by Wells Fargo, Stumpf, like so many other CEOs who are responsible for such criminogenic cultures and practices, should be sent to jail.[7] As Robert Reich observes: "Banksters like Stumpf—who raked in $19 million last year, partly because of all the products and services his employees sold— are no less responsible for the inevitable consequences of the incentive systems they establish. Banksters like Stumpf belong in jail."[8] This stuff is hard to make up.

Public spheres that once encouraged progressive ideas, enlightened social policies, democratic values, critical dialogue, and exchange have been increasingly commercialized. Or, they have been replaced by corporate settings whose ultimate fidelity is to increase profit margins and produce a vast commercial culture "that tends to function so as to erase everything that matters."[9] Since the 1980s, the scale of human suffering, immiseration, and hardship has intensified, accompanied by a theater of cruelty in which violence, especially the daily spectacle of Black men being brutalized or killed by the police, feeds the 24-hour news cycle. The tentacles of barbarism appear to be reaching into every aspect of daily life. Domestic terrorism has come home and it increasingly targets the young.

Given these conditions, an overwhelming catalogue of evidence has come into view that indicates that nation states organized by neoliberal priorities have implicitly declared war on their children, offering a disturbing index of societies in the midst of a deep moral and political catastrophe.[10] Too many young people today live in an era of foreclosed hope, an era in which it is difficult either to imagine a life beyond the dictates of a market-driven society or to transcend the fear that any attempt to do so can only result in a more dreadful nightmare. As Jennifer Silva has pointed out, this generation of especially

> young working-class men and women . . . are trying to figure out what it means to be an adult in a world of disappearing jobs, soaring education costs and shrinking social support networks . . . They live at home longer, spend more years in college, change jobs more frequently and start families later.[11]

Youth today are not only plagued by the fragility and uncertainty of the present, they are "the first post war generation facing the prospect of downward mobility [in which the] plight of the outcast stretches to embrace a generation as a whole."[12] It is little wonder that "these youngsters are called Generation Zero: A generation with Zero opportunities, Zero future," and Zero expectations.[13] Or to use Guy Standing's term, "the precariat,"[14] which he defines as "a growing proportion of our total society" forced to "accept a life of unstable labour and unstable living."[15]

Beyond exposing the moral depravity of a society that fails to provide for its youth, the symbolic and real violence waged against many young people bespeaks to nothing less than a perverse collective death wish—especially visible when youth protest their conditions. As Alain Badiou argues, we live in an era in which there is near zero tolerance for democratic protest and "infinite tolerance for the crimes of bankers and government embezzlers which affect the lives of millions."[16] This is certainly true of the United States. How else to explain the FBI's willingness to label as a "terrorist threat" youthful activists speaking against corporate and government misdeeds, while at the same time the Bureau refuses to press criminal charges against the banking giant HSBC for laundering billions of dollars for Mexican drug cartels and terrorist groups linked to al-Qaeda.[17]

If youth were once the repository of society's dreams, that is no longer true. Increasingly, young people are viewed as a public disorder, a dream now turned into a nightmare. Many youth live in a post-9/11 social order that positions them as a prime target of its governing through crime complex.[18] This is made obvious by the many "get tough" policies that now render young people as criminals, while depriving them of basic health care, education, and social services. Punishment and fear have replaced compassion and social responsibility as the most important modalities for mediating the relationship of youth to the larger social order, all too evident by the upsurge of zero tolerance laws along with the expanding reach of the punishing state in both the United States and Canada.[19] When the criminalization of social problems becomes a mode of governance and war its default strategy, youth are reduced to soldiers or targets—not social investments. As anthropologist Alain Bertho points out, "Youth is no longer considered the world's future, but as a threat to its present."[20]

Increasingly, the only political discourses available for many young people are either disciplinary or one of "emotional self-management."[21] As their future is negated, youth are now removed from any talk about democracy. Their absence is symptomatic of a society that has turned against itself, punishes its children, and does so at the risk of crippling the entire body politic. Many youth in the last few decades have been removed from any discourse about democracy and increasingly fell prey to what I have called the war on youth, a war that can be traced back to the 1970s.[22] With the rise of the Occupy movement this silence of young people gave way to a rising number of youth movements extending from Black Lives Matter to the legions of young people that joined the Bernie Sanders campaign. Sanders was able to mobilize thousands of young people who seized upon a new vision for the United States, one rooted in considerations of economic justice, police violence, and political equality. Not only did young people once again rise up to challenge the increasingly oppressive nature of American society, they refused to work within the established boundaries of established politics, a politics run by the financial elites in both major political parties. Under the Trump administration, there can be little doubt that the war on youth will be accelerated, especially with the appointment of Jeff Sessions as Attorney General.

Historically, the war on youth emerged without apology when the social contract, however compromised and feeble, came crashing to the ground around the time Margaret Thatcher "married" Ronald Reagan. Both were hard-line advocates of a market fundamentalism, and announced respectively that there was no such thing as society and that government was the problem and not the solution to citizens' woes. Within a short time, democracy and the political process were hijacked by corporations and the call for austerity policies became cheap copy for weakening the welfare state, public values, and public goods. The results of this emerging neoliberal regime included a widening gap between the rich and the poor, a growing culture of cruelty, and the dismantling of social provisions. One result has been that the promise of youth has given way to an age of market-induced angst, and a view of many young people as a threat to short-term investments, privatization, untrammeled self-interest, and quick profits.

Besides a growing inability to translate private troubles into larger and crucial social issues, what is also being lost in the current historical conjuncture is the very idea of the public good, the notion of connecting learning to social change, and developing modes of civic courage infused by the principles of social justice. Under the regime of a ruthless economic Darwinism, we are witnessing the crumbling of social bonds and the triumph of individual desires over social rights, nowhere more exemplified than in the gated communities, gated intellectuals, and gated values that have become symptomatic of a society that has lost all claims to democracy or for that matter any modestly progressive vision for the future.

As the eminent sociologist, Zygmunt Bauman, points out, "Visions have nowadays fallen into disrepute and we tend to be proud of what we should be ashamed of."[23] For instance, politicians such as the former vice president, Dick Cheney, not only refuse to apologize for the immense suffering and displacement they have imposed on the Iraqi people, but they seem to gloat in defending such unethical policies. Doublespeak took on a new register when former president Obama employed the discourse of national security to sanction a surveillance state, a kill list, and the ongoing murder of young children by drones. This expansive landscape of lies has not only produced an illegal war and justified state torture, but it has also provided a justification for the United States' slide into barbarism after the tragic events of 9/11. President Donald Trump has vowed to reinstate waterboarding and other forms of torture, effectively opening up the United States to committing war crimes. Yet, such real and proposed acts of state violence appear to be of little concern to the shameless apostles of permanent war.

Politics has become an extension of war, just as economic insecurity and state-sponsored violence increasingly find legitimation in the discourses of privatization and demonization which promote anxiety, moral panics, fear, and undermine any sense of communal responsibility for the well-being of others. Too many young people today learn quickly that their fate is solely a matter of individual responsibility, irrespective of wider structural forces. This is a much promoted hyper-competitive ideology whose message is that surviving in a society demands reducing social relations to forms of social combat. Young people today are expected to inhabit a set of relations in which the only obligation is to live for oneself and to reduce the responsibilities of citizenship to the demands of a consumer culture. Yet, there is more at work here than a flight from social responsibility, if not politics itself. Also lost is the importance of those social bonds, modes of collective reasoning, public spheres, and cultural apparatuses crucial to the formation of a sustainable democratic society.

The War Against Youth

In what follows, I want to address further the intensifying assault on young people through the related concepts of "soft war," "hard war," and "war of control."[24] The idea of the soft war considers the changing conditions of youth within the relentless expansion of a global market society. Partnered with a massive advertising machinery, the soft war targets all children and youth, devaluing them by treating them as yet another "market" to be commodified and exploited, and conscripting them into the system through relentless attempts to create a new generation of hyper-consumers. In this instance, young people are not only viewed as consumers but also as brands as their subjectivity, desires, and ways of relating to others are commodified so that their presence in the world is marked by the fact that they are either selling a product (which they inhabit) or buying one. This low-intensity war is waged by a variety of corporate institutions through the educational force of a culture that commercializes every aspect of kids' lives, and now uses the internet and various social networks along with new media technologies such as smartphones to immerse young people in the world of mass consumption in ways that are more direct and expansive than anything we have seen in the past. Commercially carpet bombed by an advertising industry that in the United States spent $170 billion in 2012, the typical child is exposed to about 40,000 ads a year and by the time they reach the fourth grade have memorized 300 to 400 brands.

An entire generation is being drawn into a world of consumerism in which commodities and brand loyalty become both the most important markers of *identity* and the primary frameworks for mediating one's relationship to the world. Increasingly, many young people, recast as commodities, can only recognize themselves in terms preferred by the market. As Bauman points out, youth are simultaneously "promoters of commodities and the commodities they promote"—defined as both brands and merchandise, on the one hand, and marketing agents on the other.[25]

Corporations have hit gold with the new media and can inundate young people directly with their market-driven values, desires, and identities, all of which fly under the radar, escaping the watchful eyes and interventions of concerned parents and other adults. The data-mining marketers make young people think they count when in fact "all they want to do is count them."[26] The dominant culture's overbearing ecology of consumption now works to selectively eliminate and reorder the possible modes of political, social, and ethical vocabularies made available to youth. Young people's most private experiences are now colonized by a consumerist ethic that deforms their sense of agency, desires, values, and hopes. Trapped within a spectacle of marketing, their capacity to be critically engaged and socially responsible citizens is greatly diminished.

At the same time, the influence of the new screen and electronic culture on young people's habits is disturbing. For instance, a 2010 study by the Kaiser Family Foundation found that young people aged 8 to 18 now spend more than seven and a half hours a day with smartphones, computers, televisions, and other electronic devices.[27] When you add the additional time youth spend texting, talking on their cell phones, and doing multiple tasks at once, such as "watching TV while updating *Facebook*—the number rises to 11 hours of total media content each day."[28] There is a greater risk here to youth than what seems to be emerging as a new form of depoliticization and thoughtlessness conveniently labeled as attention deficit disorder. The risk is that young people's lives will eventually be filled entirely by these distractions, and they will be denied the time necessary for thoughtful analysis and the pedagogical conditions necessary for them to read critically both the word and the world.

What are the consequences of the soft war? Public spaces have been transformed into neoliberal disimagination zones which makes it more difficult for young people to find public spheres where they can locate themselves and translate metaphors of hope into meaningful action. The dreamscapes that make up a society built on the promises of mass consumption translate deftly into ad copy, insistently promoting and normalizing a neoliberal order in which economic relations now provide the master script for how young people define themselves, their relations with others, and the larger world.

Of course, some youth are doing their best to resist the commercial onslaught and to stay ahead of the commodification and privatization of new media technologies. These youths are using social and digital media as creative tools to assert a range of oppositional practices and forms of protest that constitute a new realm of political activity, one that will increase in the future and be an important source of struggle and resistance. Not only are they using cell phones to post videos of police violence, they are also using a range of social media platforms such as Vine, Instagram, or Periscope to rapidly organize mass protests. Alicia Garza, one of the founders of the Black Lives Matter movement, used the #BlackLivesMatter hashtag in the summer of 2013 after George Zimmerman was acquitted for the killing of Trayvon Martin. In doing so, she put in place a "banner under which dozens of disparate organizations, new and old, and millions of individuals, loosely and tightly related, [now] press for change."[29] Online sites such as *Truthout* are being used as alternative public spheres where youth from around the globe can connect across a variety of social issues. Moreover, Moral Monday movements are springing up all over the United States and are working to both educate and mobilize people around issues such as equitable health care, a graduated income tax, preventing budget cuts that eliminate food stamps, hurt people with disabilities, and cut back on social provisions for seniors.[30] At the same time, such groups are reclaiming the language of the common good and producing visions in which people can recognize themselves and the need to struggle for economic and political justice. Rather than being in opposition to the physical commons, the online sphere functions to extend the possible sites of struggle.

The Hard War

Turning now to the hard war, this is a more serious and dangerous development for young people, especially those who are marginalized by virtue of their ethnicity, race, and class. The hard war refers to the harshest elements of a growing youth crime-control complex that operates through a logic of punishment, surveillance, and control. The young people targeted by its punitive measures are often poor minority youth who are considered failed consumers and who can only afford to live on the margins of a commercial culture that excludes anyone who lacks money, resources, and leisure time to spare. Or they are youth considered uneducable and unemployable, and therefore troublesome. The imprint of the youth crime-control complex can be traced to the increasingly popular practice of organizing schools through disciplinary practices that subject students to constant surveillance through high-tech security devices while imposing on them harsh and often thoughtless zero-tolerance policies that closely resemble measures used currently by the criminal justice system. In this instance, poor and minority youth become objects of a new mode of governance based on the crudest forms of disciplinary control. Punished if they don't show up at school and punished even if they do attend school, many of these students are funneled into what has been ominously called the "school-to-prison pipeline."[31] If middle- and upper-class kids are subject to the seductions of market-driven public relations, working-class youth are caught in the crosshairs between the arousal of commercial desire and the harsh impositions of securitization, surveillance, and policing.

How else do we explain the fact that in the United States today 500,000 young people are incarcerated and 2.5 million are arrested annually, and that by the age of 23, "almost a third of Americans have been arrested for a crime"?[32] What kind of society allows 1.6 million children to be homeless at any given time in a year? What kind of society allows one in ten youth in New York City schools to be homeless during the 2014–15 school year?[33] Or allows massive inequalities in wealth and income to produce a politically and morally dysfunctional society in which "45 percent of U.S. residents live in households that struggle to make ends meet"?[34] Current statistics paint a bleak picture for young people in the United States: 1.5 million are unemployed, which marks a 17-year high; 12.5 million are without food; and in what amounts to a national disgrace, one out of every five American children lives in poverty. Nearly half of all U.S. children and 90 percent of Black youngsters will be on food stamps at some point during childhood.[35] What are we to make of a society in which there have been more young people killed on the streets of Chicago since 2001 than there have been American soldiers killed in Afghanistan? To be more exact, 5,000 people were killed by gunfire in Chicago, many of them children, while 2,000 troops were killed between 2001 and 2012.[36] At the national level, young people are being killed by guns in numbers that suggest a national pathology. As Gary Younge points out, "Every day, on average, seven kids and teens are shot dead in America," which adds up to "2,500 dead children annually."[37]

A type of mad violence appears to be at the heart of political and everyday life in the United States. The National Rifle Association and its political lackeys support a gun culture that calls for arming students in schools while exercising an influential role in getting state legislatures to pass laws making it easier for individuals to get and carry concealed weapons. Since the passage in 1990 of the National Defense Authorization Act, which allowed the Department of Defense to transfer surplus military equipment to local police forces, the police now have access to armored troop carriers, night vision rifles, Humvees, M16 automatic rifles, grenade launchers, and other weapons designed for military tactics.[38]

As the war on terror comes home, public spaces have been militarized and police forces have taken on the role of an occupying army, especially in poor minority neighborhoods. Acting as a paramilitary force, the police have become a new symbol of domestic terrorism, harassing racialized youth by criminalizing a multitude of behaviors. This was especially true in the stop-and-frisk policies so widespread under Mayor Bloomberg in New York City. As I have mentioned in other chapters, in Ferguson, Missouri, the entire population was criminalized in what can only be described as a racist shakedown. As David Graeber puts it,

> The Department of Justice's investigation of the Ferguson Police Department has scandalized the nation, and justly so. But the department's institutional racism, while shocking, isn't the report's most striking revelation. More damning is this: in a major American city, the criminal justice system perceives a large part of that city's population not as citizens to be protected, but as potential targets for what can only be described as a shake-down operation designed to wring money out of the poorest and most vulnerable by any means they could, and that as a result, the overwhelming majority of Ferguson's citizens had outstanding warrants.[39]

The rise of the punishing state and the war on terror has emboldened police forces across the nation and in doing so feeds their use of racist violence against young people resulting in what has been called an "epidemic of police brutality." Sadly, even young minority children are not immune from such violence as the killing of Tamir Rice on November 22, 2014 by a white policeman has made clear. Once again, even more tragic is the fact that the City of Cleveland tried to blame the 12-year-old boy for his own death.[40] Rice was holding a BB gun when he was shot dead by a policeman judged unfit for duty in 2012. The killing of Black men has taken on the image of a cruel sport promoted by police forces that now hype the lawlessness and extreme violence that has replaced any viable notion of democratic idealism. Between January 2012 and December 2014, 38 unarmed Black men have been killed by the police.[41]

Many people in the United States now live in a culture that is not only being increasingly militarized, but also supports a growing indifference to such cruelty, reinforced by a notion of exaggerated self-reliance, rugged individualism, and privatization, all of which renders group solidarities repugnant and reinforces the idea that care for the other is both a pathology and a liability. Hence, it should come as no surprise that the United States currently has more police, prisons, spies, weapons, and soldiers than at any other time in its history—this coupled with a growing "army" of the unemployed and incarcerated. In addition, the military-industrial complex now joins hands with the entertainment industry in producing everything from children's toys to video games that both construct a militarized form of masculinity and serve as an enticement for recruitment. In fact, over 10 million people have downloaded *America's Army* and its various updates, including the more recent, *America's Army: Proving Grounds*, a first-person shooter video/computer game the Army uses as a recruitment tool.[42] Such representations of hyper-masculinity and aggression mimic fascism's militarization of the public sphere, through which fear and violence become the ultimate language, referent, and currency for defining the political sphere.

As David Dillard-Wright observes, Trump drowns the listener in fear, engaging in a type of verbal waterboarding by promoting a kind of panicked rage that channels anger against everyone except those who are "white, straight, male, and Christian, or holders of what Ta-Nehisi Coates recently called in *The Atlantic*, a 'badge of advantage.'"[43] Violence is woven into Trump's language, especially during the presidential primary, and was used to further normalize the language of bigotry, racism, and misogyny while furthering a politics of nihilism. His demeaning language was designed to strike fear, if not passivity, in the hearts of those who did not agree with his post-fact universe. This machinery of armed ignorance and normalization makes it more difficult to grasp how war has become a source of pride rather than alarm. As this type of legitimated violence becomes mythologized, the war on terror has been transformed into a war on society itself and the political order itself. Yet, let's be clear. This culture of militarized hardness is not confined to the United States.

Donald Trump's emphasis on law and order and his inclusion of white supremacists in his cabinet and in other high-level government positions does not augur well for poor Black youth. Trump's political playbook reeks with bigotry, hatred, and authoritarian propaganda and points to putting in place a new level of racial terror. Jason Stanley offers a frightening commentary on the emergence of an authoritarian society that will serve the wealthy elite, the well connected, and powerful corporations, all the while relegating those marginalized by class and race to a life of uncertainty, precarity, hopelessness, and despair. Stanley writes:

> What Trump is trying to convey is that there is wild disorder, because of American citizens of African-American descent, and immigrants . . . The chief authoritarian values are law and order. In Trump's value system, nonwhites and non-Christians are the chief threats to law and order. Trump knows that reality does not call for a value-system like his; violent crime is at almost historic lows in the United States. Trump is thundering about a crime wave of historic proportions, because he is an authoritarian using his speech to define a simple reality that legitimates his value system, leading voters to adopt it.[44]

The seeds of a militarized culture are growing in Europe and North America. In Canada, one child in six lives in poverty, but for Aboriginal and immigrant children that figure rises to 25 percent or more, respectively. By all accounts, the rate of incarceration for Aboriginal youth—already eight times higher than for non-Aboriginal youth—will continue to skyrocket as a result of the former Harper government's so-called Safe Streets and Community Act which emulates the failed policies of the U.S. system by, among other things, strengthening requirements to detain and sentence more youth to custody in juvenile detention centers.[45] Surely one conclusion that can be drawn from the inquest into the tragic suicide of 19-year-old Ashley Smith who spent five years of her life in and out of detention facilities tells us that incarceration for young people can be equivalent to a death sentence.[46]

Against the idealistic rhetoric of governments that claim to venerate young people lies the reality of societies that increasingly view youth through the optic of law and order, societies that appear all too willing to treat youth as criminals and when necessary make them "disappear" into the farthest reaches of the carceral state. In this context, the administration of schools and social services has given way to modes of confinement whose purpose is to ensure "custody and control."[47] As I have already suggested, many schools in the United States are modeled after prisons with their high-tech surveillance cameras, the presence of police and security guards, and punitive zero-tolerance policies. How else to explain how children as young as 12 are being subjected to stun guns, handcuffed and removed from class for doodling on a desk, or suspended from school for bringing a toy GI gun to school. John Whitehead, the president of the Rutherford Institute, has documented young girls being suspended or expelled from school for having Midol or Alka Seltzer in their purse, and children being suspended for playing cops and robbers. Instead of being sent to the principal's office for even a minor infraction such as violating dress codes, many children are handcuffed, taken from the classroom, put in a patrol car, and driven to a police station. And that is only the beginning of the nightmare for these kids and their families.

The plight of poor minority youth today also extends beyond the severity of material deprivations and violence they experience daily. Many young people have been forced to view the world and redefine the nature of their own youth within the borders of hopelessness, insecurity, and despair. There is little basis on which to imagine a better future lying just beyond the highly restrictive spaces of commodification and containment. Neoliberal austerity in social spending means an entire generation of youth will not have access to decent jobs, the material comforts, educational opportunities, or the security available to previous generations. In Canada, this is a new generation of youth who have to think, act, and talk like adults; worry about their families, which may be headed by a single parent or two out of work and searching for a job; and in the United States young people are further burdened by registers of extreme poverty that pose the dire challenge of getting enough money to buy food and face the arduous task of determining how long it will take to see a doctor in case of illness. These young people inhabit a new and more unsettling scene of suffering, a dead zone of the imagination, which constitutes a site of terminal exclusion—one that not only reveals the vast and destabilizing inequalities in neoliberal economic landscapes, but also portends a future that has no purchase on the hope that characterizes a vibrant democracy.

Politics and power are now on the side of lawlessness as is obvious in the state's endless violations of civil liberties, freedom of speech, and most constitutional rights, allegedly done in the name of national security. Lawlessness now wraps itself in government dictates. In Canada, it is evident in former prime minister Stephen Harper's support for Bill C-51, an anti-terrorism bill that would further limit civil rights through a pedagogy of fear and racist demonization—a bill that is still in existence under Prime Minister Justin Trudeau's liberal government. Such acts of lawlessness are also apparent in the United States and can be found in repressive practices that include draconian anti-immigration laws, the indiscriminate use of drone warfare, the emergence of the surveillance state, repressive law and order policies that expand the police state, the public sanctioning of state torture by President Trump, and a number of other morally and politically reprehensible practices. These would include cutting health insurance for millions of poor people, rolling back environmental protections, needlessly increasing the bloated budget for the military-industrial complex, eliminating valuable social provisions for the impoverished, especially people of color, and underfunding and privatizing public education. In addition, one can point to policies designed to reduce taxes for the rich while refusing to invest in public services and institutions vital for the pubic good.[48] The ruling corporate elites have made terror rational and fear the modus operandi of politics. Neoliberal capital is based on a Hobbesian mantra of war against all and a survival of the fittest ethic and one consequence is an aggressive politics of disposability and disappearance. Of course, this matrix of lawlessness that has been in play for decades in the United States and embraced by both major political parties will be intensified to what might be unimaginable degrees with the election of Donald Trump to the presidency. Trump has little regard for human rights and international law and has vowed that he will do whatever it takes, including the use of state-sponsored torture, to implement his ultra-nationalist world view on the global stage.

Educators, individuals, artists, intellectuals, and various social movements need to make visible both the workings of market fundamentalism "in all of its forms of exploitation whether personal, political, or economic [and they] need to reconstruct a platform" and set of strategies to oppose it.[49] Clearly, any political formation that matters must challenge the savage social costs casino capitalism has enacted and work to undo the forms of social, political, and economic violence that young people are experiencing on a daily level. This will demand more than one-day demonstrations. What is needed is a resurgence of public memory, civic literacy, and civic courage—that is, a willingness to "effectively analyze the structures and mechanisms of capitalist power [in order] to formulate a sophisticated political response" and the willingness to build long-standing oppositional movements.[50] Traces of such movements are beginning to emerge all over the globe, especially in countries such as Spain and Greece.

In North America, we have seen important, though inconclusive, attempts on the part of young people to break the hold of power. This was evident in the Occupy movement, the Quebec student movement, the Idle No More opposition, and the recent "Black Lives Matter" protests. What all of these movements have made clear is that young people aligning with like-minded others can be a vibrant source of creativity, possibility, and political struggle. Moreover, these movements in their various contemporary manifestations point to a crucial political project in which young people have raised new questions about anti-democratic forces in the United States and Canada that are threatening the collective survival of vast numbers of people. Evident in the legacy of these political movements, however slow their progression or setbacks, is a cry of collective indignation over economic and social injustices that pose a threat to humankind. They also explain how young people and others can use new technologies, develop democratic social formations, and enact forms of critical pedagogy and civil disobedience necessary for addressing the anti-democratic forces that have been corrupting North American political culture since the 1970s. Young people have shown that austerity policies can be defeated; state violence can be held accountable; collective struggles are worthwhile; and specific and isolated protests can be transformed into broad social movements that pose a fundamental challenge to neoliberal ideologies and modes of governance.[51]

Protests among young people in the United States, Canada, and elsewhere in the world illlustrate that demonstrations are not—indeed, *cannot be*—only a short-term project for reform. Young people need to enlist all generations to develop a truly global political movement that is accompanied by the reclaiming of public spaces, the progressive use of digital technologies, the development of new public spheres, the production of new modes of education, and the safeguarding of places where democratic expression, new civic values, democratic public spheres, new modes of identification, and collective hope can be nurtured and developed. A formative culture must be put in place pedagogically and institutionally in a variety of spheres extending from churches and public and higher education to all those cultural apparatuses engaged in the production of collective knowledge, desires, identities, and democratic values.

The struggles here are myriad and urgent and point to the call for a living wage, food security, accessible education, jobs programs (especially for the young), the democratization of power, economic equality, and a massive shift in funds away from the machinery of war and big banks. Any collective struggle that matters has to embrace education as the center of politics and the source of an embryonic vision of the good life outside of the imperatives of unfettered "free-market" capitalism. In addition, too many progressives and people on the left are stuck in the discourse of foreclosure and cynicism and need to develop what Stuart Hall calls a "sense of politics being educative, of politics changing the way people see things."[52] There is a need for educators, young people, artists, and other cultural workers to develop a language of both critique and hope along with an educative politics in which people can address the historical, structural, and ideological conditions at the core of the violence being waged by the corporate and repressive state, and to clarify that a government increasingly subsumed by global market sovereignty is no longer responsive to the most basic needs of young people. All the issues that matter in a substantive democratic society are under siege by the forces of neoliberalism, authoritarianism, and institutionalized racism and any viable challenge requires movement building that is a long-term project. Young people need more than demonstrations and demolition squads, they need to take on the future by merging the power of the imagination and a politics of educated hope with long-term strategies, durable organizations, and new political formations.

The issue of who gets to define the future, share in the nation's wealth, shape the parameters of the social state, steward and protect the globe's resources, and create institutional spaces for producing engaged and socially responsible citizens is no longer a rhetorical issue. This challenge offers up new categories for defining how matters of representations, education, economic justice, and politics are to be defined and fought over. This is a difficult task, but what we are seeing in cities such as Chicago, Athens, Quebec, Paris, Madrid, and other sites of massive inequality throughout the world is the beginning of a long struggle for the institutions, values, and infrastructures that make communities the center of a robust, radical democracy. At a time when democracy is fading in the United States and Europe, I realize this sounds a bit utopian, but we have few choices if we are going to struggle for a future that does a great deal more than endlessly repeat the present.

We may live in dark times, but as Slavoj Žižek rightly insists "The only realist option is to do what appears impossible within this system. This is how the impossible becomes possible."[53] As Hannah Arendt once warned, these may be dark times, but they don't have to be, and that raises serious questions about what educators, artists, youth, intellectuals, and others are going to do within the current historical climate to make sure that they do not succumb to the authoritarian forces circling American society, waiting for the resistance to stop and for the lights to go out. My friend, the late Howard Zinn, got it right in his insistence that hope is the willingness "to hold out, even in times of pessimism, the possibility of surprise."[54] Or, to add to this eloquent plea, I would say, resistance is no longer an option, it is a necessity.

Notes

1 Hannah Arendt, *The Origins of Totalitarianism* (New York: Houghton Mifflin Harcourt, 2001).
2 See, for instance, Andre Spicer, "Adults with Colouring Books, Kids with CVs—It's a World Turned Upside Down," *Guardian* (April 8, 2015). Online: www.theguardian.com/commentisfree/2015/apr/08/adults-colouring-books-kids-cvs-lego-children
3 This theme is taken up powerfully by a number of theorists. See C. Wright Mills, *The Sociological Imagination* (New York: Oxford University Press, 2000); Richard Sennett, *The Fall of Public Man* (New York: Norton, 1974); Zygmunt Bauman, *In Search of Politics* (Stanford, CA: Stanford University Press, 1999); and Henry A. Giroux, *Public Spaces, Private Lives* (Lanham, MD: Rowman and Littlefield, 2001).
4 Maggie McGrath, "Does John Stumpf Deserve to Keep His Job as Wells Fargo CEO?" *Forbes* (September 19, 2016). Online: www.forbes.com/sites/maggiemcgrath/2016/09/19/does-john-stumpf-deserve-to-keep-his-job-as-wells-fargo-ceo/#476ffe944b6e
5 For a history of the criminal behavior committed by Wells Fargo, see: Nomi Prins, "Jail Wells Fargo CEO and Chairman John Stumpf," *Moyers and Company* (September 30, 2016). Online: http://billmoyers.com/story/jail-wells-fargo-ceo-chairman-john-stumpf
6 Lucinda Shen, "Here's How Much Wells Fargo CEO John Stumpf Is Getting to Leave the Bank," *Fortune* (October 13, 2016). Online: http://fortune.com/2016/10/13/wells-fargo-ceo-john-stumpfs-career-ends-with-133-million-payday/
7 For a number of detailed stories on the history of such scandals, see Henry Finder, "Business Scandals," *New Yorker* (October 2, 2016). Online: www.newyorker.com/newsletter/issue/the-sunday-newsletter-new-york-stories?mbid=nl_Sunday%20Long reads%20(56)&CNDID=42733863&spMailingID=9613650&spUserID=MTM4NzE 1OTE4NjE5S0&spJobID=1020122397&spReportId=MTAyMDEyMjM5NwS2
8 Robert Reich, "Banksters like Wells Fargo's CEO John Stumpf Belong in Jail," *Reich's Facebook Page* (September 20, 2016). Online: www.facebook.com/RBReich/posts/1321016194577640
9 Angela Y. Davis, *Abolition Democracy: Beyond Empire, Prisons, and Torture* (New York: Seven Stories Press, 2005), p. 91.
10 J. F. Conway, "Quebec: Making War on Our Children," *Socialist Project*, E-Bulletin No. 651 (June 10, 2012). Online: www.socialistproject.ca/bullet/651.php
11 Jennifer M. Silva, "Young and Isolated," *International New York Times* (June 22, 2013). Online: http://opinionator.blogs.nytimes.com/2013/06/22/young-and-isolated/?_r=0
12 Zygmunt Bauman, *On Education* (Cambridge: Polity Press, 2012), p. 46.
13 Zygmunt Bauman, *This Is Not a Diary* (Cambridge: Polity Press, 2012), p. 64.
14 Guy Standing, *The Precariat: The New Dangerous Class* (London: Bloomsbury Academic, 2011).

15   Sara Mojtehedzadeh, "Q&A with Precarious Work Expert Guy Standing," *Toronto Star* (April 09, 2015). Online: www.thestar.com/news/gta/2015/04/09/qa-with-precarious-work-expert-guy-standing.html

16   Alain Badiou, *The Rebirth of History*, trans. Gregory Elliott (London: Verso, 2012), pp. 18–19.

17   Matt Taibbi, "After Laundering $800 Million in Drug Money, How Did HSBC Executives Avoid Jail?" *Democracy Now* (December 13, 2012). Online: www.democracynow.org/2012/12/13/matt_taibbi_after_laundering_800_million

18   On this issue, see Jonathan Simon, *Governing Through Crime: How the War on Crime Transformed American Democracy and Created a Culture of Fear* (New York, NY: Oxford University Press, 2007).

19   See, for example, David Garland, *The Culture of Control: Crime and Social Order in Contemporary Society* (Chicago: University of Chicago Press, 2002); William Ayers, Rick Ayers, and Bernardine Dohrn, eds, *Zero Tolerance: Resisting the Drive for Punishment in Our Schools: A Handbook for Parents, Students, Educators, and Citizens* (New York: New Press, 2001); Christopher Robbins, *Expelling Hope: The Assault on Youth and the Militarization of Schooling* (New York: SUNY Press, 2009); Henry A. Giroux, *Youth in a Suspect Society* (New York: Palgrave, 2009); Derek W. Black, *Ending Zero Tolerance: The Crisis of Absolute School Discipline* (New York: NYU Press, 2016); Henry A. Giroux, *The Violence of Organized Forgetting* (San Francisco: City Lights, 2014); Brad Evans and Henry A. Giroux, *Disposable Futures: The Seduction of Violence in the Age of the Spectacle* (San Francisco: City Lights, 2015).

20   Quoted in Jean-Marie Durand, "For Youth: A Disciplinary Discourse Only," trans. Leslie Thatcher, *Truthout* (November 15, 2009). Online: www.truth-out.org/11190911

21   Jennifer M. Silva, *Coming Up Short: Working-Class Adulthood in an Age of Uncertainty* (New York: Oxford Press, 2013), p. 10.

22   Jean and John Comaroff, "Reflections of Youth, from the Past to the Postcolony." In Melissa S. Fisher and Greg Downey, eds, *Frontiers of Capital: Ethnographic Reflections on The New Economy* (Durham, NC: Duke University Press, 2006), p. 267. I take this issue up in detail in Giroux, *Youth in a Suspect Society*.

23   Zygmunt Bauman, "Introduction" and "In Search of Public Space." In *In Search of Politics* (Stanford, CA: Stanford University Press, 1999), p. 8.

24   Quoted in Durand, "For Youth."

25   Zygmunt Bauman, *Consuming Life* (London: Polity, 2007), p. 6.

26   Zygmunt Bauman and David Lyons, *Liquid Surveillance* (Cambridge: Polity Press, 2013), p. 54.

27   Tamar Lewin, "If Your Kids Are Awake, They're Probably Online," *New York Times* (January 20, 2010), p. A1.

28   C. Christine, "Kaiser Study: Kids 8 to 18 Spend More than Seven Hours a Day with Media," *Spotlight on Digital Media and Learning: MacArthur Foundation* (January 21, 2010). Online: http://spotlight.macfound.org/blog/entry/kaiser_study_kids_age_8_to_18_spend_more_than_seven_hours_a_day_with_media/

29   Bijon Stephen, "How Black Lives Matter Uses Social Media to Fight the Power," *Wired* (October 15, 2015). Online: www.wired.com/2015/10/how-black-lives-matter-uses-social-media-to-fight-the-power/

30   Rev. William J. Barber, II, "We Are Witnessing the Birth Pangs of a Third Reconstruction—We Need a Moral Movement to Create Change," *ThinkProgress* (December 15, 2016). Online: https://thinkprogress.org/rev-barber-moral-change-1ad2776df7c#.jqpz3ilht

31 Nancy A. Heitzeg, *The School-to-Prison Pipeline: Education, Discipline, and Racialized Double Standards* (New York: Praeger, 2016); Christopher A. Mallett, *The School-to-Prison Pipeline: A Comprehensive Assessment* (New York: Springer, 2015).

32 Erica Goode, "Many in U.S. Are Arrested by Age 23, Study Finds," *New York Times* (December 19, 2011). Online: www.nytimes.com/2011/12/19/us/nearly-a-third-of-americans-are-arrested-by-23-study-says.html?_r=1&pagewanted=print

33 Ben Chapman, "Homelessness among NYC Schoolkids Surges as Population tops 100,000," *New York Daily News* (December 26, 2016). Online: www.nydailynews.com/new-york/exclusive-homelessness-surges-nyc-schoolkids-article-1.2834486

34 Reuters, "45% Struggle in US to Make Ends Meet," *MSNBC: Business Stocks and Economy* (November 22, 2011). Online: www.msnbc.msn.com/id/45407937/ns/business-stocks_and_economy/#.T3SxhDEgd8E

35 Lindsey Tanner, "Half of US Kids Will Get Food Stamps, Study Says," *Chicago Tribune* (November 2, 2009). Online: www.chicagotribune.com/news/chi-ap-us-med-children-food,0,6055934.story

36 Daily Mail Reporter, " 'These Kids Don't Expect to Lead a Full Life': Fears for Chicago Teens as Fatal Shootings in City Outnumber US Troops Killed in Afghanistan," *Mail Online* (June 19, 2012). Online: www.dailymail.co.uk/news/article-2161690/Chicago-crime-More-people-shot-dead-Chicago-killed-duty-Afghanistan.html

37 Gary Younge, "An All-American Slaughter: The Youthful Carnage of America's Gun Culture," *TomDispatch* (October 23, 2016). Online: www.tomdispatch.com/post/176201/tomgram%3A_gary_younge%2C_america%27s_deserving_and_undeserving_dead_children/#more

38 Taylor Wofford, "How America's Police Became an Army: The 1033 Program," *Newsweek* (August 13, 2014). Online: www.newsweek.com/how-americas-police-became-army-1033-program-264537

39 David Graeber, "Ferguson and the Criminalization of American Life," *Gawker* (March 19, 2015). Online: http://gawker.com/ferguson-and-the-criminalization-of-american-life-1692392051

40 Oliver Laughland, "Tamir Rice 'Directly and Proximately' Responsible for Own Police Shooting Death, Says City," *Guardian* (March 1, 2015). Online: www.theguardian.com/us-news/2015/mar/01/tamir-rice-directly-proximately-responsible-police-shooting-death-city

41 Rich Juzwiak and Alexander Chan, "Unarmed People of Color Killed by Police, 1999–2014," *Gawker* (December 8, 2014). Online: http://gawker.com/unarmed-people-of-color-killed-by-police-1999-2014-1666672349

42 Corey Mead, *War Play: Video Games and the Future of Armed Conflict* (New York: Houghton Mifflin, 2013). Also see, Clive Thompson, "The Making of an X Box Warrior," *New York Times Magazine* (August 22, 2004), pp. 34–7; Jeremy Hsu, "For the U.S. Military, Video Games Get Serious," *LiveScience* (August 19, 2010). Online: www.livescience.com/10022-military-video-games.html

43 David Dillard-Wright, "Explaining the Cult of Trump," *Alter Net* (December 16, 2016). Online: www.alternet.org/election-2016/explaining-cult-trump

44 Jason Stanley, "Beyond Lying: Donald Trump's Authoritarian Reality," *New York Times* (November 4, 2016). Online: www.nytimes.com/2016/11/05/opinion/beyond-lying-donald-trumps-authoritarian-reality.html?_r=1

45 Department of Justice Canada, "A One-Day Snapshot of Aboriginal Youth in Custody across Canada: Phase II." Online: www.justice.gc.ca/eng/pi/rs/rep-rap/2004/yj2-jj2/p3.html

46   Colin Perket, "Ashley Smith Inquest Slated to Finally Start in Early 2013," *CTV News* (December 27, 2012). Online: http://toronto.ctvnews.ca/local-news/ashley-smith-inquest-slated-to-finally-start-in-early-2013–1.1092580

47   Zygmunt Bauman, *Wasted Lives* (London: Polity Press, 2004), p. 82.

48   For a clear exposé of the emerging surveillance state, see Glenn Greenwald, *No Place to Hide* (New York: Signal, 2014); Julia Angwin, *Dragnet Nation: A Quest for Privacy, Security, and Freedom in a World of Relentless Surveillance* (New York: Times Books, 2014); Heidi Boghosian, *Spying on Democracy: Government Surveillance, Corporate Power, and Public Resistance* (San Francisco: City Lights Books, 2013).

49   Chris Hedges, "Tariq Ali: The Time Is Right for a Palace Revolution," *Truthdig* (March 1, 2015). Online: www.truthdig.com/report/item/tariq_ali_the_time_is_right_for_a_palace_revolution_20150301

50   Ibid.

51   Ingar Solty, "Canada's 'Maple Spring': From the Quebec Student Strike to the Movement against Neoliberalism," *Socialist Project* (December 31, 2012). Online: www.socialistproject.ca/bullet/752.php

52   Zoe Williams, "The Saturday Interview: Stuart Hall," *Guardian* (February 11, 2012). Online: www.guardian.co.uk/theguardian/2012/feb/11/saturday-interview-stuart-hall

53   Slavoj Žižek, *Demanding the Impossible*, ed. Yong-June Park (Cambridge: Polity Press, 2013), p. 144.

54   Howard Zinn, *A People's History of the United States* (New York: Harper Perennial, 2003), p. 634.

6

LYRICAL FASCISM AND THINKING DANGEROUSLY IN A TIME OF WEAPONIZED IGNORANCE

And that was what I actually meant by banality. There's nothing deep about it—nothing demonic! There's simply the reluctance ever to imagine what the other person is experiencing, right?

(Hannah Arendt)

We have come a long way from the struggles that launched the civil rights movement over 50 years ago. During that historical period, brave men and women marched, integrated white-only lunch counters, defied orders to sit in the back of buses, challenged police brutality, and put their bodies in the face of danger for civil and economic rights. Many of them were beaten, attacked by police dogs, and jailed. They fought for a higher cause, and in some cases gave their lives in opposition to insufferable injustices. They embodied an ethical grammar of hope, one that demanded courage, struggle, and the creation of social movements. One display of such collective courage took place after Emmett Till, a young 14-year-old African American boy, was mutilated and tortured by white racists in Mississippi in 1955 after he allegedly whistled at a white woman. The widely distributed image of his tortured and disfigured body made visible a vile racism that could no longer remain unchallenged. Thousands viewed the horrible image of this young boy's mutilated body and rose up in anger and determination to take part in a social movement that challenged the toxic racism that had become normalized in the United States.

It is hard to view, even contemplate, contemporary America in that historical march towards justice and democracy. We live in a historical moment when money, greed, and a culture of civic illiteracy corrupt everything from how we view social provisions and schools to what passes as entertainment and popular culture. We live at a time when politics serves the bankers, hedge fund managers, the corporate elite, and free-market fundamentalists. Evidence of such dark times has reached its most egregious example in a Trump presidency. Trump's administration represents a return to the worst politics and values of the Gilded Age and points to a future era so dark that it will be difficult to draw upon the resources of the past in order to take solace in forms of resistance that also fought against the winds of authoritarianism. The United States has lived through a number of historical periods that tested the ideals of democracy including the genocide of Native Americans, slavery, and Jim Crow in its historical and current versions. American society now faces a new threat to the ideals and promise of a viable democracy and that threat is one of an incipient authoritarianism. The United States has taken a fatal turn, one that has the feel of a "slow-motion coup,"[1] driven by an oligarchy of the rich and morally indifferent that suppresses voting rights and civil liberties, and trades in politics as theater with leaders that appear as unqualified as they are unstable and morally corrupt. Michael Brenner is on target with his comment:

> The unpalatable truth is that authoritarian movements and ideology with fascist overtones are back – in America and in Europe. Not just as a political expletive thrown at opponents, but as a doctrine, as a movement, and – above all – as a set of feelings. Against this historical backdrop, it should not be a complete surprise that due to the troubled state of the West, across Europe and now most pronounced in America, we should see recrudescence of the attitudes, the rhetoric and the inspirations that marked Fascism's rise 80 or 90 years ago. [2]

Moral witnessing and the resources of historical memory are crucial to fighting the frontal assault the Trump administration will wage on the principles, values, and institutions that give power and promise to a democracy. Yet, we live at a time in which the legacies of the past now become fodder for advertisements, revolutionary slogans are trivialized, and the pictures of modern-day heroes and freedom fighters are used to sell t-shirts. Even memory and the practice of moral witnessing are commodified, if not corrupted. One particularly egregious example comes from the rapper Lil Wayne, who in a remix version of the song *Karate Chop* by rapper Future mocked Emmett Till with the lyric: "beat the pussy up like Emmett Till." While a critical response was swift from members of the hip hop community and community leaders, it mostly focused on Lil Wayne's racist remarks. What many critics failed to do was to look at the underlying conditions that make such racist, sexist blabber and historical amnesia possible. They also largely failed to raise crucial questions about how and why such ethically and politically demeaning music, videos, and lyrics are allowed to flood the culture with so little resistance, if not moral outrage. Moreover, little was said about why such poisonous lyrics and representations are measured more for their shock value rather than for the ways in which such material denigrates history, individuals, and social movements. Lil Wayne's racist and sexist lyrics exceed bad taste. And then, of course, there is LL Cool J's "Accidental Racist" song ("If you forget my gold chains, I'll forgive the iron chains"). There is nothing accidental going on here.

What is clear is that both comments are symptomatic of a deeper order of racist ideology and commodification that was pushed to the margins of discourse in the neoliberal age of color blindness.[3] But that moment has passed. In the age of Donald Trump and the move of right-wing extremists from the fringe to the center of American culture, racism and misogyny have taken on a new and unapologetic turn. In the past, racism was ensconced in racist policies that often went unnoticed in the mainstream media such as Reagan's war on drugs and welfare queens, the poisonous legacy of President Clinton's welfare and crime bills, and Obama's deportation of over 2.4 million immigrants. In an age of armed ignorance, racism is back both as a spectacle and as a driving force of

American politics and has once again come to life as a result of a racist populist discourse that leaves nothing hidden in its blitzkrieg of rhetorical hate, bigotry, and invective. In what might have once been considered unimaginable, Trump referred in his presidential campaign to women as "pigs," "slobs," and "dogs" while suggesting that all Black neighborhoods are breeding grounds for crime and lawlessness and that one way of controlling violence in Black communities is to impose racial profiling as a national policy. This is the same candidate, Donald Trump, who headed the birther movement designed to racially slander Barack Obama during his two terms as president. As president, Trump has continued to accelerate his war against Blacks, women, unions, workers, and others that pose a threat to the financial elite who constitute the 1 percent of the new Gilded Age. Evidence of such an attack is visible in Trump's cabinet of horrors. Kali Holloway sums it up well. She writes:

> With the most recent election, we now have a vice president-elect who has repeatedly voted in favor of LGBT discrimination, pushed to defund Planned Parenthood, blocked efforts to stop the spread of AIDS while praying about it, and presided over the worst HIV outbreak in Indiana's history. Pence is joined by Tom Price, the pro-gun, anti-abortion, anti-Obamacare, anti-Medicare, anti-LGBT newly appointed Secretary of Health and Human Services. Jeff Sessions, Trump's attorney general pick, once called the NAACP "Communist-inspired," employed a staffer with white nationalist ties, and has a history of opposing voting rights. He will now head a criminal justice system that has notoriously failed black and brown people. Trump's [former] national security adviser, Michael Flynn, [was] friendly with white supremacists on social media and propagates the idea that fearing Muslims is rational. All of these people will get to spend the next few years working alongside Steve Bannon, white nationalist sympathizer and propagandist, and now chief strategist to President-elect Trump . . . Trump's cabinet selections are an unmistakable sign that this administration has zero interest in assuaging the fears of African Americans and other people of color, Muslims, women, and the

many marginalized groups who were alienated and terrified by his campaign.[4]

Such racism and sexism point to a society in which economics is divorced from ethics, profit is the ultimate measure of success, and disposable populations are now fair game for ridicule, harassment, and insulting behavior. Lil Wayne is just one example of the morally dead zone that too many artists, individuals, institutions, intellectuals, and politicians occupy in a land of massive inequality in wealth and power. Lil Wayne's allusion to Emmitt Till in his lyrics represents more than stupidity and ignorance. It represents how normalized the culture of cruelty and ignorance has become and how it wraps itself in a popular culture that is increasingly racist, misogynistic, and historically illiterate. This is neoliberalism's revenge on young people in that it elevates profits over justice and the practice of moral witnessing and in doing so creates artists and other young people who mimic a racist and authoritarian politics and are completely clueless about it. Celebrity culture is the underside of the new illiteracy in America, the soft edge of fascism with its unbridled celebration of wealth, narcissism, and glamor. My comments on Emmitt Till in the beginning of my book, *Stormy Weather: Katrina and the Politics of Disposability*, point to a different use of memory, one that engages in moral witnessing and tries to prevent justice from dying in each of us, in the public sphere, and in our relations with others. It is worth repeating as a counter-narrative to Lil Wayne's complicity with the modes of lyrical fascism that now circulate in the media like a poisonous toxin.

Emmett Till's body arrived home in Chicago in September 1955. White racists in Mississippi had tortured, mutilated, and killed the young 14-year-old African-American boy for allegedly whistling at a white woman. Determined to make visible the horribly mangled face and twisted body of the child as an expression of racial hatred and killing, Mamie Till, the boy's mother, insisted that the coffin, interred at the A. A. Ranier Funeral Parlor in the South Side of Chicago, be left open for four long days. While mainstream news organizations ignored the horrifying image, *Jet* magazine published an unedited photo of Till's face taken while he lay in his coffin. Shaila Dawn points out that "[m]utilated is the word most often used to describe the face of Emmett Till after his body was hauled out of the Tallahatchie River in Mississippi. Inhuman is more like it: melted, bloated, missing an eye, swollen so large that its patch of wiry hair looks like that of a balding old man, not a handsome, brazen 14-year-old boy." The *Jet* photos not only made visible the violent effects of the racial state; they also fuelled massive public anger, especially among blacks, and helped to launch the Civil Rights Movement.[5]

We live at a time when heroes of the civil rights generation such as Rosa Parks, Malcolm X, Martin Luther King, Jr., and Angela Davis are now replaced by business tycoons such as Lloyd Blankfein, Jamie Dimon, and Henry Paulson along with an abundance of incompetent politicians who take glee in their warmongering and racist ideologies. The older pioneers sacrificed in order to alleviate the suffering of others, while the new "celebrity heroes" of the media drawn from corporate culture live off the suffering of others. An infantilizing and hyper-masculine culture is a cesspool of greed, overpaid financial looters, and spineless media pundits who reproduce the market-driven and politically reprehensible sexist and racist grammars of suffering, state violence, and disposability. As Trump's presidential victory made clear, celebrity and reality TV based culture confers a great deal of authority and has been a major force in legitimating not just a culture of stupidity, but also in creating a deadly politics of the personal, one in which the public sphere and crucial concerns about the public good collapse into the fog of lifestyles, self-interests, and the spectacle of crass luxury.

As a master of media manipulation, Trump clearly understood the power of the spectacle, shock, and performance. As a framing mechanism of social relations, Trump pioneered the triumph of emotion over reason, the spectacle over substance. Unscripted, he used his image as a reality TV star to create a new kind of politics. This is showman politics, one designed to sell tickets by producing an array of glitz and glamor, fortified by the ever present camera that "sees but doesn't think [and] makes no meaningful or moral distinction between a bubble bath in Las Vegas staffed by pretty girls and a bloodbath in Palmyra staffed by headless corpses."[6] Trump's presidential campaign and election offer a glimpse of what happens when democracy succumbs to a culture that pits pleasure against thinking, emotion against reason, and plutocracy against the rule of law. Lewis Lapham captures this moment in which democracy withers and armed ignorance prevails. He writes:

> Upfront and fascist in his scorn for the democratic idea, he declared his candidacy on June 16, 2015, a deus ex machina descending by escalator into the atrium of Trump Tower on Manhattan's Fifth Avenue, there to say, and say it plainly, democracy is for losers. Money, ladies and gentlemen, is power, and power, my friends, is not self-sacrificing or Democratic. Never was and never will be; law unto itself, and the only one that counts. Name of the game, nature of the beast . . . His was the greatest brand on earth come to make America once again the greatest show on earth, revive it with the sweet smell of his signature men's colognes, *Empire* and *Success*. Trump didn't need briefing papers or policy positions to refine the message. He embodied it live and in person, an unscripted and overweight canary flown from its gilded cage, telling it like it is from the inside looking out.[7]

One of the ironies of the times in which we live is that a Black rap star shares with Trump the use of the brutalizing discourse of racism. Maybe Lil Wayne should read about the history of the civil rights movement before he fashions lyrics that sound as if they were written by the racists that killed this young man. Maybe the American public should go further and ask what kind of country creates people like Lil Wayne and what can be done to create pedagogical spaces that would stop this kind of racism and sexism in its tracks, rather than reward it.

In what follows, I want to provide a context for this focus on a particularly disturbing racist expression buttressed by historical amnesia and the easy comforts of a kind of manufactured ignorance. In doing so, I want to focus on ignorance not simply as the absence of knowledge, a kind of void of intelligence and information, but as something that is willed, systemically produced, and used in the interest of what can be called the violence of armed ignorance. Armed ignorance is no longer marginal to American society, but now inhabits the center of power and politics and will be used to weaponize knowledge, the social media, and the institutions in which knowledge is produced.

What happens to a society when thinking is eviscerated and disdained in favor of raw emotion? What happens when political discourse functions as a bunker rather than a bridge? What happens when the spheres of morality and spirituality give way to the naked instrumentalism of a savage market rationality? What happens when time becomes a burden for most people and surviving becomes more crucial than trying to lead a life with dignity? What happens when domestic terrorism, disposability, and social death become the new signposts and defining features of a society? What happens to a social order ruled by an "economics of contempt" that blames the poor for their condition and wallows in a culture of shaming?[8] What happens when loneliness and isolation become the preferred modes of sociality? What happens to a polity when it retreats into private silos and is no longer able to connect personal suffering with larger social issues? What happens to thinking when a society is addicted to speed and overstimulation? What happens to a country when the presiding principles of a society are violence and ignorance? What happens is that democracy withers not just as an ideal but also as a reality, and individual and social agency become weaponized as part of the larger spectacle and matrix of violence.[9]

The forces normalizing and contributing to such violence are too expansive to cite, but surely they would include: the absurdity of celebrity culture; the blight of rampant consumerism; state-legitimated pedagogies of repression that kill the imagination of students; a culture of immediacy in which accelerated time leaves no room for reflection; the reduction of education to training; the transformation of mainstream media into a mix of advertisements, propaganda, and entertainment; the emergence of an economic system that argues that only the market can provide remedies for endless social problems, while producing everything from massive poverty and unemployment to decaying schools and a war on poor minority youth; the expanding use of state secrecy and the fear-producing surveillance state; and a Hollywood fluff machine that rarely relies on anything but a non-stop spectacle of mind-numbing violence. Historical memory has been reduced to the likes of a Disney theme park and a culture of instant gratification has a lock on producing new levels of social amnesia.

As we learned in the presidential debates between Donald Trump and Hillary Clinton (a billionaire and a millionaire), ignorance is the DNA of authoritarianism, serving to subvert the truth and obscure the workings of power. Willful ignorance has become a normalized political tool and form of public pedagogy that both provides the foundation for what Noam Chomsky labels as the rise of the "stupid party" and which works incessantly to create a "stupid nation."[10] Trump, of course, proved that stupidity is in fashion and deeply entrenched within the larger culture while Hillary capitalized on her penchant for disingenuousness by claiming support for policies she really disdains, e.g. stating she will raise taxes on her buddies from Goldman Sachs and other members of the financial elite. Hardly believable from a woman who "has earned millions of dollars from speeches to Wall Street banks and investment firms (and) was paid $675,000 for a series of speeches to Goldman Sachs."[11] No hints of the radical imagination here, or the truth for that matter. What's left is the politics of stupidity and evasion and a media spectacle supporting the celebration of limited and pathologized political horizons.

Manufactured ignorance also makes invisible the corruption of the financial elite, allowing them to plunder resources and define the accumulation of capital as a divine blessing. This is aided by the voracious seductions of a commodified, corporate-driven disimagination machine that promotes a culture of empty pleasures through an endless regime of consuming and discarding. American society is now dominated by a pervasive commodified landscape of disimagination machines that extends from Hollywood movies and video games to mainstream television, magazines, news, and the social media. These mind-numbing desiring machines which thrive on speed and sensation function mostly as workstations of ignorance to create a fog of distractions that promote forms of social amnesia that erase from memory and public discourse the structural, systemic, and social forces that reinforce what can be called organized powerlessness and massive human suffering.

This is the death-dealing apparatus of a politics of disappearance and social abandonment that erases the presence of the poor, the unemployed, the "approximately 11 million Americans cycle[d] through jails and prisons each year," Black youth, immigrants, ecological disasters, class warfare, acts of state-sponsored terrorism, the rise of the police state, and the rise of the warfare state.[12] As the machinery of social death accelerates, America's most precious investment, youth, also disappear. Neoliberal disimagination machines such as Fox News make it clear that youth are no longer considered social investments and do not count in a society that disdains long-term investments and their messy calls for being included in the script of democracy. As such, the current war on youth is about erasing the future, or at least any alternative future and any notion of imagination that might summon one into view.

When coupled with an age of precarity and endless uncertainty in which young people have few decent jobs, are strangulated by debt, and face a future of career-less jobs and isolation, they have little room for politics because they are more concerned with trying to survive rather than engaging in the political act of imagining and struggling for a different future. At the same time, armies of the unemployed or underemployed are caught in a spiral of receding wages, diminished social provisions, and increasingly find themselves paralyzed by anxiety and free-floating anger. In such situations, thinking and informed action become more difficult while a politics wedded to economic and social justice is eviscerated. Moreover, politics becomes toxic when dominated by unapologetic discourses of racism and hatred as was on full display in the Trump campaign. Tapping into such anger and redirecting it away from the real problems that produce it has become the central script in the rise of the new authoritarians. The politics of manufactured ignorance is further expanded by the rise of fake news as a specific genre of the surreal.

This poisonous discourse of misrepresentation, lies, hate, and disingenuousness gains momentum and accelerates as it moves between white supremacist incantations of Trump and his zealots and the deceptive vocabulary of a financial elite who embrace a savage neo-liberalism with its false claims to freedom, choice, and the virtues of militarization. The scourge of civic death was on full display as the ideals of democracy disappeared in an election in which authoritarianism in its various forms ruled without apology. And in the aftermath of the election, thinking dangerously and acting with civic courage wane as state violence, disposability, and voicelessness become the dominant registers of an authoritarian politics that has intensified in American society producing neo-fascist movements that now occupy the center of political life.

Tragedy looms large in American society as the forces that promote powerlessness and voicelessness intensify among those elements of the population struggling just to survive the symbolic violence of a culture of cruelty and the material violence of a punishing state. The issue of losing one's voice either to the forces of imposed silencing or state repression weakens dissent and opens the door to the seductions of a dogmatism that speaks in the language of decline, making America great again, while touting the coded vocabulary of white nationalism and racial purity. How else to explain Trump's call for imposing racial profiling as a way to boost the notion of law and order.

Thinking undangerously is the first step in the triumph of formalism over substance, theater over politics, and the transformation of politics into a form of pop-idol culture. The refusal to think works in the service of a form of voicelessness, which is another marker of what it means to be powerless. Within this moral and political vacuum, the codes, rhetoric, and language of white supremacy are on the rise wrapped in the spectacle of fear mongering and implied threats of state repression. In this instance, emotion becomes more important than reason, ideas lose their grip on reality, and fashion becomes a rationale for discarding historical memory, informed arguments, and critical thought. Reflection no longer challenges the demands of common sense or the signposts of racism, hatred, and bigotry. Manufactured ignorance opens the door to an unapologetic culture of bullying and violence aimed at Muslims, immigrants, Blacks, and others who do not fit into Trump's notion of America.[13] Young children, especially those whose parents are being targeted by Trump's rhetoric, report being bullied more, hate crimes are on the rise, and state violence is accelerating against Native Americans, Black youth, and others now deemed unworthy and disposable in Trump's America.[14]

In the mainstream media, the endless and unapologetic proliferation of lies become fodder for higher ratings, informed by a suffocating pastiche of talking heads, all of whom surrender to "the incontestable demands of quiet acceptance."[15] Politics has become a spectacle, but not merely, as Neil Gabler states, "in the name of entertainment."[16] The framing mechanism that drives the mainstream media is a sink or swim individualism which accentuates and accelerates hostility, insults, and the politic of humiliation. As the discourse of the common good and compassion withers, the only vocabulary left is that of the bully. There is more at work here than a growing lack of civility in American politics. What was on full display in the presidential election of 2016 was the merging of the culture of cruelty, self-interest, anti-intellectualism, unbridled anger, disposability, and a fear of others as a driving force of collective expression and politics itself. Jessica Lustig captures this organized culture of violence, grudges, and loathing in the following comments:

> Grievance is the animating theme of this election and the natural state of at least one of the candidates; Trump is a public figure whose ideology, such as it is, essentially amounts to a politics of the personal grudge. It has drawn to him throngs of disaffected citizens all too glad to reclaim the epithet "deplorable." But beyond these aggrieved hordes, it can seem at times as if nearly everyone in the country is nursing wounds, cringing over slights and embarrassments, inveighing against enemies and wishing for retribution. Everyone has someone, or something, to resent.[17]

It gets worse. The trolling community in the age of a bullying internet culture has played a role in electing as the president one of their own. As the apostle of publicity for publicity's sake, Trump has adopted the practices of reality TV building his reputation on insults, humiliations, and a discourse of provocation and hate. According to the *New York Times*, Trump used Twitter after announcing his candidacy to insult 282 people prior to the election.[18] Not only did he hone the technique of trolling, he also made it a crucial resource in upping the ratings for the mainstream media who could not give enough coverage to Trump's insults and juvenile antics. By normalizing this culture of cruelty and ignorance, Trump has done more than bring a vicious online harassment culture into the mainstream, he has also legitimated the worst dimensions of politics and brought out of the shadows ultra-nationalists, racist militia types, misogynists, and a variety of white supremacists who have turned their hate-filled discourse into a weaponized element of political culture. Jared Keller captures perfectly the essence of Trump's politics of trolling. He writes:

> From the start, the Trump campaign has offered a tsunami of trolling, waves of provocative tweets and soundbites—from "build the wall" to "lock her up"—designed to provoke maximum outrage, followed, when the resulting heat felt a bit too hot, by the classic schoolyard bully's excuse: that it was merely "sarcasm" or a "joke." In a way, it is. It's just a joke with victims and consequences . . . Trump's behavior has normalized trolling as an accepted staple of daily political discourse . . . [quoting Whitney Philips, he continues] "When you have the presidential candidate boasting about committing sexual assault and then saying, 'Oh, it's just locker room banter' . . . it sets such an insidious, sexually violent tone for the election, and the result of that is fearfulness . . . People are being made to feel like shit."[19]

Contemporary politics has dissolved into a pit of performative narcissism and pathology and testifies to the distinctive power of neoliberal, consumer, and celebrity culture as an influential educational force being used to reconfigure not just political discourse but the nature of power itself. Rather than expressing collective anger in the face of the 2008 Wall Street collapse, the ensuing political corruption, and the consolidation of wealth and power, millions of Americans turned to the politics of misdirected resentment. Tom Engelhardt appears right on target in suggesting that the rising tide of white anger and racism gave us the presidency of Donald Trump, which is comparable to a "9/11-style shock to the body politic." He goes on to write insightfully:

> As I wrote in early October, "a significant part of the white working class . . . feels as if, whether economically or psychologically, its back is up against the wall and there's nowhere left to go . . . many of these voters have evidently decided that they're ready to send a literal loose cannon into the White House; they're willing, that is, to take a chance on the roof collapsing, even if it collapses on them." Think of Donald Trump's election, then, as the victory of the suicide bomber the white working class dispatched to the Oval Office to, as people now say politely, "shake things up" . . . The most dangerous nation on the planet will now be ours. Led by a man who knows remarkably little, other than how to manipulate the media (on which he's a natural-born genius) and, at least in part, by the frustrated generals from America's war on terror, the United States is likely to be more extreme, belligerent, irrational, filled with manias, and heavily armed, its military funded to even greater levels no other country could come close to, and with staggering powers to intervene, interfere, and repress.[20]

The collapse of the United States into an updated form of authoritarianism has been reinforced, in part, by the strange intersection of consumer culture, manufactured ignorance, and the cult of unrestrained emotion. A tsunami of manufactured thoughtlessness has produced a new register of collective resentment, which as Mark Danner points out, takes "the shape of reality television politics."[21] Within such an environment, a personalized notion of resentment drives politics while misdirecting rage towards issues that reinforce a totalitarian logic. Consequently, the long-standing forces of nativism and demagoguery drive American politics and the truth of events is no longer open to public discussion or informed judgment. All that is left is the empty, but dangerous performance of misguided hopes wrapped up in the fog of ignorance coded as theater, the haze of political and moral indifference, and the seductive appeal of the spectacle of violence.

Americans occupy a historical moment in which it is crucial to think dangerously, particularly since such thinking has the power to shift the questions, provide the tools for offering historical and relational contexts, and "push at the frontiers . . . of the human imagination."[22] Stuart Hall is right in insisting that thinking dangerously is crucial "to change the scale of magnification . . . to break into the confusing fabric that 'the real' apparently presents, and find another way in. So it's like a microscope and until you look at the evidence through the microscope, you can't see the hidden relations."[23] In this instance, the critical capacity for thinking becomes dangerous when it can intervene in the "continuity of commonsense, unsettle strategies of domination," and work to promote strategies of transformation.[24]

As Adorno observes, such thinking "speaks for what is not narrow-minded—and commonsense most certainly is."[25] As such, dangerous thinking is not only analytical in its search for understanding and truth, it is also critical and subversive, always employing the modes of self and social critique necessary to examine its own grounds and those poisonous fundamentalisms in the larger society haunting the body politic. As Michael Payne observes, thinking dangerously (or critical theory in this instance) should be cast in the language of hints, dialogue, and an openness to other positions, rather than be "cast in the language of orders."[26] Of course, this is not to suggest that thinking dangerously guarantees action, but at the same time, any action that distances itself from such thinking is bound to fail.

In an age when shouting, rage, and unchecked emotions shape public discourse, self-reflection becomes a liability and suppresses the axiom that critical thought should function to "lift . . . human beings above the evidence of our senses and sets appearances apart from the truth."[27] Salmon Rushdie is right in believing that thinking dangerously is a type of political necessity whose purpose is to "push boundaries and take risks and so, at times, to change the way we see the world."[28] As Hannah Arendt noted, thoughtfulness, the ability to think reflectively and critically, is fundamental to radical change and crucial in a functioning democracy. Put differently, formative cultures that make such thinking possible along with the spaces in which dialogue, debate, and dissent can flourish are essential to producing critically literate and actively engaged citizens.

Unfortunately, thinking undangerously cuts across ideological and political divides. For instance, there is a new kind of historical and social amnesia overtaking some elements of resistance in the United States. Many progressives have forgotten the lessons of earlier movements for real change extending from the anti-Vietnam War and Black Freedom movements to the radical feminist and gay rights movements of the sixties. These movements worked hard to make power visible, draw upon the resources of previous historical struggle—especially labor struggles— wage ideological and pedagogical struggles that enabled people to develop alternative modes of critique and narrate their problems in systemic terms, and connect a radical politics with the needs and issues people faced in their daily experience, such as offering free child care for parents, food programs for children, free early childhood education, and unrestricted health care where possible for everyone.

Too much of contemporary politics has collapsed the political into the personal, often reducing agency to the highly charged emotions of depoliticizing modes of therapy and individually embraced notions of trauma. Personal travails too often frame our grievances and in doing so confuse an embrace of personal trauma as a mode of political agency and struggle. Community drops out of this type of discourse which often confuses reform with the call "for a complete transformation of the social order."[29] What must be remembered is that the politics of historical struggles of resistance were not limited to a call for recognition and security within the confines of isolated political issues. On the contrary, they called for anti-racist struggles, activism, and economic justice. Such struggles around race, class, gay rights, and other issues were often understood in terms of their intersections, grouped not merely by their differences but what they had in common regarding their fight against an oppressive capitalist system and other modes of authoritarianism.

Thinking dangerously, in part, means embracing a historical consciousness as a repository of learning with vast resources to enable people to build on previous legacies of resistance, develop large political formations, and take seriously the pedagogical task of consciousness raising. Instead, they called for a radical transformation of capitalist and other authoritarian societies. Moreover, they understood that the truth of domination lies in understanding the totality of a society and how various issues are connected to each other. George Monbiot exemplifies this issue in arguing against responding to the varied crises associated with neoliberalism as if they emerged in isolation—a response that contributes to neoliberalism's anonymity. He writes:

> Its anonymity is both a symptom and cause of its power. It has played a major role in a remarkable variety of crises: the financial meltdown of 2007–8, the offshoring of wealth and power, of which the Panama Papers offer us merely a glimpse, the slow collapse of public health and education, resurgent child poverty, the epidemic of loneliness, the collapse of ecosystems, the rise of Donald Trump. But we respond to these crises as if they emerge in isolation, apparently unaware that they have all been either catalyzed or exacerbated by the same coherent philosophy; a philosophy that has—or had—a name. What greater power can there be than to operate namelessly?[30]

This politics of disconnection is exacerbated by the fact that mass social movements run the risk of being undermined by a politics that has collapsed into disconnected issues and the realm of the personal. For example, for too many progressives personal pain represents a retreat into an interiority that focuses on trauma. Robin Kelley provides a caveat here in pointing out that all too often "managing trauma does not require dismantling structural racism" and the larger issues of "oppression, repression, and subjugation" get replaced with "words such as PTSD, micro-aggressions, and triggers."[31] Kelley is not suggesting that the pain of personal suffering be ignored. Instead, he warns "against . . . the consequences of *framing* all grievances in the 'language of *personal* trauma.'"[32]

Personal trauma in this case can begin with legitimate calls for spaces free of racism, sexual harassment, and various other forms of hidden but morally and politically unacceptable assaults. And at its best, such a politics functions as an entry into political activism; but when it becomes less a justifiable starting point than an endpoint it begins to sabotage any viable notion of radical politics. Kelley is right in insisting that "trauma can easily slip into thinking of ourselves as victims and objects rather than agents."[33] Moreover, the language of safe spaces, personal trauma, and triggers can easily become a topsy-turvy discursive universe of trick mirrors and trapdoors that end up reproducing a politics of intimidation and conformity, while forgetting that pedagogical practices and a corresponding politics in the service of dramatic transformation are always unsettling and discomforting.

Progressives must avoid at all cost the rebirth of a politics in which how we think and act is guaranteed by the discourses of origins, personal experience, and biology. When individuals become trapped within their own experiences, the political imagination weakens, and a politics emerges that runs the risk of inhabiting a culture of exclusion and hardness that shuts down dialogue, undermines compassion, kills empathy, and makes it more difficult to listen to and learn from others. A politics that puts an emphasis on personal pain can become blind to its own limitations and can falsely offer a guaranteed access to the truth and a comforting embrace of a discourse of political certainty.

In such cases, the walls go up again as the discourses of biology and exclusion merge to guard the frontiers of moral righteousness and political absolutism. Put differently, the registers of militarization are on full display in such alleged sites of resistance such as higher education where a growing culture of political purity marks out a space in which the personal becomes the only politics there is housed within a discourse of "weaponized sensitivity" and "armed ignorance."[34] The first casualty of armed ignorance is a kind of thoughtfulness that embraces empathy for the other, a willingness to enter into public discussion, and dialogue with those who exist outside of the bunkers of imagined communities of exclusion. Leon Wieseltier is right in arguing that "grievance is sometimes the author of blindness, or worse."[35] We see examples of this kind of political purity in the academy in both students and faculty who create ideological walls around their beliefs rather than engage in dialogue with those who hold different opinions. Instead of critical exchanges people are humiliated and shamed for holding dissimilar positions or for speaking to issues from outside of a community of insiders. For instance, hard-line feminists might argue that men are not qualified to speak to women's issues or that one cannot address an issue if they are not members of an oppressed group. This is the politics of essentialism that trades in moral purity and inhabits all too gleefully circles of certainty that mimic a kind of theoretical infantilism and political immaturity.

Under such conditions, empathy wanes and only extends as far as recognizing those who mirror the self, one that endlessly narrates itself on the high ground of an unassailable moralism and stultifying orbits of self-interest. In addition, politics collapses into the privatized orbits of a crude essentialism that disdains forms of public discourse in which boundaries break down and the exercise of public deliberation is viewed as fundamental to a substantive democracy. Of course, there is more at work here than what might be called the atrophy of critical thought, self-reflection, and theory—there is also the degeneration of agency itself.

What does thinking look like when it is transformed into a pedagogical parasite on the body of democracy? At one level, it becomes toxic, blinding the ideological warriors to their own militant ignorance and anti-democratic rhetoric. At the same time, it shuts down any attempt to develop public spheres that connect rather than separate advocates of a politics walled in by suffocating notions of essentialism dressed up in the appeal to orthodoxy parading as revolutionary zeal. What must be remembered is that thinking undangerously mimics a pedagogy of repression that falsely assumes a revolutionary stance when in fact everything about it is counter-revolutionary. In the end this suggests a kind of theoretical helplessness, a replacing of the courage to think dangerously with the discourse of denunciation and a language overflowing with the comforting binary of good and evil.

Thinking dangerously can make the pedagogical more political by mapping the full range of how power is used and how it can be made accountable in all of its uses. Thinking dangerously is about more than doing a critical reading of screen culture and other texts, it is also about how knowledge, desire, and values become invaluable tools in the service of economic and political justice, how language provides the framework for dealing with power and what it means to develop a sense of compassion for others and the planet. Thinking dangerously is more than a mode of resistance, it is the basis for a formative and pedagogical culture of questioning and politics that takes seriously how the imagination can become central to the practice of freedom, justice, and democratic change.

There is more at risk here than overcoming the worst forms of thoughtlessness, particularly those that shape the interlocking registers of popular culture, celebrity-obsessed culture, and consumer culture. There is also the need to develop a politics in which theories of subjectivity and agency merge with more traditional theories of material structures of domination. How people think, invest in larger systemic structures, and define their own sense of identity and agency has to be understood in historical, political, and theoretical terms if progressives are to challenge growing public apathy, the withering of public life, and the potential undermining of any vestige of democracy. Thinking dangerously as a critical enterprise is about both a search for the truth and a commitment to the recognition that no society is ever just enough and hence is fundamental to the always unfinished struggle, making the impossible all the more possible. Not one or the other but both. Such thinking should be used to both understand and engage the major upheavals people face—racism, poverty, segregation, inequality, and a crippling sense of alienation, among others—and to connect such problems to larger political, structural, and economic issues.

Notes

1   Tom Engelhardt, "Is America Poised to Become the Most Dangerous Country on Earth?" *Nation* (December 1, 2016). Online: www.thenation.com/article/is-america-poised-to-become-the-most-dangerous-country-on-earth/

2   Michael Brenner, "How Autocracy Will Come to America," *Huffington Post* (November 30, 2016). Online: www.huffingtonpost.com/entry/how-autocracy-will-come-to-america_us_583f559ae4b0c68e047ec72f

3   On the politics of colorblindness, see David Theo Goldberg and Susan Searls Giroux, *Sites of Race* (London: Polity, 2014); Michelle Alexander, *The New Jim Crow* (New York: New Press, 2015).

4   Kali Holloway, "How 'We' Will Not Survive Trump: History Proves That Idea Has Never Been True," *AlterNet* (December 1, 2016). Online: www.alternet.org/election-2016/how-we-will-not-survive-trump

5   Henry A. Giroux, *Stormy Weather: Katrina and the Politics of Disposability* (Boulder, CO: Paradigm, 2006), pp. 1–2.

6   Lewis Lapham, "Hostile Takeover," *CounterPunch* (December 9, 2016). Online: www.counterpunch.org/2016/12/09/hostile-takeover/

7   Ibid.

8   I have borrowed this term from Jeffrey St. Clair, "The Economics of Contempt," *CounterPunch* (May 23, 2014). Online: www.counterpunch.org/2014/05/23/the-economics-of-contempt/

9   Brad Evans and I have taken up the issue of violence in its various valences in Brad Evans and Henry A. Giroux, *Disposable Futures: The Seduction of Violence in the Age of the Spectacle* (San Francisco: City Lights Books, 2015). Also, see Henry A. Giroux, *America's Addiction to Terrorism* (New York: Monthly Review Press, 2016).

10 Noam Chomsky, "Corporations and the Richest Americans Viscerally Oppose the Common Good," *Alternet* (September 29, 2014). Online: www.alternet.org/visions/chomsky-corporations-and-richest-americans-viscerally-oppose-common-good

11 Chris Cillizza, "The *New York Times* Just Perfectly Explained Hillary Clinton's Goldman Sachs Speech Problem," *Washington Post* (February 26, 2016). Online: www.washingtonpost.com/news/the-fix/wp/2016/02/26/the-new-york-times-just-perfectly-explained-why-hillary-clintons-answers-on-her-paid-speeches-dont-work/

12 Tom Engelhardt, "Tomgram: Rebecca Gordon, Arresting Our Way to 'Justice,'" *TomDispatch.com* (September 25, 2016). Online: www.tomdispatch.com/blog/176190/tomgram%3A_rebecca_gordon,_arresting_our_way_to_%22justice%22/

13 On the issue of bullying as a national pastime, see Charles Derber and Yale R. Magrass, *Bully Nation: How the American Establishment Creates a Bullying Society* (Lawrence: University of Kansas, 2016).

14 Katie Lobosco and Logan Whiteside, "In the Age of Trump, There's a New School Bully," *CNNMoney* (October 25, 2016). Online: http://money.cnn.com/2016/10/25/news/trump-rhetoric-school-bullying/

15 Brad Evans and Julien Reid, "The Promise of Violence in the Age of Catastrophe," *Truthout* (January 5, 2014). Online: http://truth-out.org/opinion/item/20977-the-promise-of-violence-in-the-age-of-catastrophe

16 Neal Gabler, "How the Media Enabled Donald Trump by Destroying Politics First," *Moyers and Company* (March 4, 2016). Online: http://billmoyers.com/story/how-the-media-enabled-donald-trump-by-destroying-politics-first/

17 Jessica Lustig, "From 'Hamilton' to Donald Trump: Are All 'Grievances' Created Equal?" *New York Times Magazine* (October 25, 2016). Online: www.nytimes.com/2016/10/30/magazine/from-hamilton-to-donald-trump-are-all-grievances-created-equal.html?rref=collection%2Fsectioncollection%2Fmagazine&action=click&contentCollection=magazine&region=rank&module=package&version=highlights&contentPlacement=6&pgtype=sectionfront

18 Jasmine C. Lee and Kevin Quealy, "The 282 People, Places and Things Donald Trump Has Insulted on Twitter: A Complete List," *New York Times* (October 23, 2016). Online: www.nytimes.com/interactive/2016/01/28/upshot/donald-trump-twitter-insults.html?_r=0

19 Jared Keller, "Trump's Grand Troll Campaign Is Just Getting Started," *Village Voice* (October 26, 2016). Online: www.villagevoice.com/news/trumps-grand-troll-campaign-is-just-getting-started-9264778?utm_source=Newsletters&utm_medium=email

20   Engelhardt, "Is America Poised to Become the Most Dangerous Country on Earth?"

21   Mark Danner, "The Magic of Donald Trump," *New York Review of Books* (May 26, 2016). Online: www.nybooks.com/articles/2016/05/26/the-magic-of-donald-trump/

22   Arundhati Roy, *Power Politics* (Cambridge, MA: South End Press, 2001), p. 1.

23   Stuart Hall and Les Back, "In Conversation: At Home and Not at Home," *Cultural Studies*, Vol. 23, No. 4 (July 2009), pp. 664–5.

24   I have taken this phrase from an interview with Homi Bhabha in Gary Olson and Lynn Worsham, "Staging the Politics of Difference: Homi Bhabha's Critical Literacy," *Journal of Composition Theory*, Vol. 18, No. 3. (1999), p. 9.

25   Zygmunt Bauman, *Liquid Life* (London: Polity Press, 2005), p. 139.

26   Michael Payne, "What Difference Has Theory Made? From Freud to Adam Phillips," *College Literature*, Vol. 32, No. 2 (Spring 2005), p. 7.

27   Bauman, *Liquid Life*, p. 151.

28   Salman Rushdie, "Whither Moral Courage?" *New York Times* (April 28, 2013). Online: www.nytimes.com/2013/04/28/opinion/sunday/whither-moral-courage.html?page wanted=all

29   Robin D. G. Kelley, "Black Study, Black Struggle," *Boston Review* (March 7, 2016). Online: http://bostonreview.net/forum/black-study-black-struggle/robin-d-g-kelley-robin-d-g-kelleys-final-response

30   George Monbiot, "Neoliberalism—the Ideology at the Root of All Our Problems," *Guardian* (April 15, 2016). Online: www.theguardian.com/books/2016/apr/15/neoliberalism-ideology-problem-george-monbiot

31   Kelley, "Black Study, Black Struggle—Final Response."

32   Ibid.

33   Ibid.

34   The notion of weaponized sensitivity is from Lionel Shriver, "Will the Left Survive the Millennials?" *New York Times* (September 23, 2016). Online: www.nytimes.com/2016/09/23/opinion/will-the-left-survive-the-millennials.html. Armed ignorance was coined by my colleague Brad Evans in personal correspondence.

35   Leon Wieseltier, "How voters' personal suffering overtook reason—and brought us Donald Trump," *Washington Post* (June 22, 2016). Online: www.washingtonpost.com/posteverything/wp/2016/06/22/how-voters-personal-suffering-overtook-reason-and-brought-us-donald-trump/

PART III

BEYOND NEOLIBERAL EDUCATION

7

DEFENDING EDUCATORS IN THE STRUGGLE FOR DEMOCRATIC RENEWAL

I should like to be able to love my country and still love justice. I don't want just any greatness for it, particularly a greatness born of blood and falsehood. I want to keep it alive by keeping justice alive.

(Albert Camus)

Authoritarian movements and ideologies with racist, xenophobic, and misogynistic overtones are back in America. As Michael Brenner[0] observes,

> Some ingredients are recognizable: racist hate; scapegoating of the alien "other"; mounting feelings of insecurity—economic, status, national; frustrated feelings of lost prowess; the scorning of elected democratic leaders condemned at once as "weak" (in not crushing the Islamic terrorists) and overbearing (in not yielding to claims of an absolute right to high caliber weaponry). Its intoxicating effects have given America over to the Tea Party and placed the Orangutan in the White House.

The institutions and public spaces that create informed citizens are in disarray as education has collapsed into training in many public schools and knowledge production in higher education is instrumentalized and wedded to the dictates of a business culture. Other sites of education, such as the various elements of mainstream media, have been reduced to cheerleaders for their corporate owners. In the absence of democratic public spheres, the need to both defend education as a public good and to make education central to politics itself becomes all the more pressing. This will not be easy, especially at a time when the Trump administration will further educational policies that will push for more charter and for-profit schools. Under such circumstances, public and higher education will be further defunded and segregated along class and racial lines. This will further exacerbate a public school system in which 51 percent of all students are from low-income families, are increasingly segregated along racial lines, are modeled after prisons, and whose classrooms are overcrowded and lack basic resources.

In addition, as a culture of hate, bigotry, and humiliation is now sanctioned at the highest levels of government, many students live in fear of being targeted and harassed by white racist students. As one report indicated, there has been a massive increase "in targeting and harassment . . . directed against immigrants, Muslims, girls, LGBT students, kids with disabilities and anyone who was on the 'wrong' side of the election," particularly in "schools with a majority of white students."[1] Under such circumstances, it is crucial to defend public and higher education not simply as places where students can receive a quality education but also as crucial sites for creating modes of agency that make a democracy possible.

In an age of intellectual and spiritual debasement, thinking is vilified as an act of subversion and ignorance translates into a political and cultural virtue. Traces of critical thought appear only at the margins of the culture as ignorance becomes the primary organizing principle of American society. For instance, two thirds of the American public believe that creationism should be taught in schools and a majority of Republicans in Congress do not believe that climate change is caused by human activity, making the U.S. the laughing stock of the world.[2]

Politicians endlessly lie knowing that the public is addicted to exhortation, emotional outbursts, and sensationalism, all of which mimic an obsessive and trivializing celebrity culture. Image selling now entails lying on principle making it all the easier for politics to dissolve into entertainment, pathology, and a unique brand of criminality. Fake news websites have become a central feature of knowledge production corresponding to and legitimated by a celebrity culture that undermines appeals to reason through an appeal to lifestyles, a marketplace of opinions, and a distrust of facts and informed arguments. The age of reason has been replaced by a new regime of illiteracy, one that uses screen culture and social media to flood the public with information while disdaining the more contemplative realm of knowledge and critical exchange for a culture of short attention spans, selfies, and immediacy. Paul Krugman claims that not only is Donald Trump, the President of the United States, ignorant, but that such ignorance is the defining feature of most of the members of the party. He writes:

> Truly, Donald Trump knows nothing. He is more ignorant about policy than you can possibly imagine, even when you take into account the fact that he is more ignorant than you can possibly imagine. But his ignorance isn't as unique as it may seem: In many ways, he's just doing a clumsy job of channeling nonsense widely popular in his party, and to some extent in the chattering classes more generally.[3]

Ignorance breeds corruption and endears us to falsehoods, venality, and carnival barking. The corruption of both the truth and politics is all the more possible since the American public have become habituated to overstimulation and live in an ever accelerating overflow of information and images. Experience no longer has the time to crystallize into mature and informed thought. Opinion outdoes reasoned and evidence-based arguments and the power of expression degenerates into a spectacle. News has become entertainment and echoes reality rather than interrogating it. Popular culture revels in the spectacles of shock and violence.[4] Too many universities have become McDonaldized and knowledge is now subject to the practice of a fast and instrumentalized education resulting in curricula that resemble a fast-food menu.[5] The university is organized increasingly to meet the needs of the market rather than to educate young people to be informed and critically engaged citizens. Lawrence Busch insightfully outlines some of the damaging market changes that have shaped higher education since the 1970s. He writes:

> Among the market-like changes that have [been] instituted (in varying degrees) are (1) shifting the cost of education from the State to individual students, (2) redefining higher education as a search for the highest paid job, (3) turning scholarly research into an individualized form of competition based on a wide range of metrics (e.g., numbers of citations, the value of grants, the numbers of patents), (4) instituting national and global competitions among universities and research institutes for funding and prestige, and (5) increasing the numbers and enhancing the power and salaries of administrators in return for pursuing these market-like objectives.[6]

Under such circumstances, higher education has lost its critical mission as a civically minded institution, and has been transformed into a commercial sphere organized by market-driven values, social relations, and financial incentives. Academics as public intellectuals with tenure have gone the way of the electric typewriter, relegated to the status of temporary Walmart workers—underpaid and overworked. Students are viewed as customers and consumers who have to be entertained and trained.[7] Critical and meaningful knowledge and scholarship are defined in accordance with the market-driven goal that they fulfill the imperatives of short-term investments and the accumulation of capital. As Noam Chomsky observes, under the reign of neoliberalism universities have been turned "into facilities that produce commodities for the job market, abandoning [their] traditional ideal[s]: fostering creative and independent thought and inquiry, challenging perceived beliefs, exploring new horizons and forgetting external constraints."[8]

There is more at stake here than redefining the meaning and purpose of higher education; there is also what the student radicals of the 1960s called the oppressive mechanizations of "the machine." That is, an institution that has become "part of a corporate business model designed to reduce labor costs and to increase labor servility."[9]

Education has lost its moral, political, and spiritual bearings just as teachers across the country are being belittled and institutions of higher education are under attack by economic and religious fundamentalists. One consequence is that higher education has become a corporate entity, which confuses training with education, employs a top-down authoritarian style of power, mimics a business culture, infantilizes students by treating them as consumers, and depoliticizes faculty by removing them from all forms of governance.[10] Clearly all of these defining relations produced by the neoliberal university have to be challenged and changed.

The slow death of public and higher education does not augur well for democracy. Americans live in a historical moment that disavows critical thinking. Rather than being an object of critique, ignorance has become an organizing principle of politics, civic culture, and society itself. Empty language and the spectacle of entertainment now expel thoughtfulness and informed judgment to the margins of American life. Some of my students tell me they don't like to talk on the phone because it is too demanding; speed dating and a hook-up culture provide the last word on the scourge of intimacy and commitment. Donald Trump takes pride in telling his aides and the American public that he does not read books and gets most of his information from Fox News. Relying on Twitter to communicate directly his simplistic messages, lies, and disparaging comments about others to the American people, Trump turns complex issues and ideas into objects of scorn, while reproducing a discourse of infantilism and fear. Fox News offers no apologies for suggesting that thinking is an act of stupidity. A culture of cruelty and a survival-of-the-fittest ethos in the United States is the new norm and one consequence is that democracy in the United States is on the verge of disappearing or has already disappeared! Andrew O'Hehir, a senior writer for *Salon*, has argued provocatively that Donald Trump represents "a domestic terrorist . . . trying to destroy America."[11] But O'Hehir does not blame Trump alone. Rather he sees the corruption and anti-democratic impulses that Trump showcased as central to a long legacy of American disorders produced in the nastiest of ideologies, practices, and policies by both parties. Yet Trump, unlike the established parties, does not represent the establishment. On the contrary, he is symptomatic of a collective anger among millions of Americans who cannot think through the conditions of their oppression and willingly have their anger directed into the explosive minefields of hate and bigotry.

What kind of society produces the person of Donald Trump? As O'Hehir observes, he is

> without doubt the most spectacularly ignorant and unqualified person ever to emerge as a major presidential candidate. . . . he's like a funhouse-mirror reflection of America's overweening pride and vanity, deadly sins for which we are now being punished. He is the ugliest possible American caricature, made flesh, and now is widely understood to be an abusive pig as well.[12]

He is the product of a culture that is proud of what it should be ashamed of—that is, a formative culture that works pedagogically to make people politically ignorant and civically thoughtless.

Where are the agents of democracy and the public spaces that offer hope in such dark times? Many are in public schools—all the more reason to praise public school teachers and to defend public and higher education as a public good. For the most part, public school teachers and higher education faculty are a national treasure and may be one of the last defenses available to undermine a growing authoritarianism, pervasive racism, permanent war culture, widening inequality, and debased notion of citizenship in American society. They can't solve these problems but they can educate a generation of students to address them. What is crucial to understand is that public and higher education are not simply about educating young people to be smart, socially responsible, and adequately prepared for whatever notions of the future they can imagine, but that education is central to democracy itself. Without the public spheres that make democracy possible, there will be no critical agents, no foundation for enabling people to force power to be liable, and no wider groundwork for challenging neoliberalism as a mode of governance and political and ideological rationality. Under Trump and his coterie of billionaires, American society is being modeled after the gambling empire of Las Vegas—a corporate rendition of the American Dream driven by a fetish for unchecked creative destruction, the celebration of bloated materialism, the financialization of everything, a suffocating individualism, and a view of everyday life based on the uncertainty and false hopes of the casino. Trump's world is one in which there are no structural problems, no systemic barriers, no history of inequality and mass exploitation, just the shining light of individual choices, responsibility, and agency.

The struggle over education and its democratic misuse cannot be separated from the struggle to undo the reign of markets, neoliberalism, and the ideologies informing this savage market fundamentalism. Neoliberal policies, values, and practices reinforce the worst dimensions of education: specialisms, a cult of distorted professionalism, a narrow empiricism, a competitive culture that reinforces the unwillingness of academics to work with others, a faculty with no governing power, deskilled teachers, a culture of punishment, and the implementation of instrumental and commodified modes of knowledge and pedagogy. All of this must change for teachers and faculty or they will continue to lose power to the corporate and managerial elite. What this suggests is that it is all the more necessary to defend educators as public intellectuals and socially concerned citizens who are crucial to the process of defending education as both a public good and a democratic public sphere.

Public school teachers, in particular, have been deskilled, forced to teach to the test, lack adequate resources, and are scorned as public servants. Yet, they are unjustly blamed by right-wing billionaires and politicians for the plight of public schools. In order to ensure their failure, schools in many cities such as Detroit and Philadelphia have been defunded by right-wing legislators. These schools are dilapidated—filled with vermin and broken floors—and they often lack heat and the most basic resources. They represent the mirror image of the culture of cruelty and dispossession produced by the violence of neoliberalism.

Under the counterfeit appeal to reform, national legislation imposes drill-and-test modes of pedagogy on teachers that kill the imagination of students. Young people suffer under the tyranny of methods that are forms of disciplinary repression. Teachers remain powerless as administrators model their schools after prisons and turn students over to the police. And in the midst of such egregious assaults, teachers are disparaged as public servants. The insecure, overworked adjunct lecturers employed en masse at most institutions of higher education fare no better. They have been reduced to an army of wage slaves, with little or no power, benefits, or time to do their research. Some states, such as Texas, appear to regard higher education as a potential war zone and have passed legislation allowing students to carry concealed weapons on campus.[13] That is certainly one way to convince faculty not to engage in controversial subjects with their students. With the exception of the elite schools, which have their own criminogenic environments to deal with, higher education is in free fall, undermined as a democratic public sphere and increasingly modeled after corporations and run by armies of administrators who long to be called CEOs.

All the while, the federal government spends billions of dollars, close to 600 billion in 2016, to fuel one of the largest defense and intelligence budgets in the world. The permanent-war death machine is overflowing with money while the public sector, social provisions, and public goods are disappearing. At the same time, many states allocate more funds to prisons than to higher education. Young children all over the country are drinking water poisoned with lead, while corporations rake in huge profits, receive huge tax benefits, and buy off politicians and utterly corrupt the political system. Trust and compassion are considered a weakness if not a liability in an age of massive inequities in wealth and power. In the midst of what can only be viewed as a blow against democracy, right-wing Republicans produce slash-and-burn policies that translate into poisonous austerity measures for the public schools and higher education. As Jane Mayer observes in *Dark Money*, the Koch brothers and their billionaire allies want to abolish the minimum wage, privatize schools, eliminate the welfare state, pollute the planet at will, break unions, and promote policies that result in the needless deaths of millions who lack adequate health care, jobs, and other essentials.[14] Public goods such as schools for these politicians and corporate lobbyists are financial investments, viewed as business opportunities. For the billionaires who are the anti-reformers, teachers, students, and unions simply get in the way and must be disciplined.

Public schools and higher education are dangerous because they hold the potential to serve as laboratories for democracy where students learn to think critically. Teachers are threatening because they refuse to view critical thinking as a burden or treat schools as if they are car dealerships. Many educators have made it clear that they regard teaching for the test and defining accountability only in numerical terms as a practice that dulls the mind and kills the spirit of students. It also kills the spirit of public school teachers. One recent survey published in 2015 found that "only 15 percent of teachers feel enthusiastic about the profession, and about three in four 'often feel' stressed by their jobs."[15] This is not surprising since teaching in the age of neoliberal tyranny has become more instrumental, feudal-like in its governing structures, and militarized in its approach to student behavior. Public schools appear in urban areas to be primarily containment centers more willing to criminalize student behavior than educate students by fulfilling the intellectual and civic purpose of critical education.[16] Such repressive requirements undermine the ability of teachers to be creative, engage with the communities in which they work, and teach in order to make knowledge critical and transformative. The claim that we have too many bad teachers is too often a ruse to hide bad policies, and unleash assaults on public schools by corporate-driven ideologues and hedge fund managers who view schools strictly as investment opportunities for big profits.

We need to praise teachers, hold them to high standards, pay them the salaries they deserve, give them control over their classrooms, reduce class sizes, and invest as much if not more in education as we do in the military-industrial complex. This is all the more reason to call attention to and join with those teachers in Chicago, Detroit, and Seattle who are collectively fighting against such attacks on public schools. We need to praise them, learn from them, and organize with them because they refuse to treat education as a commodity and they recognize that the crisis of schooling is about the crises of democracy, economic equality, and justice. This is not a minor struggle because no democracy can survive without informed citizens.

Under a Trump presidency, public schools and higher education will be subject to increasing pressure to eliminate critical scholarship and knowledge from the curriculum, dissent will be repressed and labeled as un-American, and a culture of privatization and conformity will define the future mission of public and higher education. Austerity measures will intensify as states and the federal government defund all public goods, including education. Defunding of public spheres such as schools will increase dramatically the distribution of resources between poor and wealthy schools and will reinforce segregation in American schools. A culture of austerity will be matched by a culture of fear and many educators will retreat from teaching critical ideas or teaching students how to be critical thinkers for fear of losing their jobs. Under a Trump presidency, America will enter one of the darkest periods in its history. Labor will come under intense attack, education as one of the last bastions of critical thought will weather an aggressive assault by the economic, political, and religious fundamentalists running the Trump administration. There will also be increased violence waged against Muslim students, immigrants, and people of color. As I write this chapter, according to the Southern Poverty Law Center, "more than 300 incidents of 'hateful harassment and intimidation' have been reported since election Day . . . roughly the amount they usually see in a five to six-month period."[17] According to Jack Jenkins,

> The stories behind the numbers tell an even darker story. Since Tuesday, several Muslim women have reported having their hijabs manhandled or even forcibly removed by people who made comments about Donald Trump. In Redding, California, a student recorded himself handing out fake deportation letters to students of color, and a sign promoting a Spanish-language mass at an Episcopal church was vandalized with the slogan "Trump Nation

Whites Only." An LGBT-affirming church in Blossom, Indiana was defaced with swastikas and slogans such as "Heil Trump" and "Fag church."[18]

The culture of hate, Islamophobia, anti-Semitism, and anti-immigrant fervor has become normalized under the Trump regime and this machinery of ideological fundamentalism will not only produce an increasing culture of cruelty and violence, but will also provide a powerful platform for waging an attack on any notion of the imagination, reduce faculty to a powerless and part-time labor force, and burden students with either a mind-numbing education, or enormous crippling debt, or both. If faculty and students do not resist this assault, they will have little control over the conditions of their labor, and the institutions of public and higher education will further degenerate into a repressive apparatus for producing authoritarian ideology, conformity, and a flight from any vestige of ethical and social responsibility.

With the onslaught of fake news, the emergence of websites naming alleged dangerous professors, right-wing trolling on the social media, and the call by Trump's administration for the names of people in the energy department who worked on climate change issues, there is a real threat that the United States is entering a period in which critical institutions, dissidents, and alternative media will be under threat if not censure. In addition, in the age of the domesticated simulacrum not only are the capacity for truth telling and informed judgment at risk, but politics itself is being emptied of any substance as the spectacularized forces of depoliticization go into full gear. The spectacle does more than entertain, it also pushes critical thought to the wayside as it produces endless performances of staged illiteracy and stupidity, all the while covering over the death-dealing mechanisms of the punishing state and ravages of casino capitalism. Under such circumstances, higher education and the alternative media may be some of the few places left where critical thinking can be nurtured in such dangerous times.

Clearly, it is time to revisit Mario Savio's famous University of California at Berkeley speech delivered in 1964 at Sproul Hall, which kick-started the Free Speech Movement all over the country, when he called for shutting down an educational system that had become odious. In his own words:

> [t]here comes a time when the operation of the machine becomes so odious, makes you so sick at heart, that you can't take part; you can't even passively take part, and you've got to put your bodies upon the gears and upon the wheels, upon all the apparatus, and you've got to make it stop. And you've got to indicate to the people who run it, the people who own it, that unless you're free the machine will be prevented from working at all![19]

Savio's call to resistance is more relevant today than it was then. Public schools not only mimic the injustices of an oppressive economic system, but also funnel poor youth of color into the criminal justice system. The good news is that there is an echo of outrage and resistance now emerging in the United States, especially among young people such as those in the Black Lives Matter movement.

If the major index of any democracy is measured by how a society invests in its youth, the United States is failing. Fortunately, more and more people are waking up and realizing that the fight for public schooling is not just about higher salaries for teachers, it is about investing in our children and in democracy itself. At the same time, we live in what Carl Boggs and others have called a permanent warfare state, one in which every space appears to be a battlefield, and the most vulnerable are viewed not only as an imminent threat, but also as the object of potential violence.[20] This suggests that the battle of education must become part of a wider political struggle. This is a struggle that connects assaults on education with the wide-ranging war on youth, police violence with the militarization of society, and specific instances of racist brutality with the unchecked exercise of the systemic power of finance capital.

But the struggle will not be easy. Beneath all of the current brutality, racism, and economic predation, there is some hope inspired by the generation of young people who are protesting police violence and the attack on public and higher education, and working hard to invent a politics that gets to the root of issues. There is also a glimmer of possibility in those youth who supported Bernie Sanders but are really demanding a new and more radical definition of politics: Their vision far surpasses that of the left-centrists and liberals of the Democratic Party. Elections are the ruse of capitalism, and that has never been clearer than at the present moment. Prior to Trump's electoral victory, we had on one side, a warmonger, a strong supporter of the financial elite, and a representative of a neoliberalism that is as brutal is it is cruel. On the other side we had, a circus barker inviting Americans into a den of horrors. And these are the choices that constitute democracy? I don't think so.

With the election of Donald Trump to the presidency, Americans have entered into one of the most sickening and dangerous periods of the 21st century. Trump is not only a twisted caricature of every register of economic, political, educational, and social extremism, he is the apogee of a warrior culture committed to rolling back civil rights, women's reproductive rights, denying the threat of climate change, and mocking, if not threatening, all vestiges of economic justice and democracy. As David Remnick pointed out in the *New Yorker*, Trump is a paragon of authoritarianism, a crude misogynist, liar, and racist who gives a new, bold, and unapologetic face to the dark specter of authoritarianism.[21] Actually, it gets worse. Trump is the fascist shadow that has been lurking in the dark since Nixon's Southern Strategy. A ghostly reminder of the price to be paid when historical consciousness and public values are lost in a culture of instant information, anxiety-producing precarity, a comforting ignorance, and a flight from social and political responsibility.

Authoritarianism has now become viral in America, spreading its toxic ideology into every facet of American life. The threat of total-itarianism with its legions of neo-fascist political zombies has now exposed itself, without apology, knowing full well that it no longer has to code or apologize for its hatred of all those who do not fit into its white-supremacist and ultra-nationalist script. Neo-fascist rhetoric and passions now animate many of Trump's appointees to the highest reaches of government. As I have mentioned previously, these are individuals such as Stephen Bannon and Jeff Sessions, who believe that whites are victims, Blacks inhabit a criminal culture, who long for the good old days when segregation was widespread, and believe in the superiority of a demagogue who renounces reason for his own instincts. In many ways, a significant number of Trump's cabinet appointments—filled with generals, billionaires, white supremacists, xenophobes, and anti-intellectuals—would fall comfortably into Robert Paxton's definition of fascism:

> Fascism may be defined as a form of political behavior marked by obsessive preoccupation with community decline, humiliation, or victim-hood and by compensatory cults of unity, energy, and purity, in which a mass-based party of committed nationalist militants, working in uneasy but effective collaboration with traditional elites, abandons democratic liberties and pursues with redemptive violence and without ethical or legal restraints goals of internal cleansing and external expansion.[22]

With America tipping over into authoritarianism, we have learned that liberalism sabotaged itself as it morphed into third-way market-driven economic and political policies, transforming itself into nothing more than an ugly corpse decomposing on the national and global landscape. Its commitment to corporate power and the financial elite has helped to provoke a wave of unchecked anger among the dispossessed, which Trump has tapped into in order to turn misfortune into hatred. In doing so, he has helped to undermine the most sacred democratic ideals and has pushed America into a mirror image of those European countries which have been transformed into gated sites of social abandonment for refugees and a petri dish for right-wing extremists.

Of course, power is never entirely on the side of domination, and in this coming era of acute repression, we will have to redefine politics, reclaim the struggle to educate, change individual and collective consciousness, engage in meaningful dialogue with people left out of the political landscape, and construct large social movements. There are hints of this happening among youth of color and we need to be attentive to these struggles.

This is a time for those who believe in democracy to both talk back and fight back. It will not be easy but it can happen and there are historical precedents for this. The main vehicle of change and political agency has to be young people. They are the beacon of the future and we have to learn from them, support them, contribute where possible, and join in their struggles.

The lights are going out in America and in many European countries and the time to wake up from this nightmare is today. Forget depression, look ahead, get energized, read, build alternative public spheres, and learn how to make authority responsible. There are no guarantees in politics, but there is no politics that matters without hope—that is, educated hope. What is happening in the United States can happen in any country, including Canada. America's move into authoritarianism is a warning for all of us, regardless of where we live.

Collective self-delusion will only go so far in the absence of an education system that offers a space for critical learning, dissent, and functions as a laboratory for democracy. There is a tendency to forget in an age dominated by the neoliberal celebration of self-interest and unchecked individualism that public goods matter, that critical thinking is essential to an informed public, and that education at the very least should provide students with unsettling ruptures that display the fierce energy of outrage and the hope for a better world. But a critical education has the capacity to do more. It also has the power not only to prevent justice from going dead in ourselves and the larger society but also, in George Yancy's poetic terms, to teach us how to "love with courage."[23] Hopefully, while education cannot solve such problems, it can produce the pedagogical spaces necessary to enable a generation of young people to create a robust third party—a party fueled by social movements demanding the economic and political justice that could allow a radical democracy to come to life.

Hannah Arendt was right in stating that "the aim of totalitarian education has never been to instill convictions but to destroy the capacity to form any," suggesting that totalitarianism was as much about the production of thoughtlessness as it was about the imposition of brute force, gaping inequality, corporatism, and the spectacle of violence.[24] Totalitari-anism destroys everything that democracy makes possible and in doing so thrives by stoking mass insecurity, fear, and rage; all of which are marshaled to demonize the Other—the Immigrant, the Black, the Mus-lim, the intellectual, and the young protesters. We live in an age in which the crucial notion that democracies need informed citizens who can think critically and act with a sense of civic responsibility is being forgotten, at great peril to democracy. Yet power, however tyrannical, is never without resistance. The dark clouds of authoritarianism are not ahead, they are upon us, but that does not mean that they are here to stay.

Notes

0   Michael Brenner, "The Essence of Fascism," *Huffington Post* (March 29, 2017). Online: htp://www.huffingtonpost.com/michael-brenner/essence-of-fascism_b_9557198.html

1   Maureen B. Costello, "The Trump Effect: The Impact of the 2016 Presidential Election on Our Nation's Schools," *Southern Poverty Law Center* (November 28, 2016). Online: www.splcenter.org/20161128/trump-effect-impact-2016-presidential-election-our-nations-schools

2   Sean Cockerham, "Senate Not Ready to Tie Climate Change to Mankind," *McClatchy Washington Bureau* (January 21, 2015). Online: www.mcclatchydc.com/news/politics-government/congress/article24778816.html; Kristen Ellingboe and Ryan Koronowski, "Most Americans Disagree with Their Congressional Representative on Climate Change," *Thinkprogress* (March 8, 2016). Online: http://thinkprogress.org/climate/2016/03/08/3757435/climate-denier-caucus-114th-new-research/

3   Paul Krugman, "The Making of an Ignoramus," *New York Times* (May 10, 2016). Online: www.nytimes.com/2016/05/09/opinion/the-making-of-an-ignoramus.html?_r=0

4   Brad Evans and Henry A. Giroux, *Disposable Futures: The Seduction of Violence in the Age of the Spectacle* (San Francisco: City Lights, 2016).

5   Ulrich Beck, *Twenty Observations on a World in Turmoil* (London: Polity Press, 2010), especially pp. 53–9.

6   Lawrence Busch, *Knowledge for Sale: The Neoliberal Takeover of Higher Education* (Cambridge, MA: The MIT Press, 2017), p. xvii.

7   I have taken these themes up in detail in Henry A. Giroux, *Neoliberalism's War on Higher Education* (Chicago: Haymarket Books, 2014).

8   Noam Chomsky, "Academic Freedom and the Corporatization of Universities," Lecture, University of Toronto, Scarborough (April 6, 2011). Online: http://chomsky.info/talks/20110406.htm

9   Noam Chomsky, "The Death of American Universities," *Reader Supported News* (March 30, 2015). Online: http://readersupportednews.org/opinion2/277-75/29348-the-death-of-american-universities

10 On the transformation of the university into a capitalist entity, see Henry Heller, *The Capitalist University* (London: Pluto Press, 2016).

11 Andrew O'Hehir, "Donald Trump, Domestic: The Man Who Tried to Kill Democracy —and Why We Had It Coming," *Salon* (October 22, 2016). Online: www.salon.com/

2016/10/22/donald-trump-domestic-terrorist-the-man-who-tried-to-kill-democracy-and-why-we-had-it-coming/

12   Ibid.

13   Simone Gubler, "Philosophizing with Guns," *New York Times* (April 11, 2016). Online: http://opinionator.blogs.nytimes.com/2016/04/11/philosophizing-with-guns/

14   Jane Mayer, *Dark Money: The Hidden History of the Billionaires behind the Rise of the Radical Right* (New York: Doubleday, 2016).

15   Jeff Bryant, "We Won't Improve Education by Making Teachers Hate Their Jobs," *CommonDreams* (April 22, 3016). Online: www.commondreams.org/views/2016/04/22/we-wont-improve-education-making-teachers-hate-their-jobs. The particular study mentioned here can be found at: www.aft.org/sites/default/files/worklifesurveyresults2015.pdf

16   Henry A. Giroux, *Youth in a Suspect Society* (New York: Palgrave Macmillan, 2010); Annette Fuentes, *Lockdown High: When the Schoolhouse Becomes a Jailhouse* (New York: Verso, 2013).

17   Jack Jenkins, "There Have Been More than 300 Reported Hate Incidents since Election Day," *Think Progress* (November 14, 2016). Online: https://thinkprogress.org/300-hate-incidents-since-election-day-bf9fd91edbd6#.g76e82iar

18   Ibid.

19   See: www.fsm-a.org/stacks/mario/mario_speech.html

20   Carl Boggs, *Origins of the Warfare State* (New York: Routledge, 2017).

21   David Remnick, "An American Tragedy," *New Yorker* (November 9, 2016). Online: www.newyorker.com/news/news-desk/an-american-tragedy-donald-trump

22   Robert Paxton, *The Anatomy of Fascism* (New York: Vintage, 2005), p. 218.

23   Brad Evans and George Yancy, "The Perils of Being a Black Philosopher," *New York Times* (April 18, 2016). Online: http://opinionator.blogs.nytimes.com/2016/04/18/the-perils-of-being-a-black-philosopher/

24   Hannah Arendt, "Ideology and Terror: A Novel Form of Government." In *The Origins of Totalitarianism* (New York: Houghton Mifflin Harcourt, 2001), p. 468.

8
TOWARDS A POLITICS OF COURAGE IN DARK TIMES

> We decide whether we love the world enough to assume responsibility for it.
>
> (Hannah Arendt)

During his presidential campaign, Donald Trump made it clear that he liked the illiterate masses and that once he assumed the presidency, he would appoint a range of incompetent people to high-ranking positions that would ensure that many people remained poorly educated, uninformed, and impoverished. A few examples make the point. Betsy DeVos, the current Secretary of Education, is a multimillionaire, has no experience in higher education, supports for-profit charter schools, and is a strong advocate for private school vouchers. Without irony, she has described her role in education as one way to "advance God's kingdom."[1] She is anti-union and her motto for education affirms Trump's own educational philosophy to "defund, devalue, and privatize."[2] Ben Carson, Trump's choice for Secretary of Housing and Urban Development, has never run a federal agency and has no experience in government, policy making, or in public housing and has described housing policy pejoratively as a form of social engineering and a socialist experiment.

New York City council member and chair of the city's Housing and Buildings Committee described Carson's appointment as "ill-advised, irresponsible and hover[ing] on absurdity."[3] Carson will run a $48 billion agency that oversees public housing and ensures that low-income families have access to housing that is safe and affordable. He believes people can escape from poverty through hard work alone and has argued that government regulations resemble forms of totalitarian rule comparable to what existed in communist countries.[4] Andrew F. Puzder, Trump's initial choice for Secretary of Labor, has less experience in government "than any secretary since the early 1980s."[5] He is a critic of worker protections, opposes raising the minimum wage, and appears to share Trump's disparaging views of women. As the *New York Times* pointed out, the advertisements that Mr. Puzder's companies run "to promote its restaurants frequently feature women wearing next to nothing while gesturing suggestively."[6] When asked about the ads, Mr. Puzder replied "I like our ads. I like beautiful women eating burgers in bikinis. I think it's very American."[7] I am sure Trump agrees. Puzder eventually withdrew his nomination to be labor secretary.

It is hard to believe that this gaggle of religious fundamentalists, conspiracy theory advocates, billionaires, and retrograde anti-communists, who uniformly lack the experience to take on the jobs for which they were nominated, could possibly be viewed as reasonable candidates for top government positions. As Representative Jared Huffman cited in the *Hill* observed,

> most of Trump's appointees are "The greatest collection of stooges and cronies and misfits we have ever seen in a presidential administration . . . Some of these people's only qualifications for the jobs they are being appointed for is that they have attempted to dismantle and undermine and destroy the very agencies they are now hoping to run."[8]

What these appointments suggest is that one element of the new authoritarianism is a deep embrace of ignorance, anti-intellectualism, crony capitalism, and a disdain for the institutions that give legitimacy to the social contract and the welfare state. Most of Trump's appointees to top cabinet positions are a mix of incompetent and mean-spirited billionaires and generals. This alliance of powerful representatives of predatory financial capitalists and right-wing supporters of the immense military-industrial-surveillance complex makes clear Trump's support of the worst elements of neoliberalism—a war on education, support for austerity policies, and an attack on social provisions, the poor, workers, unions, and the most vulnerable. As Eric Sommer wrote in *CounterPunch*, "These ministerial level cabinet selections are a warning that far greater attacks on the social and economic rights of American workers, and greater militarism and military aggression abroad are being prepared."[9] Trump's affirmation of an updated version of the Gilded Age and his attempts to accelerate America's slide into authoritarianism are an assault on reason, compassion, and human dignity. Its underside is a political mix of militarism and rule by the financial elite, both of which are central features of a savage neoliberal assault on democracy. Trump's government of billionaires and militarists makes clear that the next few years will be governed by a ruthless financial elite who will give new meaning to the state-sanctioned war culture that will impose forms of domestic terrorism across a wide swath of American society.

Thus far, Trump has appointed three generals to join his cabinet—James Mattis and Michael Flynn for Secretary of Defense and National Security Advisor, along with retired general John Kelly to head the Department of Homeland Security. Kelly is infamous for defending the force-feeding of prisoners held at Guantanamo Bay and wants to expand the prison population there. Retired general Mattis, whose nickname is "Mad Dog," stated in 2003, the year that Iraq was invaded, that "It's fun to shoot some people, you know, it's a hell of a hoot."[10] He once told marines under his command "Be polite. Be professional. But have a plan to kill everybody you meet."[11] As difficult as it is to imagine, it gets worse. Lieutenant General Michael T. Flynn, Trump's choice for national security advisor [now resigned], considers Islam, with its population of 1.3 billion, a terrorist threat. He has also used the social media to spread fake news stories "linking Mrs. Clinton to underage sex rings and other serious crimes [while pushing] unsubstantiated claims about Islamic laws spreading in the United States."[12] Because of his illegal dealings with Russia, he was forced to resign 24 days after his appointment. At work here is an emerging political–social formation in which fake news becomes an accepted mode of shaping public discourse, inexperience and incompetence become revered criteria for holding public office, and social responsibility is removed from any vestige of politics. All of these appointments point to the emergence of a new political order in which the dystopian fears of George Orwell and Aldous Huxley are merged with the comic grotesquery of the tyrannical systems lampooned by the Marx brothers.

Under the reign of right-wing governments and social movements spreading throughout the world, thinking has become dangerous. Increasingly, neoliberal regimes across Europe and North America have waged a major assault on critical pedagogy, public pedagogy, and the public spheres in which they take place. For instance, public and higher education are being defunded, turned into accountability factories, and now largely serve as adjuncts of an instrumental logic that mimics the values of a business culture. But, of course, this is not only true for spaces in which formal schooling takes place, it is also the case for those public spheres and cultural apparatuses producing knowledge, values, subjectivities, and identities through a range of media and sites. This applies to a range of creative spaces including art galleries, museums, diverse sites that make up screen culture, and various elements of mainstream media.[13]

Such sites have come under increasing fire since the 1970s and the war against dissident journalism, in particular, will intensify under a Trump presidency. Attacking the media was a central feature of Trump's presidential campaign and speaks to a coming age of repression, posing a dire threat to freedom of speech. As Christopher Hass observes:

> But more importantly, he threatened to "open up" libel laws so that he and others can more easily sue publications that are critical of them. Those kinds of attacks are designed to burn money and hours that independent publications don't have—and sometimes they can be fatal.[14]

What the apostles of neoliberalism have learned is that alternative media outlets along with diverse forms of artistic production can change how people view the world, and that such forms of public pedagogy can be dangerous because they not only hold the potential for creating critically engaged students, intellectuals, and artists, but can strengthen and expand the general public's imagination, give them critical tools to enable them to think otherwise in order to act otherwise, and hold to power accountable. Such thinking is also a prerequisite for developing social movements willing to rethink the vision and tactics necessary to fight against an authoritarian state.

In the face of Trump's draconian assault on democracy, it is crucial to rethink mechanisms of a repressive politics not only by highlighting its multiple registers of economic power, but also through the ideological pedagogical mechanisms at work in creating modes of agency, identities, and values that both mimic and surrender to authoritarian ideologies and social practices. In this instance, education as it works through diverse institutions, cultural apparatuses, and sites is crucial to both understand and appropriate as part of the development of a radical politics. Reclaiming radical pedagogy as a form of educated and militant hope begins with the crucial recognition that education is not solely about job training and the production of ethically challenged entrepreneurial subjects but is primarily about matters of civic literacy, critical thinking, and the capacity for liberatory change. It is also inextricably connected to the related issues of power, inclusion, and social responsibility.[15] If young people, workers, educators, and others are to develop a keen sense of the common good, as well as an informed notion of community engagement, pedagogy must be viewed as a cultural, political, and moral force, if not formative culture, that provides the knowledge, values, and social relations to make such democratic practices possible.

In this instance, pedagogy as a central element of politics needs to be rigorous, self-reflective, and committed not to the suffocating discourse of instrumental rationality but to the practice of freedom and liberation for the most vulnerable and oppressed. It must also cultivate a critical sensibility capable of advancing the parameters of knowledge, stretching the imagination, addressing crucial social issues, and connecting personal concerns to systematic social problems. Any viable notion of critical pedagogy must overcome the image of education as purely instrumental, a dead zone of the imagination, and a normalized space of oppressive discipline and imposed conformity.

A neoliberal and anti-democratic pedagogy of management and conformity not only undermines the critical knowledge and analytical skills necessary for students to learn the practice of freedom and assume the role of critical agents, it also reinforces deeply authoritarian practices while reproducing deep inequities in the educational opportunities that different students acquire. As Sara Robinson points out,

> In the conservative model, critical thinking is horrifically dangerous, because it teaches kids to reject the assessment of external authorities in favor of their own judgment—a habit of mind that invites opposition and rebellion. This is why, for much of Western history, critical thinking skills have only been taught to the elite students—the ones headed for the professions, who will be entrusted with managing society on behalf of the aristocracy. (The aristocrats, of course, are sending their kids to private schools, where they will receive a classical education that teaches them everything they'll need to know to remain in charge.) Our public schools, unfortunately, have replicated a class stratification on this front that's been in place since the Renaissance.[16]

Pedagogies of repression and conformity impose punishing forms of discipline not just on students, but on the general public, deadening their ability to think critically; how else to explain the refusal of large segments of the public to think through and challenge the lies, misrepresentations, and contradictions that Trump used during his campaign? Repressive forms of public pedagogy empty out politics of any substance and further a modern-day pandemic of loneliness and alienation. Such pedagogies emphasize aggressive competition, unchecked individualism, and cancel out empathy for an exaggerated notion of self-interest. Solidarity and sharing are the enemy of these pedagogical practices, which are driven by a withdrawal from sustaining public values, trust, and goods and serve largely to eliminate a democratic future for young

people. This type of pedagogical tyranny poses a particular challenge
for progressives who are willing to acknowledge that the crisis of politics
and economics has not been matched by a similar crisis of critical
thought and informed judgment, resulting in a new age of authoritarianism. This is especially true for those educators who want to take
up the role of engaged public intellectuals, especially at a time when
higher education has become corporatized and is intent on reproducing
a toxic emphasis on careerism, a narrow commercialism, a demeaning
view of students as consumers, the reduction of faculty to an inden-
tured labor force, and a neoliberal mode of governance.[17] What is often
forgotten by theorists criticizing higher education is that not only have
students been reduced to clients and consumers and business models
taken over many administrations in higher education, but the faculties
in many schools have been decimated, reduced to contingent labor,
barely able to provide for themselves and reduced to living in fear about
doing or saying anything both in and out of class that may threaten
their jobs. As Michael Meranze observes:

> One of the most glaring, if also most often ignored in public debate,
> is the working conditions of precarious faculty and its relation-
> ship to questions of academic freedom. It is no secret that the
> large majority of teaching in colleges and universities is done
> by contingent labor (either graduate students or non-tenure track
> faculty) ... the particular threats that contingency poses to
> academic freedom have been largely ignored. Yet there can be little
> question that it is contingent faculty, not tenure track, let alone
> tenured, faculty who face the greatest dangers regarding their
> freedom to teach and to write. After all, the very point of hiring
> contingent faculty is to preclude obligations to ensure them long-
> term or full-time employment.[18]

Under such circumstances, critical pedagogical work becomes more
difficult and risky; yet such work is necessary if public and higher education are to remain viable sites of struggle. A new age of monstrosities

is emerging that necessitates that we rethink the connection between politics and democracy, on the one hand, and education and social change on the other. More specifically, we might begin with the following questions: What institutions, agents, and social movements can be developed capable of challenging the dark times ahead? Moreover, what pedagogical conditions need to be exposed and overcome in order to create the cultural experiences and institutions that would make such a challenge successful?

At stake here is the need for artists, educators, and others to create pedagogical practices that encourage militant dreamers, people capable of envisioning a more just and democratic world and those who are willing to struggle for it. In this instance, pedagogy becomes not only central to politics but also a practice dedicated to creating a sense of belonging, community, empathy, and practices that address changing the way people think and navigate conflicts emotionally—practices that awaken passion and energize forms of identification that speak to the conditions in which people find themselves. In the shark-like world of neoliberal-driven values, excessive competition, uncertainty, and deep-seated fears of the other, there is no room for empathetic conversations that focus on the common good, democratic values, or the pedagogical conditions that would further critical dialogue and the potential for students to learn how to interrogate and change oppressive power relations. Nor is there room for the institutions, including public and higher education, that connect knowledge to social change and the call for a society and world defined by the imperatives of economic and social justice.

Domination is at its most powerful when its mechanisms of control and subjugation hide in the discourse of common sense, and its elements of power are made to appear invisible. Public intellectuals in a wide variety of sites can take up the challenge not only of relating their specialties and modes of cultural production to the intricacies of everyday life but also of rethinking how politics works, and how power is central to such a task. Bruce Robbins articulates the challenge well in both his defense of the intellectual and his reference to how other theorists such as Foucault provide a model for such work. He writes:

> But I also thought that intellectuals should be trying, like Foucault, to relate our specialized knowledge to things in general. We could not just become activists focused on particular struggles or editors striving to help little magazines make ends meet. We also had a different kind of role to play: thinking hard, as Foucault did, about how best to understand the ways power worked in our time. Foucault, like Sartre and Sontag and Said, was an intellectual, even at some points despite himself. He helped us understand the world in newly critical and imaginative ways. He offered us new lines of reasoning while also engaging in activism and political position-taking. Why, then, is there so much discomfort with using the term "intellectual" as an honorific?[19]

Power is fundamental to any discourse about education and raises critical questions about what role education should play in a democracy and what role academics, artists, and other cultural workers might assume in order to address important social issues, in part, through the liberatory functions of education. This would suggest not only a relentless critique of dominant discourses, social practices, and policies, but also the need to engage in collective attempts to invent a new way of doing politics. Those concerned about the future of democracy have to rethink how power informs and shapes, and can be resourceful in both understanding and challenging power under the reign of global neoliberalism. This is especially true at a time in which a full-scale attack is being waged by the Trump administration and other neoliberal societies on the public good, social provisions, and the welfare state. As Pierre Bourdieu has argued,

> This is where the . . . intellectual can play its irreplaceable role, by helping to create the social conditions for the collective production of realist utopias. It can organize or orchestrate joint research on new forms of political action, on new ways of mobilizing

and making mobilized people work together, on new ways of elaborating projects and bringing them to fruition.[20]

For those academics who have tenure, the issue of assuming a sense of moral and political responsibility in a time of tyranny becomes imperative. By breaking out of the academic microcosm and other corporatized spaces, academics, artists, and other cultural workers can highlight the fact that power is not just a theoretical abstraction. That is, they can spell out how it shapes the spaces in which everyday life takes place and touches people's lives in multiple registers, all of which represent in part a struggle over their identities, values, views of others, and the larger world. In this instance, the role of the public intellectual, within a variety of sites and institutions, becomes crucial in engaging in a permanent critique of authority all the while making clear the role that critical pedagogy plays in the indispensable task in developing such a criticism. Utilizing a discourse of persuasion, critical pedagogy can be made meaningful in order to become an object of critique and transformation. That is, it should be cosmopolitan and imaginative—a public-affirming pedagogy that demands a critical and engaged interaction with the world we live in mediated by a responsibility for challenging structures of domination and for alleviating human suffering.

This is a pedagogy that addresses the needs of multiple publics. As an ethical and political practice, a public pedagogy of wakefulness rejects modes of education removed from political or social concerns, divorced from history and matters of injury and injustice. At issue here is a pedagogy that includes "lifting complex ideas into the public space," recognizing human injury inside and outside of the academy, and using theory as a form of criticism to change things.[21] This is a pedagogy in which artists, educators, and other cultural workers are afraid of neither controversy nor the willingness to make connections between isolated and personal issues and systemic elements of society's problems that are otherwise hidden. Nor should they be afraid of using their work to address the challenges of the day.

As the practice of freedom, critical pedagogy arises from the conviction that artists, educators, and other cultural workers have a responsibility to unsettle power, trouble consensus, and challenge common sense. This is a view of pedagogy that should disturb, inspire, and energize a vast array of individuals and publics. Critical pedagogy comes with the responsibility to view intellectual and artistic work as public, assuming a duty to enter into the public sphere unafraid to take positions and generate controversy, functioning as moral witnesses, raising political awareness, making connections to those elements of power and politics often hidden from public view, and reminding "the audience of the moral questions that may be hidden in the clamor and din of the public debate."[22]

As I have pointed out in Chapter 7, pedagogy is not a method but a moral and political practice, one that recognizes the relationship between knowledge and power, and at the same time emphasizes that central to all pedagogical practice is a struggle over agency, power, politics, and the institutional spheres that make a radical democracy possible. This view of pedagogy does not mold, but inspires, and at the same time it is directive, capable of imagining a better world, the unfinished nature of agency, and the need to consistently reimagine a democracy that is never finished. In this sense, critical pedagogy is a form of educated hope committed to producing young people capable and willing to expand and deepen their sense of themselves, to think the "world" critically, "to imagine something other than their own well-being," to serve the public good, take risks, and struggle for a substantive democracy that is now in a state of acute crisis as the dark clouds of totalitarianism increasingly threaten to destroy democracy itself on a global scale.[23]

Pedagogy is always the outcome of struggles, especially in terms of how pedagogical practices produce particular notions of citizenship and an inclusive democracy. Pedagogy looms large in this instance not as a technique or a priori set of methods but as a political and moral practice. As a political practice, pedagogy illuminates the relationship among power, knowledge, and ideology, while self-consciously, if not self-critically, recognizing the role it plays as a deliberate attempt to influence how and what knowledge and identities are produced within particular sets of social relations. As a moral practice, pedagogy recognizes that what cultural workers, artists, activists, media workers, and others teach cannot be abstracted from what it means to invest in public life, presuppose some notion of the future, or locate oneself in a public discourse.

The moral implications of pedagogy also suggest that our responsibility as cultural workers cannot be separated from the consequences of the knowledge we produce, the social relations we legitimate, and the ideologies and identities we offer up to students. Refusing to decouple politics from pedagogy means, in part, that teaching in classrooms or in any other public sphere should not simply honor the experiences people bring to such sites, including the classroom, but should also connect their experiences to specific problems that emanate from the material contexts of their everyday life. Pedagogy in this sense becomes performative in that it is not merely about deconstructing texts but about situating politics itself within a larger set of relations that addresses what it might mean to create modes of individual and social agency that enables rather than shuts down democratic values, practices, and social relations. Such a project recognizes not only the political nature of pedagogy, but also situates it within a call for artists, intellectuals, and others to assume responsibility for their actions, to link their teachings to those moral principles that allow us to do something about human suffering, as Susan Sontag once suggested.[24]

Part of this task necessitates that cultural workers anchor their own work, however diverse, in a pedagogical project that seriously engages the promise of an unrealized democracy against its really existing and radically incomplete forms. Of crucial importance to such a project is rejecting the assumption that theory can understand social problems without contesting their appearance in public life. Any viable cultural politics needs to make visible and address the diverse mechanisms of injustice if we are to take seriously what it means to fight for the idea of the good society. I think Zygmunt Bauman is right in arguing that "If there is no room for the idea of *wrong* society, there is hardly much chance for the idea of good society to be born, let alone make waves."[25]

Artists and other cultural workers should consider being more forceful in, if not committed to, linking their overall politics to modes of critique and collective action that address the presupposition that democratic societies are never too just or just enough, and such a recognition means that a society must constantly nurture the possibilities for self-critique, collective agency, and forms of citizenship in which people play a fundamental role in critically discussing, administrating, and shaping the material relations of power and ideological forces that bear down on their everyday lives. This is particularly important at a time when ignorance provides a sense of community; the brain has migrated to the dark pit of the spectacle and the only discourse that matters is about business. Trump has legitimated a spirit of ignorance, anti-intellectualism, and corruption. Thought now chases after emotions that obliterate it and actions are no longer framed against any viable notion of social responsibility.

At stake here is the task, as Jacques Derrida insists, of viewing the project of democracy as a promise, a possibility rooted in an ongoing struggle for economic, cultural, and social justice.[26] Democracy in this instance is not a sutured or formalistic regime, it is the site of struggle itself. The struggle over creating an inclusive and just democracy can take many forms, offers no political guarantees, and provides an important normative dimension to politics as an ongoing process of democratization that never ends. Such a project is based on the realization that a democracy that is open to exchange, question, and self-criticism never reaches the limits of justice.

Theorists such as Raymond Williams and Cornelius Castoriadis recognized that the crisis of democracy was not only about the crisis of culture but also the crisis agency, values, and education. Cultural workers would do well to take account of the profound transformations taking place in the public sphere and reclaim pedagogy as a central category of politics itself. Pierre Bourdieu was right when he stated that cultural workers have too often "underestimated the symbolic and pedagogical dimensions of struggle and have not always forged appropriate weapons to fight on this front."[27] He goes on to say in a later conversation with Gunter Grass that

> left intellectuals must recognize that the most important forms
> of domination are not only economic but also intellectual and

pedagogical, and lie on the side of belief and persuasion. Important to recognize that intellectuals bear an enormous responsibility for challenging this form of domination.[28]

These are important pedagogical interventions and imply rightly that critical pedagogy in the broadest sense is not just about understanding, however critical, but also provides the conditions, ideals, and practices necessary for assuming the responsibilities we have as citizens to expose human misery and to eliminate the conditions that produce it.

Matters of responsibility, social action, and political intervention do not simply develop out of the practice of social criticism but also through forms of self-critique. The relationship between knowledge and power, on the one hand, and creativity and politics, on the other, should always be self-reflexive about its effects, how it relates to the larger world, whether or not it is open to new understandings, and what it might mean pedagogically to take seriously matters of individual and social responsibility. In short, this project points to the need for cultural workers to address critical pedagogy not only as a mode of educated hope and a crucial element of an insurrectional educational project, but also as a practice that addresses the possibility of interpretation as intervention in the world.

Critical pedagogy can neither be reduced to a method nor is it non-directive in the manner of a spontaneous conversation with friends over coffee. As public intellectuals, authority must be reconfigured not as a way to stifle curiosity and deaden the imagination, but as a platform that provides the conditions for students to learn the knowledge, skills, values, and social relationships that enhance their capacities to assume authority over the forces that shape their lives both in and out of schools. Power and authority are always related; such a relationship, however, must never operate in the service of domination or the stifling of autonomy but in the service of what I have called the practice of freedom. The notion that authority is always on the side of repression and that pedagogy should never be directive is for all practical purposes a political and theoretical flight from the educator assuming a sense of moral and political responsibility.

For artists and educators willing to be voiceless, to renounce the knowledge that benefits a wider social order, or to assume that a wider public need not be exposed to diverse legacies of struggle is to allow themselves to become accomplices of an authoritarian society. By making the political more pedagogical, educators and artists can provide critical pedagogical practices and modes of teaching that inspire and energize, while introducing a wider audience to the resources necessary for them to learn how to govern rather than be governed. If politics is about the appropriation and use of power, pedagogy is its moral underside providing the lens and practices to ensure that education is always about the struggle over knowledge, desire, identity, values, and agency in the service of a democratic and just future.

Critical pedagogy for public intellectuals must always be attentive to addressing the democratic potential of engaging how experience, knowledge, and power are shaped in the classroom in different and often unequal contexts, and how teacher authority might be mobilized against dominant pedagogical practices as part of the practice of freedom, particularly those practices that erase any trace of subaltern histories, historical legacies of class struggles, and the ever persistent historical traces and current structures of racial and gender inequalities and injustices. In this sense, teacher authority must be linked both to a never-ending sense of historical memory, existing inequities, and a "hopeful version of democracy where the outcome is a more just, equitable society that works toward the end of oppression and suffering of all."[29] As I have said previously:

> Authority in this perspective is not simply on the side of oppression, but is used to intervene and shape the space of teaching and learning to provide students with a range of possibilities for challenging a society's commonsense assumptions, and for analyzing the interface between their own everyday lives and those expansive social formations that bear down on them. Authority, at best, becomes both a referent for legitimating a commitment to a particular vision of pedagogy and a critical referent for a kind of auto critique.[30]

Any viable understanding of the artist and educator as a public intellectual must begin with the recognition that democracy begins to fail and civic life becomes impoverished when power is relegated to the realm of common sense and critical thinking is no longer viewed as central to politics itself. The election of Donald Trump to the presidency is a case study in how politics has been emptied of any viable meaning and civic illiteracy has been normalized. Trump's claim that he loves the uniformed appears to have paid off for him just as his victory makes clear that ignorance rather than reason, emotion rather than informed judgment, and the threat of violence rather than critical exchange appear to have more currency in the age of civic collapse.

This political tragedy ushered in with Trump's election signifies the failure of the American public to recognize the educative nature of how agency is constructed, to address the necessity for moral witnessing, and the need to create educational spaces that produce critically engaged and socially responsible citizens. Reality TV bombast and a celebrity dominated culture confer enormous power and influence in America and in doing so empty civil society and democracy of any meaning. Neoliberalism's culture of consumerism, immediate satisfaction, and unchecked individualism both infantilizes and depoliticizes. As I stated earlier, the election of Donald Trump cannot simply be dismissed as an eccentric and dark moment in the history of American politics. His election proves that collective self-delusion can be dangerous when the spaces for critical learning, dissent, and informed judgment begin to wither or disappear altogether.

As Trump's presidency gets under way, neoliberalism's hired intellectuals and celebrity pundits have already ushered in a discourse that will increasingly normalize the regime of a dangerous demagogue, glossing over the ideological, economic, and religious fundamentalists he has chosen to fill top government positions. Such actions represent more than a flight from political and social responsibility, they also represent a surrender to the dark forces of authoritarianism. Charles Blow, an opinion writer for the *New York Times*, argues strongly against normalizing Trump's administration. According to Blow, Trump not only represents "an unstable, unqualified, undignified demagogue," but also he has surrounded himself with "a rogue's gallery of white supremacy sympathizers, anti-Muslim extremists, devout conspiracy theorists, anti-science doctrinaires and climate-change deniers," all of which pose a singular threat to the nation that is not normal.[31] Yet, there are many people more than willing to return to the old normal of the forces of hatred, misogyny, and bigotry. Dierdre Fulton, a writer for the *Nation*, is right in arguing that the process of normalization has already begun since Trump's election. She writes:

> Oprah Winfrey, in an interview with *Entertainment Tonight*, said Trump's recent visit to the White House gave her "hope" and suggested he has been "humbled" by the experience ... The Guardian's Simon Jenkins told his readers to "calm down" and that Trump wasn't the "worst thing." His colleague, Nouriel Roubini, insisted the Oval Office will "tame" Trump. *People Magazine* ran a glowing profile of Trump and his wife Melania (though a former *People* writer accused Trump of sexual assault). The *New York Times'* Nick Kristof dubiously added that we should "Grit our teeth and give Trump a chance." The mainstay—*Washington Post*, *New York Times*, and CNN—while frequently critical, are covering Trump's transition as they would any other.[32]

Normalizing the toxic poison of racist exclusion, white supremacy, and reactionary populism turns civic courage upside down, justice into injustice, and politics into a dangerous spectacle. Trump is not ordinary and his politics forebode the dark clouds of an American version of totalitarianism. Thus, it is all the more surprising that Lesley Stahl's *60 Minutes* interview with Trump portrayed him less as a demagogue than as a transformed politician who was "subdued and serious."[33] NBC's Andrea Mitchell, who was endlessly critical of Hillary Clinton during the presidential primary "reported approvingly upon the transition as if proposed White House counselor Steve Bannon and proposed attorney general Jeff Sessions, two men with racism in their pasts, were ordinary appointments."[34] Such actions by the mainstream press indicate clearly not just a retreat from responsible reporting, but also the collapse of serious journalism into the corrupt world of a corporate-controlled media empire. Mainstream media now functions largely as a vehicle for trivial entertainment, increased ratings, and a desiring machine for consumerism. At the same time, it aligns itself to the willing role of an obedient, if not slavish, adjunct serving the power of the ultra-rich and financial elite.[35] Normalizing the Trump regime does more than sabotage the truth, moral responsibility, and justice, it also cancels out the future and undermines democracy itself.

Democracy should be a way of thinking about education in a variety of spheres and practices, one that thrives on connecting equity to excellence, learning to ethics, and agency to the imperatives of the public good.[36] The question regarding what role education and pedagogy should play in democracy becomes all the more urgent at a time when the dark forces of authoritarianism are being normalized in the mainstream media. Central to such a discourse are hidden structures of critique and power attempting to normalize a full-frontal attack on public values, trust, solidarities, and modes of liberatory education. As such, the discourses of hate, humiliation, rabid self-interest, and greed are exercising a poisonous influence in many Western societies. This is most evident at the present moment in the discourse of the right-wing extremists vying to consolidate their authority within a Trump presidency, all of whom sanction a war on immigrants, women, young people, poor Black youth, and so it goes. One consequence is that democracy is on life support. This is all the more reason to heed the late Edward Said's call for cultural workers and others to take seriously the need "to uncover and elucidate the contest, to challenge and defeat both an imposed silence and the normalized quiet of unseen power, wherever and whenever possible."[37] In spite of the dark forces now threatening many societies around the globe, it is crucial for intellectuals, artists, and others to renounce any form of normalization of power, the toxic public pedagogies of neoliberalism, and to take on radical democracy as both a pedagogical project and unfinished ideal. Such a challenge will be all the easier if progressives and others can create the public spheres and pedagogical conditions that can produce an individual and collective sense of moral and political outrage, a new understanding of politics, and the pedagogical projects needed to allow democracy to breathe once again.

Trump's presence in American politics has made visible a plague of deep-seated civic illiteracy, a corrupt political system, and a contempt for reason; it also points to the decline of civic attachments, the collapse of politics into the spectacle of an infantilizing culture, the decline of public life, the use of violence and fear to numb people into shock, and a willingness to transform politics into a pathology. Trump's administration will produce a great deal of violence in American society, particularly among the ranks of the most vulnerable: poor children, minorities of color, immigrants, women, climate change advocates, Muslims, and those protesting a Trump presidency.

Trump will use screen culture to humiliate, criticize, and attempt to suppress dissent of his administration. As cyberbully in chief, he has taken to Twitter to launch tirades against the cast of the play *Hamilton*, *Saturday Night Live*, and Chuck Jones, President of United Steelworkers Local 1999. Trump's verbal takedown of the union chief was the result of Jones accusing Trump of lying about the number of jobs he claimed he saved in Indiana at Carrier Corporation from being shipped to Mexico. Actually, 350 jobs were slated to stay in the U.S. before Trump's intervention; hence, the number of jobs saved by Trump was 850 rather than 1,100. To some this may seem like a trivial matter, but Trump's weaponizing of Twitter against critics and political opponents functions not only to produce a chilling effect on critics, but gives legitimacy to those willing to suppress dissent through various modes of harassment and even the threat of violence. Frank Sesno, Director of the School of Media and Public Affairs at George Washington University, is right in stating that "Anybody who goes on air or goes public and calls out the president has to then live in fear that he is going to seek retribution in the public sphere. That could discourage people from speaking out."[38] Such actions could also threaten their lives, as Chuck Jones found out. After the President called him out, he received an endless stream of harassing phone calls and online insults, some even threatening him and his children. According to Jones, "Nothing that says they're gonna kill me, but, you know, you better keep your eye on your kids," he told O'Donnell. "We know what car you drive. Things along those lines."[39] It seems more probable that his right-wing advisors, including Steve

Bannon, view the tweets as part of a legitimate tool to attack their perceived political foes and in this case the attack was not simply on Jones but on unions that may rebel against Trump's policies in the future. Trump is at war with democracy and his online attacks will take place not only in conjunction with ongoing acts of state repression, but also with the production of violence in the culture at large, which Trump will orchestrate as if he is producing a reality TV show.

What must be made clear is that Trump's election and the damage he will do to American society will stay and fester in American society for quite some time because he is only symptomatic of the darker forces that have been smoldering in American politics for the last 40 years. What cannot be exaggerated or easily dismissed is that Trump is the end result of a long-standing series of attacks on democracy and that his presence in the American political landscape has put democracy on trial. This is a challenge that artists, educators, and others must address. While mass civil demonstrations have erupted and continue to erupt over Trump's election, what is more crucial to understand is that something more serious needs to be addressed. Those who believe in economic and social justice have to acknowledge that at this particular moment in American history the real issue is not simply about resisting Donald Trump's insidious values and anti-democratic policies but whether a political system can be reclaimed in which democracy is not on trial but is deepened, strengthened, and sustained. This will not happen unless new modes of representation challenge the aesthetics, culture, and discourse of neo-fascism.

Yet, under a Trump presidency, it will be more difficult to sustain, construct, and nurture those public spheres that sustain critique, inform dialogue, and work to expand the radical imagination. If democracy is to prevail in and through the threat of "dark times," it is crucial that the avenues of critique and possibility become central to any new understanding of politics. If the authoritarianism of the Trump era is to be challenged, it must begin with a politics that is comprehensive in its attempts to understand the intersectionality of diverse forces of oppression and resistance. That is, it must move towards developing analyses that address the existing state of authoritarianism through a totalizing lens that brings together the diverse registers of oppression and how they are both connected and mutually reinforce each other. It is worth repeating that such a politics must, as Robin D. G. Kelley has noted, "move beyond stopgap alliances"[40] and work to unite single-issue movements into a more comprehensive social movement that can make a viable claim to a resistance that is as integrated as it is powerful. For too long progressive cultural workers and activists have adhered to a narrative about domination that relies mostly on remaking economic structures and presenting to the public what might be called a barrage of demystifying facts and an aesthetics of transgression. What they have ignored is that people also internalize oppression and that domination is about not only the crisis of economics, images that deaden the imagination, and the misrepresentation of reality, but also about the crisis of agency, identification, meaning, and desire.

The failure to develop a crisis of consciousness is deeply rooted in a society that suffers from a plague of atomization, loneliness, and despair. Neoliberalism has undermined any democratic understanding of freedom limiting its meaning to the dictates of consumerism, hatred of government, and a politics where the personal is the only emotional referent that matters. Freedom has collapsed into the dark abyss of a vapid and unchecked individualism and in doing so has canceled out that capacious notion of freedom rooted in the bonds of solidarity, compassion, social responsibility, and the bonds of social obligation. The toxic neoliberal combination of unchecked economic growth is a discourse that legitimates plundering the earth's resources and exhibits a pathological disdain for community and public values that has weakened democratic pressures, values, and social relations and opened the door for the dark side of politics under Donald Trump's presidency.

The collapse of democratic politics points to an absence in progressive movements and among various types of public intellectuals about how to address the importance of emotional connections among the masses, take seriously how to connect with others through pedagogical tools that demand respect, empathy, a willingness to listen to other stories, and to think seriously about how to change consciousness as an educative task.

The latter is particularly important because it speaks to the necessity of politically addressing the challenge of awakening modes of identification coupled with the use of language not merely to demystify but to persuade people that the issues that matter have something to do with their lived realities and daily lives. Pressing the claim for social justice and economic equality means working hard to develop alternative modes of consciousness, promoting the proliferation of democratic public spheres, creating the conditions for modes of mass resistance, and making the development of sustainable social movements central to any viable struggle for economic, political, and social justice. No viable democracy can exist without citizens who value and are willing to work towards the common good. That is as much a pedagogical question as it is a political challenge.

Notes

1   Yesmin Villarreal, "Betsy DeVos: Education Reform Can 'Advance God's Kingdom,'" *Advocate* (December 3, 2016). Online: www.advocate.com/politics/2016/12/03/antigay-betsy-devos-education-reform-can-advance-gods-kingdom

2   Catherine Brown, "Point: Trump's Education Plan—Defund, Devalue and Privatize Our School System," *Inside Sources* (December 5, 2016). Online: www.insidesources.com/point-trumps-education-plan-defund-devalue-privatize-school-system/

3   Amy Goodman, "Housing Advocate: It's Scary that Trump HUD Secretary Pick Ben Carson Thinks Poverty Is a Choice," *Democracy Now* (November 16, 2016). Online: www.democracynow.org/2016/12/7/housing_advocate_its_scary_that_trump

4   Brendan Gauthier, "HUD Secretary Front-Runner Ben Carson Recently Called Fair Housing 'Communist,'" *Salon* (November 28, 2016). Online: www.salon.com/2016/11/28/hud-secretary-front-runner-ben-carson-recently-called-fair-housing-communist/

5   Noam Scheiber and Maggie Haberman, "Trump's Likely Labor Pick, Andrew Puzder, Is Critic of Minimum Wage Increases," *New York Times* (December 8, 2016). Online: www.nytimes.com/2016/12/08/us/politics/andrew-puzder-labor-secretary-trump.html

6   Ibid.

7   Ibid.

8   Mike Lillis, "Liberal Dems: Trump Filling Cabinet with 'Stooges,'" *Hill* (December 8, 2016). Online: http://thehill.com/homenews/house/309455-liberal-dems-trump-filling-cabinet-with-stooges

9   Eric Sommer, "Team Trump: A Government of Generals and Billionaires," *CounterPunch* (December 7, 2016). Online: www.counterpunch.org/2016/12/07/team-trump-a-government-of-generals-and-billionaires

10 Cited in Dahr Jamail, "Trump Nominee for Homeland Security John Kelly Favors Draconian Immigration Policy," *Real News* (December 8, 2016). Online: http://thereal news.com/t2/index.php?option=com_content&task=view&id=31&Itemid=74&jumival=17874

11 Ibid.

12   Matthew Rosenberg, "Trump Adviser Has Pushed Clinton Conspiracy Theories," *New York Times* (December 5, 2016). Online: www.nytimes.com/2016/12/05/us/politics/-michael-flynn-trump-fake-news-clinton.html?_r=0

13   Henry A. Giroux, *On Critical Pedagogy* (New York: Bloomsbury, 2011).

14   Christopher Hass, "This Is Serious," *In These Times* (December 7, 2016). Online: https://mail.google.com/mail/u/0/?ui=2&ik=eaf3b5986f&view=pt&search=inbox&th=158daeb c10733820&siml=158daebc10733820

15   On this issue, see Henry A. Giroux, *Neoliberalism's War on Higher Education* (Chicago: Haymarket Press, 2014); Susan Searls Giroux, "On the Civic Function of Intellectuals Today." In Gary Olson and Lynn Worsham, eds, *Education as Civic Engagement: Toward a More Democratic Society* (Boulder, CO: Paradigm Publishers, 2012), pp. ix–xvii.

16   Sara Robinson, "How the Conservative Worldview Quashes Critical Thinking—and What That Means for Our Kids' Future," *AlterNet* (May 20, 2012). Online: www.alternet.org/education/155469/how_the_conservative_worldview_quashes_critical_thinking_and_what_that_means_for_our_kids%27_future?page=entire

17   See, for instance, Giroux, *Neoliberalism's War on Higher Education* and Henry Heller, *The Capitalist University* (London: Pluto Press, 2016).

18   Michael Meranze, "On Self-Inflicted Wounds: Precarious Faculty and Academic Freedom," *Remaking the University* (December 29, 2017). Online: http://utotherescue.blogspot.com/2016/12/on-self-inflicted-wounds-precarious.html?m=0. See also the invaluable book: Christopher Newfield, *The Great Mistake: How We Wrecked Public Universities and How We Can Fix Them* (Baltimore, MD: Johns Hopkins University Press, 2016); Gaye Tuchman, *Wannabe U: Inside the Corporate University* (Chicago: University of Chicago Press, 2009); Christopher Newfield, *Unmaking the Public University* (Cambridge, MA: Harvard University Press, 2008).

19   Bruce Robbins, "A Starting Point for Politics," *Nation* (October 22, 2016). Online: www.thenation.com/article/the-radical-life-of-stuart-hall

20   Pierre Bourdieu, "For a Scholarship with Commitment," *Profession* (2000), pp. 42–3.

21   Edward Said, *Out of Place: A Memoir* (New York: Vintage, 2000), p. 7.

22   Edward Said, "On Defiance and Taking Positions," *Reflections on Exile and Other Essays* (Cambridge, MA: Harvard University Press, 2001), p. 504.

23   See, especially, Newfield, *Unmaking the Public University.*

24   Susan Sontag, "Courage and Resistance," *Nation* (May 5, 2003), pp. 11–14.

25   Zygmunt Bauman, *Society under Siege* (Malden, MA: Blackwell, 2002), p. 170.

26   Jacques Derrida, "Intellectual Courage: An Interview," trans. Peter Krapp, *Culture Machine*, Volume 2 (2000), pp. 1–15.

27   Pierre Bourdieu, *Acts of Resistance* (New York: Free Press, 1998), p. 11.

28   Pierre Bourdieu and Gunter Grass, "The 'Progressive' Restoration: A Franco-German Dialogue," *New Left Review*, Vol. 14 (March–April 2002), p. 2.

29   Richard Voelz, "Reconsidering the Image of Preacher-Teacher: Intersections between Henry Giroux's Critical Pedagogy and Homiletics," *Practical Matters* (Spring 2014), p. 79.

30   Giroux, *On Critical Pedagogy*, p. 81.

31   Charles Blow, "Donald Trump, This Is Not Normal," *New York Times* (December 19, 2016). Online: www.nytimes.com/2016/12/19/opinion/donald-trump-this-is-not-normal.html?_r=0

32   Deirdre Fulton, "There's No Normalizing President-Elect Trump," *Nation* (November 14, 2016). Online: www.commondreams.org/news/2016/11/14/theres-no-normalizing-president-elect-trump-or-least-there-shouldnt-be

33   Neil Gabler, "And So It Begins: Normalizing the Election," *Moyers and Company* (November 24, 2016). Online: http://billmoyers.com/story/media-normalizing-election/

34   Ibid.

35   Robert W. McChesney, *Rich Media, Poor Democracy: Communication Politics in Dubious Times* (New York: New Press, 2015).

36   Henry A. Giroux, *Dangerous Thinking in the Age of the New Authoritarianism* (New York: Routledge, 2015).

37   Edward Said, "The Public Role of Writers and Intellectuals," *The Nation* (October 1, 2001), p. 31.

38   Michael D. Shear, "Trump as Cyberbully in Chief? Twitter Attack on Union Boss Draws Fire," *New York Times* (December 8, 2016). Online: www.nytimes.com/2016/12/08/us/politics/donald-trump-twitter-carrier-chuck-jones.html

39   Madeline Farber, "Union Leader Says He's Getting Threats after Donald Trump Attacked Him on Twitter," *Fortune* (December 8, 2016). Online: http://fortune.com/2016/12/08/carrier-union-leader-threats-donald-trump/

40   Robin D. G. Kelley, "After Trump," *Boston Review* (November 15, 2016). Online: http://bostonreview.net/forum/after-trump/robin-d-g-kelley-trump-says-go-back-we-say-fight-back

PART IV

RESISTING NEOLIBERALISM'S DYSTOPIAN FUTURE

9
ISOLATION AND LOSS IN TRUMP'S DYSTOPIA

> There are no dangerous thoughts; thinking itself is dangerous.
> (Hannah Arendt)

In August 2016, Donald Trump lowered the bar even further than he has in the past when he called Mexicans who illegally entered the country rapists and drug dealers, stated he wanted to ban Muslims from coming into the United States, defamed Fox News host Megyn Kelly by referring to her menstrual cycle, and questioned the heroism and bravery of former prisoner of war Senator John McCain. In what can only be described as unimaginable, Trump urged Russia to hack Hillary Clinton's emails and attacked the Muslim parents of Captain Humayan Khan, who was killed in 2004 by a suicide bomber while he was trying to save the lives of the men in his unit. In addition, during a campaign rally in North Carolina, Trump suggested that "Second Amendment people" would take care of Hillary Clinton for picking Supreme Court judges who favor stricter gun laws. The Clinton campaign and many others saw this as a veiled endorsement of an assassination attempt.[1]

These inflammatory, if not dangerous, comments are part of a wider movement in American politics to empty political discourse of any meaningful substance, turning it mostly into a form of rhetorical theater of hate, bigotry, humiliation, and shame designed to mimic a larger culture of stupidity, insecurity, and spectacle. The spectacle of a titillating and infantilizing consciousness that floods public discourse with shocks, sensations, and simplistic views has become the hallmark of a broken political system now largely controlled by ideological extremists who inhabit big corporations, hedge funds, and the ranks of the ultra-rich. What is particularly disheartening is that these extremists under the presidency of Donald Trump will be in charge of the most powerful, if not most dangerous, government in the world. As might be expected, a range of supine politicians, media pundits, and mainstream journalists are tying themselves "in apologetic knots" while they "desperately look for signs that Donald Trump will be a pragmatic, recognizable American president once he takes the mantle of power."[2] It has become increasingly clear that the most dangerous powers of the state will be unleashed under Trump on the environment, public and higher education, protesters, poor Blacks, Muslims, and illegal immigrants. Americans may be on the verge of witnessing how democracy comes to an end.

Civic attachments in the Unites States are disappearing in the age of precarity, isolation, and shame. As Adam Haslett has brilliantly argued, we live in a political world marked by "endless acts of public verbal violence" that capitalizes on the national glut of shame in order to weaponize its effects by getting people to enjoy the shame of others.[3] Trading in shame is a national pastime and is not simply limited to politicians such as Donald Trump. The mainstream media also manipulates misery and humiliation in order to attract viewers and drive up ratings. Reality TV shows such as *The Jerry Springer Show*, *The Biggest Loser*, *Toddlers and Tiaras*, and *The Apprentice* are symptomatic of a tsunami of verbal and cinematic violence that allows people to identify with shame less to understand the economic and political conditions that produce it, such as widespread poverty, economic distress, and unemployment, than to use it cathartically to displace their own anger onto others or to enjoy the spectacle of humiliation being imposed on others.

As Haslett rightly argues, shame has indeed become weaponized and is part of a new kind of warfare in which critical agency is turned against itself, its possibilities for solidarity, and its promise of collective struggles in the name of economic, cultural, and political justice.[4] Donald Trump has brought shame out of the entertainment realm, made it a centerpiece of his political campaign, and, given his relentless use of Twitter during his term as president-elect, will continue to do so during his presidency. At the same time, the fog of shame moves from politics to a kind of sickening spectacle of voyeurism that sadistically makes "entertainment out of people's weaknesses . . . and [has] made a culture of humiliation the key to prime time audience ratings."[5]

Neoliberalism defines itself through a culture of cruelty by disdaining any form of compassion, legitimizing the discourse of rabid individualism, and insisting that everything is for sale, including human dignity. Competitive attitudes saturate political discourse and screen cultures. Commenting on the culture of cruelty and shame that now dominates American culture as entertainment, Nicolaus Mills writes:

> Indeed, the overriding lesson that humiliation TV offers is that people will do anything for money, and that we are living in an America in which the only way to get ahead is to behave as ruthlessly as possible. Forget cooperation. Forget fairness. Think zero-sum society. That is the vision that television's new culture of humiliation holds out. Our high schools and colleges may be bastions of "political correctness," teaching students to refrain from judging each other on the basis of differences in appearance or beliefs, but in humiliation TV, judging dismissively is the name of the game. Excluding someone from sharing the top prize is the ultimate triumph.[6]

While thinking about these issues, I have recently returned to reading Leo Lowenthal, particularly his insightful essay, "Terror's Atomization of Man," first published in *Commentary* on January 1, 1946 and reprinted in his book, *False Prophets: Studies in Authoritarianism.*[7] He writes about the atomization of human beings under a state of fear that approximates a kind of updated fascist terror. What he understood with great insight, even in 1946, was that democracy cannot exist without the educational, political, and formative cultures and institutions that make it possible. He observed that atomized individuals are not only prone to the forces of depoliticization, but also to the poisonous visions and spirit of demagogues, discourses of hate, emotionally charged appeals to violence, and racist rhetoric that demonize and objectify the Other. While he did not write about the contemporary ways in which such isolation is depoliticized through the updated uses of shame, he did provide a searing critique of isolation's centrality in producing a neo-fascist culture and society.

Lowenthal is helpful in illuminating the relationship between the underlying isolation individuals feel in an age of precarity, uncertainty, and disposability and the dark shadows of authoritarianism threatening to overcome the United States.[8] Within this new historical conjuncture, finance capital produces extremes of wealth for the 1 percent, promotes cuts to government services, and defunds investments in public goods, such as public and higher education, in order to offset tax reductions for the ultra-rich and big corporations.[9] Meanwhile, millions are plunged into either the painful experience of poverty or become part of the mass incarceration state. Mass fear is normalized as violence increasingly becomes the default logic for handling social problems. In an age where everything is for sale, and the Trump administration appears intent on purging facts and evidence of their legitimacy, ethical accountability is rendered a liability and the vocabulary of empathy is viewed as a weakness. Moreover, as the United States enters what Oliver Munday calls the "dark cave of civic and moral depravity,"[10] such actions are reinforced by the neoliberal view that individual happiness and its endless search for instant gratification are more important than supporting the public good and embracing an obligation to care for others. Americans are now pitted against each other as casino capitalism puts a premium on competitive cage-like relations that degrade collaboration and the public spheres that support it. Under such circumstances, shared citizenship falls by the wayside and civic culture withers.

Within neoliberal ideology, an emphasis on competition in every sphere of life promotes a winner-takes-all ethos that finds its ultimate expression in the assertion that fairness has no place in a society dominated by winners and losers. As William Davies points out, competition in a market-driven social order allows a small group of winners to emerge while at the same time sorting out and condemning the vast majority of institutions, organizations, and individuals "to the status of losers."[11]

As has been made clear in the much publicized language of Donald Trump, both as a former reality TV host of *The Apprentice* and as a presidential candidate, calling someone a "loser" has little to do with them losing in the more general sense of the term. On the contrary, in a culture that trades in cruelty and divorces politics from matters of ethics and social responsibility, "loser" is now elevated to a pejorative insult that humiliates and justifies not only symbolic violence, but also (as Trump has made clear in many of his rallies) real acts of violence waged against his critics, such as members of the movement Black Lives Matter. As Greg Elmer and Paula Todd observe, "to lose is possible, but to be a 'loser' is the ultimate humiliation that justifies taking extreme, even immoral measures."[12] They write:

> We argue that the Trumpesque "loser" serves as a potent new political symbol, a caricature that Trump has previously deployed in his television and business careers to sidestep complex social issues and justify winning at all costs. As the commercial for his 1980s board game "Trump" enthused, "It's not whether you win or lose, but whether you win!" Indeed, in Trump's world, for some to win many more must lose, which helps explain the breath-taking embrace by some of his racist, xenophobic, and misogynist communication strategy. The more losers—delineated by Trump based on every form of "otherism"—the better the odds of victory.[13]

These pejorative notions of loser and losing make it all the more difficult to critically engage the claims that loss has upon history, memory, politics, and life itself. There is no attempt to understand how daily experiences are mediated by loss and its relationship to power, particularly how loss signals "the end station of poverty," the emergence of zones of social abandonment, "inscriptions of invisibility," and states of terminal exclusion.[14]

In the friend/enemy distinction that the pejorative notion of loser connotes, there is no remorse or compassion for loss as a staggering experience due to loss of income, security, ecological destruction, economic displacement, the loss of partners due to war, or sons killed by the police. Under such circumstances, loss becomes the object of scorn and denigrates any display of compassion, sorrow, empathy, and grief. The poor, Blacks, immigrants, and others marginalized by class and race in Trump's world become an updated version of vermin. As Sheldon Wolin observes, the task of theory pertaining to the notion of loss is to raise questions regarding "What survives of the defeated, the indigestible, the unassimilated, the 'cross-grained,' the 'not wholly obsolete' is what should interest the theorist."[15]

This discourse of the loser reinforces a notion of atomization and shaming fueled by a fervor for unbridled individualism and produces a pathological disdain for community, public values, and the public good. In this context, fear is militarized and both creates and legitimates a toxic air of misplaced rage and hatred. How else to explain comments by veteran political operative Roger Stone, a top Trump aid in which he "called a CNN commentator a 'stupid Negro' and accused the Gold Star parents of Capt. Humayun Khan of being Muslim Brotherhood agents."[16] As democratic pressures are weakened, authoritarian societies resort to fear so as to ward off any room for ideals, visions, and hope. Efforts to keep this space open are made all the more difficult by the ethically tranquilizing presence of a celebrity and commodity culture that works to depoliticize people. The realms of the political and the social imagination wither as shared responsibilities and obligations give way to an individualized society that elevates selfishness, avarice, and militaristic modes of competition as its highest organizing principles.

Unsurprisingly, neoliberal values also support and amplify what the late historian Richard Hofstadter called the "paranoid style in American politics."[17] Writing in the 1960s in the aftermath of the McCarthy period, Hofstadter made clear that the animosities, anger, "heated exaggerations, suspiciousness, and conspiratorial fantas[ies]" that characterize such a style were deeply rooted in American politics and history and did not simply apply "to men with profoundly disturbed minds."[18] Such a paranoid style could only be understood within a larger social, cultural, and political context specific to a distinctive historical era. Hofstadter has performed a theoretical service in providing a language for unpacking the new authoritarianism in American society. What is distinct about the current era is that such extremism has moved to the center of politics and has become the hallmark of a period characterized by the destruction of civil liberties, the emergence of what Mike Lofgren calls *The Deep State*,[19] mass surveillance, the militarization of everyday life, the widespread spectacle of violence, and a culture steeped in the mobilization of mass fear, humiliation, and cruelty.

Donald Trump's takeover of the Republican Party and the United States government alone cannot explain the emergence and embrace of right-wing populism among millions of Americans who, as Beverly Bandler observes: "sport idiocy as a 'badge of honor,' cling to the discredited, silly birtherism, brazenly support serial lying, rampant xenophobia, racism, misogynism, [and] suggest that [Trump's] political opponent is 'the devil.'"[20] We live in an era when knowledge has been replaced by information, and billions of dollars provided by advertisers, the Koch brothers, hedge fund criminals, bankers, the ultra-rich, and big corporations provide the pedagogical parameters for what can be considered acceptable ideas, views, and frames of reference. Screen culture is the new force of politics and it is signed, sealed, and delivered by powerful corporate interests, with some exceptions in the mainstream media and certainly a sprinkling of alternative views in online progressive sites such as *Truthout*, *Truthdig*, *CounterPunch*, and others, though such sites are highly marginalized. Couple the latter control of commanding cultural apparatuses with the Supreme Court ruling, *Citizens United*, which allowed politics to be flooded and controlled by big money, and you have what Tom Engelhardt has rightly called the "first 1% elections" coupled with a dominant public pedagogy infused with insults, stupidity, racism, and a toxic "sea of words and images."[21]

As a result, the foundations for stability and democracy are being destroyed with jobs being shipped overseas, social provisions eliminated, the social state hollowed out, public servants and workers under a relentless attack, students burdened with the rise of a neoliberal debt machine, and many groups considered disposable. And given the war culture that Trump will initiate under his regime, these problems will be intensified. At the same time, these acts of permanent repression are coupled with new configurations of power and militarization normalized by a neoliberal regime in which an ideology of political and economic savagery has become unaccountable; amidst these conditions, one dispenses with any notion of compassion and holds others responsible for problems they face, problems over which they have no control. In this case, shared responsibilities and hopes have been replaced by the isolating logic of individual responsibility, a false notion of resiliency, and a growing resentment toward those viewed as strangers.[22]

We live in an age of death-dealing loneliness, isolation, and militarized atomization. If you believe the popular press, loneliness is reaching epidemic proportions[23] in advanced industrial societies. A few indices include the climbing suicide rate of adolescent girls;[24] the rising deaths of working-class, less-educated white men;[25] and the growing drug over-dose crises raging across small towns and cities throughout America.[26] Meanwhile, people often interact more with their cell phones, tablets and computers than they do with embodied subjects. Disembodiment in this view is at the heart of a deeply alienating neoliberal society in which people shun in-person relationships for virtual ones. According to this perspective, the warm glow of the computer screen can produce and reinforce a new type of alienation, isolation, and sense of loneliness. At the same time, it is important to note that in some cases digital technologies have also enabled young people who are hyper-connected to their peers online to increase their face-to-face time by coordinating spontaneous meet-ups, in addition to staying connected with each other near constantly virtually. How this dialectic plays out will in part be determined by the degree to which young people can be educated to embrace modes of agency in which a connection to other human beings, however diverse, becomes central to their understanding of the value of creating bonds of sociality.

Needless to say, however, blaming the internet alone—which has also helped forge connections, has facilitated movement building, and has made information widely accessible—is too easy. We live in a society in which notions of dependence, compassion, mutuality, care for the other, and sociality are undermined by a neoliberal ethic in which self-interest and greed become the organizing principles of one's life and a survival-of-the fittest ethic breeds a culture that at best promotes an indifference to the plight of others and at worst a disdain for the less fortunate and support for a widespread culture of cruelty. Isolated individuals do not make up a healthy democratic society.

New Forms of Alienation and Isolation

A more theoretical language produced by Marx talked about alienation as a separation from the fruits of one's labor. While that is certainly truer than ever, the separation and isolation is now more extensive and governs the entirety of social life in a consumer-based society run by the demands of commerce and the financialization of everything. Isolation, privatization, and the cold logic of instrumental rationality have created a new kind of social formation and social order in which it becomes difficult to form communal bonds, deep connections, a sense of intimacy, and long-term commitments.

Neoliberalism fosters the viewing of pain and suffering as entertainment, warfare as a permanent state of existence, and militarism as the most powerful force shaping masculinity. Politics has taken an exit from ethics and thus the issue of social costs is divorced from any form of intervention in the world. For example, under casino capitalism, economic activity is removed from its ethical and social consequences and takes a flight from any type of moral consideration. This is the ideological metrics of political zombies. The key word here is atomization, and it is a defining feature of neoliberal societies and the scourge of democracy.

At the heart of any type of politics wishing to challenge this flight into authoritarianism is not merely the recognition of economic structures of domination, but something more profound—a politics which points to the construction of particular identities, values, social relations, or more broadly, agency itself. Central to such a recognition is the fact that politics cannot exist without people investing something of themselves in the discourses, images, and representations that come at them daily. Rather than suffering alone, lured into the frenzy of hateful emotion, individuals need to be able to identify—see themselves and their daily lives—within progressive critiques of existing forms of domination and how they might address such issues not individually but collectively. This is a particularly difficult challenge today because the menace of atomization is reinforced daily not only by a coordinated neoliberal assault against any viable notion of the social but also by an authoritarian and finance-based culture that couples a rigid notion of privatization with a flight from any sense of social and moral responsibility.

The cultural apparatuses controlled by the 1 percent, including the mainstream media and entertainment industries, are the most power-ful educational forces in society and they have become apparatuses of misrecognition and brutality. Collective agency is now atomized, devoid of any viable embrace of the democratic social imaginary. Under such circumstances, domination does not merely repress through its apparatuses of terror and violence, but also—as Pierre Bourdieu argues—through the realm of ideology, consciousness, values, and ideas. These are intellectual and pedagogical practices which register their own forms of internalized domination.[27] For instance, in an age in which the term "loser" denotes language in the service of humiliation, there is also a deeper structure of meaning that is indebted to the current fascistic embrace of "total war" and a "survival-of-the fittest" ethos in which winning and losing become the central organizing principles of an armed neoliberal society. As the discourse of war and excessive com-petition moves into the realm of the market place, consumption also serves to reward winners and debase losers based upon a fetishistic notion of consumerism. Subjecting the majority of the polity to the discourse of humiliation and disdain and praise for the small number of winners who constitute the criminogenic 1 percent of the population serves to create an affective economy of misdirected rage, resentment, and retaliation, which finds its most egregious overt expression in the hateful and racist discourses of authoritarianism. An allegedly less offensive and comforting weaponizing of ignorance and shame can be found in the shaming industries and political discourses I have mentioned earlier in this chapter.

The economic and pedagogical forces at work in the production of atomization, loneliness, and humiliation provide fertile ground for the rise of the fascistic sovereign. This was evident at the 2016 Republican National Convention when Donald Trump told his adoring crowd that only he could speak for them, address their problems, and "restore law and order." As Yoni Appelbaum points out in *The Atlantic*, Trump "did not appeal to prayer, or to God. He did not ask Americans to measure him against their values, or to hold him responsible for living up to them. He did not ask for their help. He asked them to place their faith in him."[28] According to Appelbaum,

> when Trump said, "I am your voice," the delegates on the convention floor roared their approval. When he said, "I alone can fix it," they shouted their approbation. The crowd peppered his speech with chants of "USA!" and "Lock her up!" and "Build the wall!" and "Trump!" It booed on cue, and cheered when prompted.[29]

And in doing so, he was greeted with sporadic emotional outbursts that amounted to disturbing expressions of racism, hyper-nationalism, and calls for lawlessness. More is on display here than the fascistic celebration of the heroic leader; there is also a systemic attempt to empty politics of its democratic impulses, repress debate and dialogue, and construct an anti-politics that thrives on conflict, on an enemy/friend divide, fueled by a rhetoric of demonization, objectification, and hatred.

Under such circumstances, language becomes militarized, serving as an expression of politics in which persuasion becomes armed, wedded to the production of desires, modes of agency, and forms of identification compatible with political and economic forms of authoritarian domination. Trump's rhetoric echoes Hannah Arendt's insight that totalitarianism is produced, in part, by making human beings superfluous, ignoring their voices, and silencing them in fascistic discourses of certainty, absolutes, and unaccountability that allow no space for critical thinking and informed agency. Trump's speeches and off-the-cuff comments bear an eerie resemblance to what Arendt once called in her famous book on Adolf Eichmann "the banality of evil," which she defines as a type of thoughtlessness, the inability to think, and the disavowal of any form of self-reflection and critical inquiry.[30] For some theorists, such as Richard J. Bernstein, Arendt was largely interested in understanding how ordinary people with banal motives can commit horrendous crimes and how such actions were connected making human beings superfluous as critical, thinking agents.[31] He is only partly right. Arendt connected the dethroning of the political to the emergence of a kind of anti-politics based on the inability or reluctance of individuals to "imagine what the other person is experiencing . . . a kind of stupidity (in which) obedience is idealized."[32]

What can be learned from the rise of the political and economic structures of domination is that they are deeply dependent upon the educative nature of a politics that undermines consciousness, stunts any viable notion of agency, and embraces a view of war that thrives on demonization, exclusion, and the production of losers. Too many people on the left have defaulted on this enormous responsibility for recognizing the educative nature of politics and the need for appropriating the tools, if not weapons, provided by the symbolic and pedagogical for challenging various forms of domination, working to change consciousness, and making education central to politics itself. Vital to such a task is expanding the notion of the political to include a notion of pedagogy that would be fundamental to addressing matters of identity, consciousness, and agency. The inability to think, the elimination of institutions and public spheres that make thinking possible, and the connection between non-thinking, thoughtlessness, and the routinization of misery, human suffering, and the destruction of the ecosystem should be at the heart of any theory willing to address the distinctive challenges posed by the emergence of a digital age in which culture, power, and politics become more integrated and serve to reconstitute the ways in which people relate to themselves, others, and the larger world. The task of theory in the age of an overabundance of information and knowledge is not to redcue pedagogy to a method but to theorize education as a holistic political project of which pedagogy is central to how human beings understand, address, and shape the world.

Donald Trump's Media Strategy

Donald Trump plays the media because he gets all of this. His media strategy is aimed at erasing memory, informed judgment, and critical dialogue. For Trump, miseducation is the key to getting elected. The issue here is not about the existing reign of civic illiteracy, it is about the crisis of agency, the forces that produce it, and the failure of progressives and the left to take such a crisis seriously by working hard to address the ideological and pedagogical dimensions of struggle. All of which is necessary in order to get people to be able to connect individual troubles with larger systemic considerations. The latter may be the biggest political and educational challenge facing those who wish to convince Trump supporters that he alone not only cannot solve their problems but also that he is a dishonest mouthpiece and agent for the ruling elite he dismisses as being part of the establishment.

At the same time, it is important to recognize that Trump represented the more immediate threat, especially for people of color. As the apotheosis of a brutal, racist, fascist expression of neoliberalism, Trump has promised to eliminate 22 million people from the ranks of those insured under Obamacare, would deport 11 million undocumented immigrants, restrict or jail dissident journalists, "withdraw U.S. from the Paris agreement on global warming, end enforcement of the voting rights act," legitimate state-sanctioned torture, encourage the spread of nuclear weapons, and stack the Supreme Court with right-wing ideologues who would implement reactionary policies for the next few decades. All of which he has done a short time into his presidency. And that is only the beginning of what would amount to a reign of terror and a series of events that could lead to an unimaginable nightmare for American democracy.[33] A nightmare that began with Trump's ascendancy to the presidency on January 20, 2017.

At stake here is a different type of conflict between those who believe in democracy and those who don't. The election did not address the ensuing crisis, which is really a fight for the soul of democracy. One consequence will be that millions one way or another will once again bear the burden of a society that hates democracy and punishes all but the financial elite. Both Trump and Clinton and the economic and political forces they represent are part of the problem and offer up different forms of domination. What is crucial for progressives to recognize is their responsibility to highlight that neoliberal economic structures register only one part of the logic of repression. The other side is the colonization of consciousness, the production of modes of agency complicit with their own oppression.

This dual register of politics, which has been highlighted by theorists extending from Hannah Arendt and Antonio Gramsci to Raymond Williams and C. Wright Mills, has a long history but has been pushed to the margins under neoliberal regimes of oppression. Once again, any viable notion of collective resistance must take matters of consciousness, identity, desire, and persuasion seriously so as to speak to the underlying conditions of atomization that depoliticize and paralyze people within orbits of self-interest, greed, resentment, misdirected anger, and spiraling violence.

Addressing the affective and ideological dimensions not only of casino capitalism but also of the social imagination is crucial to waking us all up to our ability to work together, recognize the larger economic, cultural, and systemic structures that dominate our lives, and provide each other with the tools to situate isolated problems into a more comprehensive landscape of power and politics. The power of solidarity does not only come together in social movements; it is also central to the educative force of a politics that embraces democratic social relations as the foundation for collective action.

Overcoming the atomization inherent in neoliberal regimes means making clear how they destroy pedagogically and politically every vestige of solidarity in the interest of amassing huge amounts of wealth and power while successfully paralyzing vast numbers of people in the depoliticizing orbits of privatization and self-interest. Of course, we see examples of movements that embrace solidarity as an act of collective resistance—most visibly the Black Lives Matter movement. This is a model that needs to take on a more general political significance in which the violence of apparatuses of oppression can be connected to a politics of atomization that must be addressed as both an educational and political issue. Neoliberal precarity, austerity, and the militarization of society inflict violence not just on the body but on the psyche as well. This means that the dual crisis of economic structures must be understood as part of the crisis of memory, thinking, hope, and agency itself.

Beyond Disimagination Machines

The election of Donald Trump to the American presidency exemplifies how resentment mediated by ignorance breeds irrationality and endears a large number of people to falsehoods, venality, and carnival barking. The corruption of both the truth and politics is made all the easier since the American public have become habituated to over-stimulation and live in an ever accelerating overflow of information and images. Experience no longer has the time to crystallize into mature and informed thought. Leon Wieseltier is right in stating that "words cannot wait for thoughts and patience [becomes] a liability."[34] Opinion outdoes reasoned and evidence-based arguments and the power of expression degenerates into a spectacle. This was evident throughout Donald Trump's presidential campaign given that he lied incessantly, and rather than being held accountable for his falsification, he used his continuous attacks on the truth to drive the news cycle and receive billions of dollars in free advertising from the mainstream media. Popular culture revels in the spectacles of shock and violence.[35] Universities now labor under the burden of a neoliberal regime that celebrates the corporate model made famous by McDonald's. Knowledge has been commodified, standardized, and collapses the distinction between education and training. Knowledge is packaged for easy consumption resulting in curricula that resemble a fast-food menu.[36]

Many of the commanding institutions that produce and distribute ideas—from the media to higher education—have become disimagination machines, tools for legitimating ignorance, and central to the formation of an authoritarian politics that is gutting any vestige of democracy from the ideology, policies, and institutions that now shape American society. This is particularly evident in higher education. Governed by a neoliberal model of business, knowledge has become instrumentalized, students are viewed as customers, and the bottom line now determines what courses will be taught.[37] Education has lost its moral, political, and spiritual bearings just as teachers and other public servants across the country are being belittled and attacked by economic and religious fundamentalists. One consequence is that an increasing number of public spheres have become corporatized, employ a top-down authoritarian style of power, mimic market-driven values, and infantilize the larger polity by removing the public from all forms of governance. In addition, the connection between public and higher education has been lost and as a result the common good is now subordinated to the realms of the private and the personal. Clearly all of these defining relations have been produced in a neoliberal social order that has to be challenged and changed.

The rise of thoughtlessness and the inability to think has become a political epidemic and does not augur well for democracy. Americans live in a historical moment that attempts to annihilate thoughtfulness and critical thinking. For instance, while on the campaign trail, Donald Trump declared, he liked "the uneducated"—implying that it is better that they stay ignorant than be critically engaged agents. Trump's love affair with ignorance became visible once again when he boasted that he didn't read books, a declaration that needs no commentary. On the media front, Fox News offers no apologies for suggesting that thinking is an act of stupidity. Couple the latter with the fact that a culture of cruelty and a survival-of-the-fittest ethos in the United States is the new norm and one consequence is that democracy is on the verge of disappearing or has already disappeared!

We have seen this demagogic script play out before in Nazi Germany. Hitler was an egomaniac who collapsed the distinction between the truth and falsehoods. He defined himself through superlatives suggesting only he could solve Germany's problems and save the world. He bombarded his audience with the discourse of law and order and endlessly insisted in his speeches that he would overturn a long period of decline and return

Germany to national greatness. He deplored reason and argued in *Mein Kampf* that "propaganda must appeal to the emotions—not the reasoning powers—of the crowd." He also loved the illiterate masses and that the only thing they could grasp were sensationalist slogans. Like Donald Trump, he was also viewed initially as a clown and dismissed until it was too late, and his discourse of cultural pessimism, hate, and national greatness along with his thugs and the cowards that supported him ushered him into power.[38]

Where are the agents of democracy and the public spaces that offer hope in such dark times? What role will theory play at a time when the very ability of the public's capacity to discern informed arguments from opinions is disappearing? What role should theory play as a pedagogy force in a time of increasing violence? What role should intellectuals, cultural workers, artists, writers, journalists, and others play as part of a bigger struggle to reclaim a democratic vision and exercise a collective sense of civic courage? Theorists such as Antonio Gramsci, C. Wright Mills, Hannah Arendt, and Raymond Williams understood the importance of the educative force of the wider culture and how such an understanding posed a challenge to those theories that relegated pedagogy to the lower depths of theorizing. What is now clear is that pedagogy is not only linked to social change but also to the production of modes of agency and the institutions that make such change possible. Education as a political force makes us both the subjects of and subject to relations of power. The key is to expand that insight theoretically so as to make pedagogy central to politics itself. That is a lesson we can learn from both Arendt and Hofstadter.

Notes

1   Surprisingly, a good take on this issue can be found in Thomas L. Friedman, "Trump's Wink to 'Second Amendment People,'" *New York Times* (August 9, 2016). Online: www.nytimes.com/2016/08/10/opinion/trumps-ambiguous-wink-wink-to-second-amendment-people.html?_r=0; see also, David S. Cohen, "Trump's Assassination Dog Whistle Was Even Scarier than You Think," *Rolling Stone Magazine* (August 9, 2016). Online: www.rollingstone.com/politics/features/trumps-assassination-dog-whistle-was-scarier-than-you-think-w433615
2   Tom Engelhardt, "Tomgram: Rebecca Gordon, No 'New Normal,'" *TomDispatch* (November 20, 2016). Online: www.tomdispatch.com/blog/176212/

3   Adam Haslett, "Donald Trump, Shamer in Chief," *Nation* (October 4, 2016). Online: www.thenation.com/article/donald-trump-shamer-in-chief/

4   Ibid.

5   Nicolaus Mills, "Television and the Politics of Humiliation," *Dissent* (Fall 2016). Online: www.dissentmagazine.org/article/television-and-the-politics-of-humiliation

6   Ibid.

7   Leo Lowenthal, "Atomization of Man." In *False Prophets: Studies in Authoritarianism* (New Brunswick, NJ: Transaction Books, 1987), p. 181.

8   His colleague Erich Fromm also wrote brilliantly on the discourse of isolation and atomization. See, for instance, his *Escape from Freedom* (New York: Avon, 1972).

9   See, for instance, Paul Buchheit, "The Real Terrorists: The .01%," *CommonDreams* (January 11, 2016). Online: www.commondreams.org/views/2016/01/11/real-terrorists-01. For a full-length treatment of the issue of inequality, see Anthony B. Atkins, *Inequality: What Can Be Done?* (Cambridge, MA: Harvard University Press, 2015); Joseph E. Stiglitz, *The Price of Inequality* (New York: Norton, 2012). And for the political forces driving inequality, see Mike Lofgren, *The Deep State: The Fall of the Constitution and the Rise of a Shadow Government* (New York: Viking, 2016).

10   Oliver Munday, "Truth and Lies in the Age of Trump," *New York Times* (December 10, 2016). Online: www.nytimes.com/2016/12/10/opinion/truth-and-lies-in-the-age-of-trump.html

11   William Davies, "How 'Competitiveness' Became One of the Great Unquestioned Virtues of Contemporary Culture," *Evonomics* (July 24, 2016). Online: http://evonomics.com/how-competitiveness-became-one-of-the-great-unquestioned-virtues/?utm_source=Newsletter&utm_medium=Mailchimp&utm_campaign=Email

12   Greg Elmer and Paula Todd, "Don't Be a Loser: Or How Trump Turned the Republican Primaries into an Episode of The Apprentice," *Television and New Media* (June 29, 2016), p. 1.

13   Ibid.

14   João Biehl, *Vita: Life in A Zone of Social Abandonment* (Los Angeles: University of California Press, 2005), pp. 2–3, 10.

15   Sheldon Wolin, "Political Theory: From Vocation to Invocation." In Jason Frank and John Tambornino, eds, *Vocations of Political Theory* (Minneapolis: University of Minnesota Press, 2000), p. 4.

16   Cited in Timothy Egan, "The Sore Loser Uprising," *New York Times International* (August 13–14, 2016), p. 14.

17   Richard Hofstadter, *The Paranoid Style in American Politics: And Other Essays* (Cambridge, MA: Harvard University Press, 1996).

18   Richard Hofstadter, "The Paranoid Style in American Politics," *Harper's* (November 1964). Online www.harpers.org/archive/1964/11/0014706

19   Lofgren, *The Deep State*.

20   Beverly Bandler, "Paranoid Right-Wing Extremism," email posting on August 12, 2016 (personal correspondence).

21   Tom Engelhardt, "Better than Reality Television: The 2016 Election Is Proving to Be the Greatest Show on Earth," *Salon* (August 10, 2016). Online: www.salon.com/2016/08/10/better-than-reality-televisio_partner/

22   For a brilliant critique of the concept of resiliency, see Brad Evans and Julian Reid, *Resilient Life: The Art of Living Dangerously* (London: Polity, 2014).

23   Michael Bader, "How Can We Stop America's Deadly Epidemic of Loneliness?" *AlterNet* (December 22, 2015). Online: www.alternet.org/news-amp-politics/how-can-we-stop-americas-deadly-epidemic-loneliness

24   Rae Ellen Bichell, "Suicide Rates Climb In U.S., Especially among Adolescent Girls," *NPR Org* (April 22, 2016). Online: www.npr.org/sections/health-shots/2016/04/22/ 474888854/suicide-rates-climb-in-u-s-especially-among-adolescent-girls

25   Gina Kolatanov, "Death Rates Rising for Middle-Aged White Americans, Study Finds," *New York Times* (November 2, 2015). Online: www.nytimes.com/2015/11/03/ health/death-rates-rising-for-middle-aged-white-americans-study-finds.html

26   Nadja Popovich, "A Deadly Crisis: Mapping the Spread of America's Drug Overdose Epidemic," *Guardian* (May 25, 2016). Online: www.theguardian.com/society/ng-interactive/2016/may/25/opioid-epidemic-overdose-deaths-map

27   Pierre Bourdieu and Gunter Grass, "The 'Progressive' Restoration: A Franco-German Dialogue," *New Left Review*, Vol. 14 (March–April, 2002), p. 2.

28   Yoni Appelbaum, "I Alone Can Fix It," *Atlantic* (July 21, 2016). Online: www.the atlantic.com/politics/archive/2016/07/trump-rnc-speech-alone-fix-it/492557/

29   Ibid.

30   Hannah Arendt's notion of the banality of evil was first used in her 1963 book, *Eichmann in Jerusalem: A Report on the Banality of Evil* (New York: Penguin, 2006). Hofstadter's phrase 'the paranoid style of politics' gained prominence in his book of the same title.

31   Richard J. Bernstein, *The Abuse of Evil: The Corruption of Politics and Religion since 9/11* (Cambridge: Polity Press, 2005).

32   Hannah Arendt, *Hannah Arendt: The Last Interview and Other Conversations* (Brooklyn, NY: Melville House Publishing, 2013), p. 50.

33   Mark Kleiman, "How Much Damage Could Donald Trump Really Do, After All?" *Huffington Post* (August 9, 2016). Online: www.huffingtonpost.com/mark-kleiman/ donald-trump-damage_b_11402038.html. Also, see: Philip Bump and Aaron Blake, "Donald Trump's Dark Speech to the Republican National Convention, Annotated," *Washington Post* (July 21, 2016). Online: www.washingtonpost.com/news/the-fix/wp/ 2016/07/21/full-text-donald-trumps-prepared-remarks-accepting-the-republican-nomination; John Halle, "Noam Chomsky's 8-Point Rationale for Voting for the Lesser Evil Presidential Candidate," *Alter Net* (July 25, 2016). Online: www.alternet. org/election-2016/noam-chomskys-8-point-rationale-voting-lesserevil-presidential-candidate

34   Leon Wieseltier, "Among the Disrupted," *International New York Times* (January 7, 2015). Online: www.nytimes.com/2015/01/18/books/review/among-the-disrupted. html?_r=0

35   Brad Evans and Henry A. Giroux, Disposable Futures: *The Seduction of Violence in the Age of the Spectacle* (San Francisco: City Lights, 2016).

36   Ulrich Beck, *Twenty Observations on a World in Turmoil* (London: Polity Press, 2010), especially pp. 53–9.

37   See, for instance, Henry A. Giroux, *Neoliberalism's War on Higher Education* (Chicago: Haymarket Books, 2014).

38   These themes are taken up in Volker Ullrich, *Hitler: Ascent, 1889–1939* (New York: Knopf, 2016).

10

RECLAIMING THE RADICAL IMAGINATION UNDER NEOLIBERAL AUTHORITARIANISM

Historically, the most terrible things; war, genocide, and slavery, have resulted not from disobedience, but from obedience.

(Howard Zinn)

The threat of George Orwell's nightmarish vision of a totalitarian society seems more imminent today than when he first published his dystopian warnings. The looming specter of authoritarianism in American society has undercut the most progressive elements of modernity, deformed an emancipatory notion of civic life, and contributed to the emptying out of the political.[1] As the United States has moved from a welfare to a warfare state, the institutions that were once meant to further justice, limit human suffering and misfortune, and protect the public from the excesses of the market have been either weakened or abolished.[2] With the weakening, if not evisceration, of the social contract, the discourse of social responsibility has been removed from the practices of democratic reform. Disdained by right-wing extremists, democratic principles are withering under a social order marked by a growing lawlessness, a hardening of the culture towards society's most vulnerable, and the emergence of an unprecedented survival-of-the fittest ethos. This mean-spirited ethos rails against any notion of solidarity and compassion that embraces a respect for others. The consequences of this emerging form of domestic terrorism point to a distinctive mode of authoritarianism emerging in the United States in the 21st century. Mike Lofgren is right to insist that "The rise of authoritarian populism in the West is a very real, clear and present danger."[3] The crucial issue here is not to highlight simply the replication of anti-democratic ideologies, policies, and practices from the past but to raise serious questions about what this heralds for the future.[4]

After a decade and a half of war abroad, war has come home mobilized through a culture of fear, surveillance, and violence. As David Packer has observed, violence has become inseparable from justice and lawlessness now defines the commanding political, military, and economic institutions of the United States.[5] The very idea of violence has metamorphosed into a solution for addressing social problems. For instance, as everyday behavior is criminalized, school children are assaulted by security personnel, Black youth are killed by the police for making eye contact, and under the pretext of a war on terror the distinction between civilians and combatants is blurred. Public spheres once considered safe spaces have been transformed into war zones, turning poor urban schools into prisons, cities into training grounds for paramilitarized police forces, and airports into sites of intensive surveillance and security. Hannah Arendt's notion that the protean origins of totalitarianism have survived "the passing of Hitler and Stalin" and are capable of crystallizing into new forms appears difficult to contest as the United States moves closer to a police state. John Whitehead captures this perfectly. He writes:

> You might walk past a police officer outfitted in tactical gear, holding an assault rifle, or drive past a police cruiser scanning license plates. There might be a surveillance camera on the street corner tracking your movements. At the airport, you may be put through your paces by government agents who will want to either pat you down or run scans of your body. And each time you make a

call or send a text message, your communications will most likely be logged and filed. When you return home, you might find that government agents have been questioning your neighbors about you, as part of a "census" questionnaire. After you retire to sleep, you might find yourself awakened by a SWAT team crashing through your door (you'll later discover they were at the wrong address), and if you make the mistake of reaching for your eyeglasses, you might find yourself shot by a cop who felt threatened.[6]

As I have argued throughout this book, the basic elements of this new neoliberal authoritarianism can also be seen in the ongoing and ruthless assault on the social state, unions, higher education, workers, students, poor minority youth, and any vestige of the social contract. Free-market policies, values, and practices with their emphasis on the privatization of public wealth, the elimination of social protections, and the deregulation of economic activity now shape practically every commanding political and economic institution in the United States, and this control will intensify under the Trump administration. Markets now use their economic and ideological resources to weaponize and militarize all aspects of everyday life. This militarized status quo is increasingly held in place by a culture of fear, a pedagogy of repression, an ongoing spectacle of violence, game show aesthetics, and a politics of precarity, control, and mass surveillance. A world of shadows, secrecy, and lawlessness now characterizes an authoritarian state that is ruthless in its pursuit of wealth and power and indifferent to its plundering of both humanity and the planet.[7] Depoliticization is nearly all-encompassing and disguises itself in the normalization of greed, the celebration of self-interest as national ideal, and the corporate-controlled consumer-soma machine that inoculates the public with an addiction to instant gratification and the commodification of practically everything.[8] We don't see the work camps or death camps that characterized the catastrophes of mid-century totalitarian regimes. However, Trump's pledge to run his administration around what he calls a regime of law and order will only strengthen the forces of repression and authoritarianism in the United States. Yet, one doesn't have to be in jail to feel imprisoned, especially when it is increasingly difficult to take control of one's life in a meaningful way.

We live at a time when politics is nation-based and power is global.[9] Global markets now trump the national rendering of the political culture and democratic institutions of modernity making them nearly obsolete. The financial elite now float beyond national borders and no longer care about the welfare state, the common good, or for that matter any institution not subordinate to the dictates of finance capitalism. Hence, the ruling elites make no concessions in their pursuit of power and profits. The social contract of the past, especially in the United States, is now on life support as social provisions are cut, pensions are decimated, and the certainty of a once-secure job disappears. Many neoliberal societies are now governed by politicians and financial elites who no longer believe in social investments and are more than willing to condemn young people and others—often paralyzed by the precariousness and instability that haunts their lives and future—to a savage form of casino capitalism.

Deregulation, privatization, commodification, and the unimpeded flow of capital now drive politics and concentrate power in the hands of the 1 percent. Class warfare has merged with neo-conservative policies to eliminate or weaken crucial social provisions such as food stamp programs or Medicaid. There are no safe spaces free from the rich hoarders of capital and the tentacles of the surveillance and punishing state. The basic imperatives of casino capitalism have become the new common sense—extending from eliminating corporate taxes and shifting wealth from the public to the private sector to dismantling corporate regulations and insisting that markets should govern all of social life. Any viable notion of the social, solidarity, and shared democratic values is now viewed as a pathology, replaced by a survival-of-the-fittest ethic, the celebration of self-interest, and a notion of the good life entirely tied to a vapid consumerist ethic.[10]

With the return of the new Gilded Age, not only are democratic institutions, values, and social protections at risk in many countries, but the civic, pedagogical, and social formations that make them central to democratic life are in danger of disappearing altogether. Poverty, joblessness, low-wage work, and the threat of state-sanctioned violence produce among many populations the ongoing fear of a life of perpetual misery and an ongoing struggle simply to survive. Insecurity coupled with a climate of fear and surveillance dampens dissent and promotes a political paralysis fed daily by the mobilization of moral panics, whether they reference the violence of lone domestic terrorists, immigrants swarming across borders, or poor Black youth in run-down urban neighborhoods.

Neoliberalism's War against Critical Thought

Underlying the rise of the authoritarian state and the forces that hide in the shadows is a politics indebted to promoting historical and social amnesia. The new authoritarianism is strongly indebted to what Orwell once called a "protective stupidity" that negates political life and divests language of its critical content.[11] Neoliberal authoritarianism has changed the language of politics and everyday life through a malicious public pedagogy that turns reason on its head and normalizes a culture of fear, war, surveillance, and exploitation. That is, the heavy hand of Orwellian control is evident in those dominant cultural apparatuses that extend from schools to print, audio, and screen cultures, which now serve as repressive forms of public pedagogy attacking any critical notion of politics that makes a claim to be educative in its attempts to enable the conditions for changing "the ways in which people might think critically."[12]

Higher education represents one area where casino capitalism wages war on any field of study that might encourage students to think critically. One egregious example was on full display in North Carolina where the Republican Party members who control the Board of Governors decimated higher education by voting to cut 46 degree programs. One member defended such cuts with the comment: "We're capitalists, and we have to look at what the demand is, and we have to respond to the demand."[13] This is more than an example of crude economic instrumentalism, it is also a recipe for instituting an academic culture of thoughtlessness and a kind of stupidity receptive to what Hannah Arendt once called totalitarianism. In Wisconsin, Governor Scott Walker has worked hard to eliminate tenure at Wisconsin's public universities as well as eviscerate any vestige of shared governance.[14]

He also cut $200 million from the state higher education budget, which is not surprising given his hatred of public education.

Both of these examples point to a new breed of politician waging war on higher education, critical pedagogy, the public good, and any viable notion of the social state. Like many of their politically extremist colleagues, they reflect a crudely harsh authoritarian era that exhibits zero tolerance for economic, social, and racial justice and a boundless tolerance to overlook the crimes committed by CIA torturers, mortgage lenders who cheated millions of homeowners, and Wells Fargo bankers who engaged in illegalities such as creating false bank accounts for their customers.[15] Under such conditions, material violence is now matched by symbolic violence, as made evident by the proliferation of images, institutions, and narratives that legitimate not only the manufactured ignorance of market-driven culture and its corollary worship of wealth, greed, and a political and consumer culture that craves instant gratification, but also what might be called an expanding politics of disposability.

Rendered redundant as a result of the collapse of the welfare state, a pervasive racism, a growing disparity in income and wealth, and a take-no-prisoners market-driven ideology, an increasing number of individuals and groups—especially young people, low-income groups, and people of color—are being demonized, criminalized, or simply abandoned either by virtue of their inability to participate in the rituals of consumption or due to low-paying jobs, poor health, or pressing family needs. What Joao Biehl has called "zones of social abandonment" now accelerate the disposal of the unwanted.[16] The injuries of class are now compounded by injuries directed at immigrants, gays, poor minorities, and women. Daily debasements create a perpetual climate of fear, insecurity, and a range of illnesses extending from heart attacks and suicide, to mental illness and imprisonment. For example, low-income youth and youth of color, especially, are often warehoused in schools that resemble boot camps, dispersed to dank and dangerous workplaces, incarcerated in prisons that privilege punishment over rehabilitation, or consigned to the increasing army of the permanently unemployed. Human misery and systemic violence are now built into the nervous system of America. No one is compelled to stare; there is no shock of recognition; no inclination to act against a perceived injustice. There is just the fog of resignation, complacency, and normalcy waiting to be ruptured by the rage that comes with people being humiliated, exploited, assaulted, bound, and gagged for too long.

People who were once viewed as facing dire problems in need of state intervention and social protection are now seen as a problem threatening society. With successive waves of get-tough-on-crime policy, the war on poverty has become a war against the poor. Even the plight of the homeless is defined less as a political and economic issue in need of social reform than as a matter of law and order. Yet criminalizing the homeless for crimes such as falling asleep in public "does nothing to break the cycle of poverty or prevent homelessness in the future."[17] If mass incarceration is one index of an emerging punishing state, another register is when government budgets for prison construction eclipse funds for higher education.

Already disenfranchised by virtue of their age, young people are under assault in ways that are entirely new because they now face a world that is far more precarious than at any other time in recent history. Not only do many of them live in a space of social homelessness in which austerity and a politics of uncertainty lock them out of a secure future, they also find themselves inhabiting a society that seeks to silence them as it makes them invisible. Victims of a neoliberal regime that smashes their hopes and attempts to exclude them from the fruits of democracy, young people are now told not to expect too much. Written out of any claim to the economic and social resources of the larger society, they are increasingly told to accept the status of being "stateless, faceless, and functionless" nomads, a plight for which they alone have to accept responsibility.[18] Increasing numbers of youth suffer mental anguish and overt distress, including among the college-bound, debt-ridden, and unemployed whose numbers are growing exponentially. Many reports claim that "young Americans are suffering from rising levels of anxiety, stress, depression and even suicide." For example, "One out of every five young people and one out of every four college students . . . suffers from some form of diagnosable mental illness."[19]

The politics of disposability with its expanding machineries of civic and social death, terminal exclusion, and zones of abandonment represent a dangerous historical moment and must be addressed within the context of a market-driven society that is rewriting the meaning of common sense, agency, desire, and politics itself. Post-2008 recession, the capitalist dream machine is back with huge profits for hedge fund managers, major players in the financial service industry, and the denizens of the ultra-rich. In these new landscapes of wealth, exclusion, and fraud, the commanding institutions of casino capitalism promote a winner-takes-all ethos and aggressively undermine a more egalitarian distribution of wealth via corporate taxation. In addition, the financial elite defund crucial social services such as the food stamp programs for poor children, attack labor unions, gay rights, and women's reproductive rights, while waging a counter-revolution against the principles of social citizenship and democracy. In this instance, the war on the poor, women, Black youth, immigrants, and labor is part of the war on democracy, and signifies a new thrust toward what might be called the authoritarian rule of corporate sovereignty and governance.

Sanctioned Violent Lawlessness and Cruelty

Politics and power are now on the side of legally protected lawlessness, as is evident in the state's endless violations of civil liberties, freedom of speech, and many constitutional rights, mostly done in the name of national security. Violent lawlessness wraps itself in government dictates in such policies as the Patriot Act, the National Defense Authorization Act, the Military Commissions Act, former President Obama's kill list, and a host of other legal illegalities. These would include the right of the president "to order the assassination of any citizen whom he considers allied with terrorists,"[20] to use secret evidence to detain individuals indefinitely, to develop a massive surveillance apparatus to monitor every audio and electronic communication used by citizens who have not committed a crime, to employ state torture against those considered enemy combatants, and to block the courts from prosecuting those officials who commit such heinous crimes.[21] All of these legal illegalities will be expanded under the Trump administration given his repeated false claim that "enhanced interrogation" works and that there is nothing wrong with using waterboarding against enemy combatants. In fact, Trump's comments on state-sanctioned torture made during his constitutional campaign legitimate what can be called his willingness to commit what the international community would label as war crimes. According to Trump:

> Torture works. OK, folks? You know, I have these guys—'Torture doesn't work!'—believe me, it works. And waterboarding is your minor form. Some people say it's not actually torture. Let's assume it is. But they asked me the question: What do you think of waterboarding? Absolutely fine. But we should go much stronger than waterboarding.[22]

In reading Orwell's dystopia, what becomes clear is that his nightmarish future has become our present and there is more under assault than simply the individual's right to privacy.

Power in its most oppressive form is deployed not only by various repressive government policies and intelligence agencies but also through a predatory and market-driven culture that turns violence into entertainment, foreign aggression into video games, and domestic terrorism into a goose-stepping celebration of masculinity and the mad values of unbridled militarism. At the same time, the increasing circulation of public narratives and public displays of cruelty and moral indifference continue to maim and suffocate the exercise of reason and social responsibility. What we have been witnessing in the United States since the 1980s and the Reagan–Thatcher disavowal of all things social is an increasing turn to a punitive and militarized society marked by an increasing indifference to matters of empathy and an erasure of ethical considerations.

Evidence of such cruelty is everywhere. We see it in the words of West Virginia Republican lawmaker, Ray Canterbury, who added a requirement to a bill—without irony—intended to end child hunger in which school children would be forced to work in exchange for free school meals. As he put it, "I think it would be a good idea if perhaps we had the kids work for their lunches: trash to be taken out, hallways to be swept, lawns to be mowed, make them earn it."[23] Newt Gingrich has made a similar argument; one that is even crueler, if that is possible. At a 2011 speech given at Harvard University, he argued that it was time to relax child labor laws, which he called "truly stupid."[24] He linked this suggestion to the call for "getting rid of unionized janitors . . . and paying local students to take care of the school. The kids would actually do work, they would have cash, they would have pride in the school."[25] This policy suggestion is more than "Dickensian," it is draconian and suggests a deep disrespect for working people and a lack of knowledge regarding what school janitors actually do. Gingrich mimics a neoliberal ideology that separates economic actions from social costs. He seems to be clueless about whether 9 and 13 year olds could perform work that is often back breaking, brutalizing, and sometimes dangerous, including tasks such as working with hazardous chemicals, fixing basic plumbing work, and cleaning floors and toilets. To impose this type of work on poor children who allegedly need it to teach them something about character borders on insanity. Gingrich appears to be unaware about either the vindictive nature or the lapse in moral judgment regarding his call to keep poor children in school. In addition, he has no qualms about putting school janitors out of work as if they don't need to make a living wage to pay hospital bills and "put food on the table for their own children."[26]

Neoliberalism has produced a broad landscape of cruelty, precarity, and disposability. We see and hear it in the words of Ben Carson, Trump's Secretary of Housing and Urban Development, who stated without irony that "poverty is a state of mind" reducible to a "poverty of spirit." He has also mischaracterized US slaves as "immigrants."[27] There is also the now infamous examples provided by President Donald Trump who infamously revealed with pride while running for office that he was a racist, Islamophobic, misogynistic, xenophobic, lying, bloviating, narcissistic charlatan, and alleged serial groper of women.[28] The culture of cruelty and the hatred that promotes it appear to be completely divorced from any sense of reality, social responsibility, or reason. For instance, Andy Kessler, a wealthy hedge fund operator, insisted that homeless shelters generate poverty because they bring people into a web of dependency.[29] As Eleanor Goldberg states, "So, according to Kessler, the reason why 1.6 million people in America don't have a place to sleep at night is because spoiled teens determined to get into Brown University (with their service-heavy résumés) are giving them enough food to eat to keep them from needing to get jobs."[30]

There is more at stake here than the ignorant babble of insulated rich folks, there is also a type of psychotic behavior on display reminiscent of Christian Bale's character Patrick Bateman, the wealthy investment banker in the film *American Psycho*. In addition, there was the egregious case of the insufferable Martin Shkreli, the 33-year-old chief executive of Turing Pharmaceuticals who raised by 5,000 percent the cost of a drug used by patients affected with HIV and cancer. The price of a pill went from $13.50 to $750.00, imposing an enormous financial hardship on patients requiring the drug to fight potentially deadly infections. Shkreli, who has been quoted as saying he likes money more than people, responded initially to criticism of price gouging with a quote from an Eminem song. In a verse that now passes for public exchange, he tweeted: "And it seems like the media immediately points a finger at me. So I point one back at em, but not the index or pinkie."

Another instance of the culture of cruelty can be seen in the high-octane and unethical grammars of violence that now offer the only currency with any enduring value for mediating relationships, addressing problems, and offering instant pleasure in the larger culture. This is evident in the transformation of local police forces into paramilitarized militias, schools being increasingly transformed into punishing factories, and in the ongoing criminalization of social behaviors, especially of poor minority youth. Brute force and savage killing replayed over and over in various media platforms now function as part of an auto-immune system that transforms the economy of genuine pleasure into a mode of sadism that saps democracy of any political substance and moral vitality, even as the body politic appears to weaken itself by cannibalizing its own young. Needless to say, extreme violence is more than a spectacle for upping the pleasure quotient of those disengaged from politics; it is also part of a punishing machine that spends more on putting poor minorities in jail than on educating them.

As American society becomes more militarized, "civil society organizes itself for the production of violence."[31] As a result, the capillaries of militarization feed and mold social institutions extending across the body politic—from the schools to local police forces. In the United States, local police forces, in particular, have been outfitted with full riot gear, submachine guns, armored vehicles, and other lethal weapons imported from the battlefields of Iraq and Afghanistan, reinforcing their mission to assume battle-ready behavior. Is it any wonder that violence rather than painstaking neighborhood police work and community outreach and engagement becomes the norm for dealing with many youth, especially at a time when more and more behaviors are being criminalized?

The police in too many cities have been transformed into soldiers just as dialogue and community policing have been replaced by military-style practices that are way out of proportion to the crimes the police are trained to address. For instance, *The Economist* reported that "SWAT teams were deployed about 3,000 times in 1980 but are now used around 50,000 times a year. Some cities use them for routine patrols in high-crime areas. Baltimore and Dallas have used them to break up poker games."[32] Such egregious uses of police time and taxpayer dollars would appear idiotic if they weren't so savage.

In the advent of the recent display of police force in Ferguson, Missouri and Baltimore, Maryland, it is not surprising that the impact of the rapid militarization of local police on poor Black communities is nothing short of terrifying and yet deeply symptomatic of the violence that takes place in authoritarian societies. For instance, Michelle Alexander exposes the racist nature of the punishing state by pointing out that "There are more African American adults under correctional control today—in prison or jail, on probation or parole—than were enslaved in 1850, a decade before the Civil War began."[33] When young Black boys and girls see people in their neighborhood killed by the police for making eye contact, holding a toy gun, walking in a stairway, or for selling cigarettes while "the financial elite go free for a bookmaking operation that almost brought the country to economic ruin," not only do the police lose their legitimacy, so do established norms of lawfulness and modes of governance.[34]

Neo-Darwinist Ethics

In terms reminiscent of Orwell, morality loses its emancipatory possibilities and degenerates into a pathology in which individual misery is denounced as a moral failing. Under the neo-Darwinian ethos of survival of the fittest, the ultimate form of entertainment becomes the pain and humiliation of others, especially those considered disposable and powerless. They populate the stories we are now hearing from U.S. politicians who disdain the poor and see poverty as a matter of morality; in this world view, the poor are viewed as moochers who don't need social assistance but stronger morals. Jeb Bush echoed this argument in his claim that if he were elected president, he wouldn't be giving Black people "free stuff", [35] drawing on racist stereotypes about Black Americans being lazy and "plagued by pathological dependence."[36]

These narratives can also be heard from conservative pundits such as *New York Times* columnist David Brooks, who insists that poverty is a matter of the poor lacking virtue, middle-class norms, and decent moral codes.[37] For Brooks, the problems of the poor and disadvantaged can be solved "through moral education and self-reliance . . . high-quality relationships and strong familial ties."[38] This logic is really code for the racist notion that the culture of blackness is synonymous with the culture of criminality and that all types of problems ranging from living in poverty and homelessness to being unemployed in the end are about a lack of personal responsibility. The view that people who are impoverished or held back from getting ahead are mainly responsible for their fate is central to the normalization of neoliberal ideology. Blaming the victim has been taken to a new level under the regime of neoliberalism, which wages a fierce pedagogical struggle in order to convince people that the only way to understand and analyze the effects of inequality, mass incarceration, segregated schools, racism, and extreme poverty is to view such problems through the lens of bad character, individual irresponsibility, and the absence of middle-class norms. Keeanga-Yamahtta Taylor brilliantly dissects this blaming-the-victim ideology when it is used to rationalize Black inequality. She writes:

The point is that explanations for Black inequality that blame Black people for their own oppression transform material causes into subjective causes. The problem is not racial discrimination in the workplace or residential segregation: it is Black irresponsibility, erroneous social mores, and general bad behavior. Ultimately this transformation is not about "race" or even "white supremacy" but about "making sense" of and rationalizing poverty and inequality in ways that absolve the state and capital of any culpability.[39]

In this discourse, soaring inequality in wealth and income, high levels of unemployment, stagnant economic growth, and low wages for millions of working Americans are willfully covered over and covered up. What Brooks, Carson, Trump, and other conservatives consistently obfuscate is the racist nature of the drug war, police violence, the stranglehold of the criminal justice system on poor Black communities, the egregious effect of "racially skewed patterns of mass incarceration," mass unemployment for underserved youth, and poor-quality education in low-income neighborhoods.[40] Paul Krugman gets it right in rebutting the argument that all the poor need are the virtues of middle-class morality and a good dose of resilience.[41] He counters: "The poor don't need lectures on morality, they need more resources—which we can afford to provide—and better economic opportunities, which we can also afford to provide through everything from training and subsidies to higher minimum wages."[42]

As the claims and promises of a neoliberal utopia have been transformed into an Orwellian nightmare, the United States continues to succumb to the pathology of financial speculation, political corruption, the redistribution of wealth upward into the hands of the 1 percent, the rise of the surveillance state, and the use of the criminal justice system as a way of dealing with social problems. At the same time, Orwell's sinister fantasy of an authoritarian future continues without enough opposition. Students, low-income whites, and poor minority youth are exposed to a low-intensity war in which they are held hostage to a number of forces including: a future of low expectations, increasing police violence, an atomizing consumer culture, a growing anti-intellectualism, religious fundamentalism, corporate government modes of surveillance, and the burden of extreme debt. Higher education no longer models itself, however weakly, after a public good or as a protective space to think critically, question, engage in thoughtful dialogue, and learn how to question power. It now functions as part of the "higher education-to-corporate pipeline."[43]

No democracy can survive the kind of inequality in which "the 400 richest people ... have as much wealth as 154 million Americans combined, that's 50 percent of the entire country [while] the top economic 1 percent of the U.S. population now has a record 40 percent of all wealth and more wealth than 90 percent of the population combined."[44] On a global scale, according to a study by anti-poverty charity Oxfam, "the wealthiest 1% [are expected] to own more than 50% of the world's wealth by 2016."[45] Within such iniquitous conditions of power, access, and wealth, a society cannot foster a sense of organized responsibility fundamental to a democracy. Instead, it encourages a sense of organized irresponsibility—a practice that underlies the economic Darwinism and civic corruption at the heart of a debased politics.

The Role of Education

I want to return to an issue that I have developed throughout the book. What role might education and critical pedagogy have in a society in which the social has been individualized, emotional life collapses into the therapeutic, and education is relegated to either a personal affair or to a kind of algorithmic mode of regulation in which everything is reduced to a desired measurable outcome? How might education function to reclaim a notion of the democratic imagination and the importance of the social under a system that celebrates and normalizes the assumption that individuals are "greedy, self-interested animals [and that] we must reward greedy, self-interested behaviour to create a rational and efficient economic system"?[46] There is more at work here than a pedagogy of repression, there is a market-driven ideology that flirts dangerously with irrationality and removes itself from any vestige of solidarity, compassion, and care for the other or the planet.

Feedback loops now replace politics and the concept of democracy is defined through the culture of measurement and efficiency.[47] In a culture drowning in a new love affair with empiricism and data collecting, that which is not measurable—such as compassion, vision, the imagination, care for the other, and a passion for justice—withers. In its place emerges an insight from what Goya called in one of his engravings "The Sleep of Reason Produces Monster." Goya's title is richly suggestive particularly about the role of education and pedagogy in compelling students to be able to recognize, as my colleague David Clark points out,

> that an inattentiveness to the never-ending task of critique breeds horrors: the failures of conscience, the wars against thought, and the flirtations with irrationality that lie at the heart of the triumph of everyday aggression, the withering of political life, and the withdrawal into private obsessions.[48]

What is not so hidden about the tentacles of power that are clumsily tucked behind the vacuous claims to democratic governance manifests in the rise of a punishing state and a totalitarian paranoia in which everyone is considered a potential terrorist or criminal. How else to explain the increasing criminalization of social problems such as homelessness and the failure of the poor to pay off court costs, to say nothing of arresting students for trivial infractions such as doodling on a desk or throwing peanuts at a bus, all of which can land the most vulnerable in jail? As I mentioned in Chapter 5, there is a hard and soft war being waged against young people. The hard war is taking place in many schools, which now resemble prisons in light of their lockdown procedures, zero-tolerance policies, metal detectors, and the increasing presence of police in schools.[49]

The soft war is the war of consumerism and finance. Partnered with a massive advertising machinery and variety of corporate institutions, the soft war targets all youth by treating them as yet another "market" to be commodified and exploited, while attempting to create a new generation of hyper-consumers. The soft war is waged by a commercial culture that commodifies every aspect of kids' lives, while teaching them that their only responsibility to citizenship is to consume. A subtler form of this type of repression burdens and normalizes them with a lifetime of debt and does everything possible to depoliticize them and remove them from being able to imagine a different and more just society. In the United States, the average student graduates with a loan debt of $27,000. Debt bondage is the ultimate disciplinary technique of casino capitalism that robs students of the time to think, dissuades them from entering public service, and reinforces the debased assumption that they should simply be efficient cogs in a consumer economy.

The Promise of Radical Democracy

If neoliberal authoritarianism is to be challenged and overcome, it is crucial that intellectuals, unions, workers, young people, and various social movements unite to reclaim democracy as a central element in fashioning a radical imagination. Such action necessitates interrogating and rupturing the material and symbolic forces that hide behind a counterfeit claim to participatory democracy. This requires rescuing the promises of a radical democracy that can provide a living wage, quality health care for all, public works, and massive investments in education, child care, housing for the poor, along with a range of other crucial social provisions that can make a difference between living and dying for those who have been relegated to the ranks of the disposable.

The growing global threat of neoliberal authoritarianism signals both a crisis of politics and a crisis of beliefs, values, and agency. One indication of such a crisis is the fact that the economic calamity of 2008 has not been matched by a shift in ideas about the nature of finance capital and its devastating effects on American society. Banks got bailed out, and those everyday Americans who lost their houses bore the brunt of the crisis. The masters of finance capital were not held accountable for their crimes and many of them received huge bonuses paid for by American taxpayers. Revenge against the establishment was to come later with a growing right-wing populist movement that railed against the notion of insiders controlling the government and a call for the overthrow of establishment politics in Washington. What emerged was a neo-fascist government led by Donald Trump, an overt racist, misogynist, and ultra-nationalist. The dark political implications of Trump's victory cannot be overstated. As Cornel West observes:

> The political triumph of Donald Trump shattered the establish-
> ments in the Democratic and Republican parties—both wedded
> to the rule of Big Money and to the reign of meretricious politicians.
> The Bush and Clinton dynasties were destroyed by the media-
> saturated lure of the pseudo-populist billionaire with narcissist
> sensibilities and ugly, fascist proclivities. The monumental election
> of Trump was a desperate and xenophobic cry of human hearts for
> a way out from under the devastation of a disintegrating neoliberal
> order—a nostalgic return to an imaginary past of greatness. This
> lethal fusion of economic insecurity and cultural scapegoating . . .
> unleashed a hate-filled populism and protectionism that threatens
> to tear apart the fragile fiber of what is left of US democracy. And
> since the most explosive fault lines in present-day America are first
> and foremost racial, then gender, homophobic, ethnic and religious,
> we gird ourselves for a frightening future.[50]

West believes that neoliberalism ended with the triumph of neo-fascism in America, but I believe it is an outgrowth and extension of neoliberal ideology, pedagogy, and policies.[51] Neo-fascism is the endpoint of a political and economic system in which social costs are removed from human activity and disposability is applied not only to goods but to human lives. Neoliberalism is an intensified form of class and racial warfare, its modus operandi is state violence and its most visible symbol of cruelty and disposability is the prison. In light of the United States tipping over into authoritarianism, the issue of education becomes all the more essential as a central aspect of political organizing and raising individual and collective consciousness. Matters of education must be at the heart of any viable notion of politics, meaning that education must be at the center of any attempt to change consciousness, not just the ways in which people think, but also how they act, and construct relationships to others and the larger world. Americans seem to have forgotten that the fate of democracy is inextricably linked to the profound crisis of knowledge, critical thinking, and agency. As education is removed from the demands of civic culture, it undermines the political, ethical, and governing conditions for individuals and social groups to participate in politics. Under such circumstances, knowledge is commodified, contingent faculty replace full-time tenured faculty, governance is removed from faculty control, the culture of higher education is replaced by the culture of business, and students are viewed as customers. Consequently, higher education is no longer viewed as a public good or a place where students can imagine themselves as thoughtful and socially responsible citizens and furthers the destruction of the underlying ideals and practices that make a democratizing politics possible.

Politics is an imminently educative task and it is only through such recognition that initial steps can be taken to challenge the powerful ideological and affective spaces through which market fundamentalism produces the desires, identities, and values that bind people to its forms of predatory governance. The noxious politics of historical, social, and political amnesia and the public pedagogy of the disimagination machine must be challenged and disassembled if there is any hope of creating meaningful alternatives to the dark times in which we live. Young people need to think otherwise in order to act otherwise, but in addition they need to become cultural producers who can create their own narratives about their relationship to the larger world and what it means to sustain public commitments and develop a sense of compassion for others, locally and globally.

But the question remains regarding how a public largely indifferent to politics and often paralyzed by the need to survive, and caught in a crippling cynicism, can be moved from "an induced state of stupidity" to a political formation willing to engage in various modes of resistance extending from "mass protests to prolonged civil disobedience."[52] This terrifying intellectual and moral paralysis must be offset by the development of alternative public spheres in which educators, artists, workers, young people and others can change the terms of the debate in American culture and politics. Ideas matter, but they wither without institutional infrastructures in which they can be nourished, debated, and acted upon. Any viable struggle against casino capitalism must focus on those forms of domination that pose a threat to public spheres, such as public and higher education and the new media, that are essential to developing the critical visions, identities, and desires that nourish modes of engaged thinking necessary for the production of critically engaged citizens.

If such a politics is to make any difference, it must be worldly; that is, it must incorporate a critical disposition that both addresses social problems and tackles the conditions necessary for modes of democratic political exchange that enable new forms of agency, power, and collective struggle. Until the language of politics can give meaning and a sense of identification to those considered invisible, if not disposable, there will be no significant opposition to casino capitalism.

Reviving the Radical Imagination

Following up on initiatives I have made throughout this book, I want to suggest a few initiatives, though incomplete, that might mount a challenge to the current oppressive historical conjuncture in which many Americans now find themselves.[53] In doing so, I want to address what I have attempted to map as a crisis of memory, agency, and education and reclaim what I call a pedagogy of educated hope that is central to any viable notion of change that I am suggesting.

First, there is a need for what can be called a revival of the radical imagination and the defense of the public good, especially higher education, in order to reclaim its egalitarian and democratic impulses. This call would be part of a larger project "to reinvent democracy in the wake of the evidence that, at the national level, there is no democracy— if by 'democracy' we mean effective popular participation in the crucial decisions affecting the community."[54] One step in this direction would be for young people, intellectuals, scholars, and others to go on the offensive against a conservative-led campaign "to end higher education's democratizing influence on the nation."[55] Higher education should be harnessed neither to the demands of the warfare state nor to the instrumental needs of corporations. Clearly, in any democratic society, education should be viewed as a right, not an entitlement. We need to produce a national conversation in which higher education can be defended as a public good and the classroom as a site of engaged inquiry and critical thinking, a site that makes a claim on the radical imagination and a sense of civic courage. At the same time, the discourse on defining higher education as a democratic public sphere would provide the platform for moving onto the larger issue of developing a social movement in defense of public goods.

For instance, we might begin with Felix Guattari's question, "How do you bring a classroom to life as if it were a work of art?" and its reformulation as a different question: "How do you bring a work of art to life as if it were a classroom?" In actuality, these are two questions that mutually inform each other by extending the meaning of pedagogy as a political, moral, and social practice that underlies the production not only of knowledge, ideas, and values, but also the production of subjectivities, identities, and modes of identification. In both cases, pedagogy defies its reduction to a methodology and form of instrumental rationality, usually one designed to both deaden the imagination and serve the disciplinary needs of a hyper-capitalist economy and social order. Pedagogy in both cases is troubling, unsettling, and is meant to inspire, energize, and expand both the imagination and the capacity to be critically engaged actors in the world. Where they differ is that bringing a classroom to life by making pedagogy meaningful in order to make it critical and transformative is usually ascribed to what goes on in institutional forms of schooling, specifically public and higher education.

On the other hand, bringing a work of art to life as if it were a classroom I read as a recognition that the pedagogy is central to acknowledging the powerful educational force of the culture and more generally the role of education as being central to politics itself. Pedagogy works through the ideological and affective spaces that a society makes available and should always be viewed as a site of struggle. Art suggests a mix of performance, uncertainty, risk taking, being self-reflective, emboldening the creative process, learning to think outside of established sensibilities, and recognizing that one cannot act otherwise unless one can think otherwise. In this sense, art as a critical pedagogical practice and space shares a deep commitment to both matters of agency, politics, and the ongoing process of democratization as an unfinished journey, if not an ongoing struggle over matters of moral witnessing, historical memory, agency, and politics itself. The two questions inspired by Guattari's work signal how pedagogy operates in different sites across various landscapes that extend from the school and alternative media to mainstream journalism and newly emerging screen cultures.

What connects these two questions and understanding of education as a work of art is the need for what can be called a revival of the radical imagination and the defense of the public good in order to reclaim pedagogy's egalitarian and democratic impulses. One step in this direction would be for artists, young people, intellectuals, scholars, and others to go on the offensive against conservative-led campaigns to end the democratizing influence of a vast array of public spheres that extend from schooling to the alternative media.

Politically, this suggests defining pedagogy, if not education itself, as central to producing those democratic public spheres capable of producing an informed citizenry public, and enabling critical modes of thought that advance thinking against the grain.[56] Thinking against the grain implies a willingness to be thoughtful, experience the other as a work of art with his or her own specificity and stories, and to learn how to listen reflectively and to be able to imagine otherwise. Pedagogies that push against the grain speak to the need for students to be reflective, willing to listen to the views of others, subordinate ideology to rigorous acts of self-reflection, and to aid in expanding the spaces in which diverse views can be articulated and critically interrogated. Guattari's understanding of education is rich with possibilities not only for understanding the classroom as an artistic production fused with the power of pedagogical practices that rupture, engage, unsettle, and inspire, but also extending the meaning of the classroom into wider cultural apparatuses in which education functions often by stealth to shape subjects, identities, and social relations, often so as to mimic the values of a market-driven society.

These insights are particularly important at a time when the fragmentation of the left is due to its inability to develop a wide political and ideological umbrella to address a range of problems extending from extreme poverty, the assault on the environment, the emergence of the permanent warfare state, and the roll-back of voting rights to the war on public servants, women's rights, and social provisions, and a range of other issues that erode the possibilities for a radical democracy. With the election of Donald Trump the attack on these issues and higher education as a public good will intensify. This is not to suggest that single-issue movements are not important but it is crucial for educators and others to understand their limits in developing a more comprehensive understanding of politics and the international social formations to address the new space of global politics and the growing authoritarianism in the United States under a Trump presidency. The dominating mechanisms of casino capitalism in both their symbolic and material registers reach deeply into every aspect of society. Any successful movement for the defense of democracy itself will have to struggle against this new mode of authoritarianism rather than isolating and attacking specific elements of its anti-democratic ethos. Such a challenge must combine politics and art, pedagogy and desire, imagination, and a notion of pedagogical grace with a discourse of critique and possibility. This adds up to developing what I have called a politics of the totality, a comprehensive politics that refuses a politics of disconnect and fragmentation.

Given the assault on critical thinking, civic literacy, and public goods that will occur under a Trump administration, it is all the more crucial to define higher education as a democratic public sphere and reject the notion that the culture of education is synonymous with the culture of business. Pedagogically, this points to modes of teaching and learning capable of producing an informed citizenry, enacting and sustaining a culture of questioning, that advances what Kristen Case calls moments of classroom grace.[57] Pedagogies of classroom grace should provide the conditions for students and others to reflect critically on common-sense understandings of the world, and begin to question, however troubling, their sense of agency, relationships to others, and their relationships to the larger world. This can be linked to wide-ranging pedagogical imperatives that ask why we have wars, massive inequality, and a surveillance state. There is also the issue of how everything has become commodified, along with the decline of political participation by the public and a growing lack of faith in democracy itself as a mode of governance. This is not merely a methodical consideration but also a moral and political practice because it presupposes the creation of critically engaged students who can imagine a future in which justice, equality, freedom, and democracy matter. In this instance, the classroom should be a space of grace—a place to think critically, ask troubling questions, and take risks, even though that may mean transgressing established norms and bureaucratic procedures.

Second, young people and progressives need to develop a comprehensive educational program that would include a range of pedagogical initiatives from developing a national online news channel to creating alternative schools for young people in the manner of the diverse democratically inspired schools such as Highlander under Miles Horton, the Workers College in New York, and a host of other alternative educational institutions. Such a pedagogical task would enable a sustained critique of the transformation of a market economy into a market society along with a clear analysis of the damage it has caused both at home and abroad. What is crucial to recognize here is that it is not enough to teach students to be able to interrogate critically screen culture and other audio, video, and visual forms of representation. They must also learn how to be cultural producers. This suggests developing alternative public spheres such as online journals, television shows, newspapers, magazines, and any other platform in which different positions can be developed. In addition, such tasks can be done by mobilizing the technological resources and platforms they already have. It also means working with one foot in existing cultural apparatuses in order to promote unorthodox ideas and views that would challenge the affective and ideological spaces produced by the financial elite who control the commanding institutions of public pedagogy in North America. What is often lost by many educators and progressives is that popular culture is a powerful form of education for many young people and yet it is rarely addressed as a serious source of knowledge. As Stanley Aronowitz has observed, "theorists and researchers need to link their knowledge of popular culture, and culture in the anthropological sense—that is, everyday life, with the politics of education."[58]

Third, academics, artists, community activists, young people, and parents must engage in an ongoing struggle for the right of students to be given a free, formidable and critical education not dominated by corporate values, and for young people to have a say in the shaping of their education and what it means to expand and deepen the practice of freedom and democracy. Young people have been left out of the discourse of democracy. They are the new disposable people who lack jobs, a decent education, hope, and any semblance of a future better than the one their parents inherited. Facing what Richard Sennett calls the "specter of uselessness," they are a reminder of how finance capital has abandoned any viable vision of the future, including one that would support future generations. This is a mode of politics and capital that forces young people to fight against their sense of invisibility and throws their fate to the vagaries of the market. The ecology of finance capital only believes in short-term investments because they provide quick returns. Under such circumstances, young people who need long-term investments are considered a liability. If any society is in part judged by how it views and treats its children, the United States by all accounts is truly failing in a colossal way. If young people are to receive a critical and comprehensive education, academics must take on the role of public intellectuals, capable of the critical appropriation of a variety of intellectual traditions and also able to relate their scholarship to wider social problems.

Fourth, as I have argued previously and cannot stress enough, casino capitalism is so widespread that progressives need to develop a comprehensive vision of politics that "does not rely on single issues."[59] It is only through an understanding of the wider relations and connections of power that young people and others can overcome uninformed practice, isolated struggles, and modes of singular politics that become insular and self-sabotaging. In short, moving beyond a single-issue orientation means developing modes of analyses that connect the dots historically and relationally. It also means developing a more comprehensive vision of politics that can be helpful in connecting a range of issues so as to be able to build a united front in the call for a radical democracy.

This is a particularly important goal given that the fragmentation of the left has been partly responsible for its inability to develop a wide political and ideological umbrella to address a range of problems extending from extreme poverty, the assault on the environment, the emergence of the permanent warfare state, the roll-back of voting rights, to the assault on public servants, women's rights, and social provisions. The dominating mechanisms of casino capitalism in both their symbolic and material registers are inscribed deeply into every aspect of American society. Any successful movement for the defense of public goods and democracy itself will have to struggle against this new mode of authoritarianism rather than isolating and attacking specific elements of its anti-democratic ethos.

One important development is that Black youth, among other concerned young Americans, are currently making real strides in moving beyond sporadic protests, short-lived demonstrations, and non-violent street actions in the hope of building sustained political movements. Groups such as Black Lives Matter, Black Youth Project, We Charge Genocide, and Dream Defenders represent a new and growing political force that is not only connecting police violence to larger structures of militarism throughout society, but is also reclaiming public memory by articulating a direct link "between the establishment of professional police systems in the United States [and] the patrolling systems that maintained the business of human bondage in chattel slavery."[60]

Fifth, another serious challenge facing advocates of a new truly democratic social order is the task of developing a discourse of both critique and possibility, or what I have called a discourse of educated hope. Critique is important and is crucial to break the hold of common-sense assumptions that legitimate a wide range of injustices. The language of critique is also crucial for making visible the workings of unequal power and the necessity of holding authority accountable. But critique is not enough and, without a discourse of hope, it can lead to a paralyzing despair or, even worse, a crippling cynicism. Hope speaks to imagining a life beyond capitalism, and combines a realistic sense of limits with a lofty vision of demanding the impossible. Reason, justice, and change cannot blossom without hope because educated hope taps into our deepest experiences and longing for a life of dignity with others, a life in which it becomes possible to imagine a future that does not mimic the present. I am not referring to a romanticized and empty notion of hope, but to a notion of informed hope that faces the concrete obstacles and realities of domination but continues the ongoing task of "holding the present open and thus unfinished."[61]

The discourse of possibility not only looks for productive solutions, it is also crucial in defending those public spheres in which civic values, public scholarship, and social engagement allow for a more imaginative grasp of a future that takes seriously the demands of justice, equity, and civic courage. Democracy should encourage, even require, a way of thinking critically about education, one that connects equity to excellence, learning to ethics, and agency to the imperatives of social responsibility and the public good. Casino capitalism is a toxin that has created a predatory class of unethical zombies, who are producing dead zones of the imagination that even Orwell could not have envisioned, while waging a fierce fight against the possibilities of a democratic future. The time has come to develop a political language in which civic values, social responsibility, and the institutions that support them become central to invigorating and fortifying a new era of civic imagination, a renewed sense of social agency, and an impassioned international social movement with a vision, organization, and set of strategies to challenge the neoliberal nightmare engulfing the planet. Educators, artists, youth, intellectuals, and others must refuse to succumb to the authoritarian forces that are circling American society, waiting for the resistance to stop and for the lights to go out. History is open and as James Baldwin once insisted, "Not everything that is faced can be changed; but nothing can be changed until it is faced."[62]

Notes

1 This theme has long been argued by Hannah Arendt. Also, see Michael Halberstam, *Totalitarianism and the Modern Conception of Politics* (New Haven, CT: Yale University Press, 1999).

2 This theme is taken up powerfully by a number of theorists. See C. Wright Mills, *The Sociological Imagination* (New York: Oxford University Press, 2000); Richard Sennett,

The Fall of Public Man (New York: Norton, 1974); Zygmunt Bauman, *In Search of Politics* (Stanford, CA: Stanford University Press, 1999); and Henry A. Giroux, *Public Spaces, Private Lives* (Lanham, MD: Rowman and Littlefield, 2001).

3   Mike Lofgren, "Maybe This Is How Democracy Ends," *Moyers and Company* (January 11, 2016). Online: http://billmoyers.com/story/maybe-democracy-ends/

4   Elisabeth Young-Bruehl, *Why Arendt Matters* (New York: Integrated Publishing Solutions, 2006), p. 17.

5   George Packer, "Dark Hours," *New Yorker* (July 20, 2015). Online: www.newyorker.com/magazine/2015/07/20/dark-hours

6   John Whitehead, "Paranoia, Surveillance and Military Tactics: Have We Become Enemies of the Government?" *Rutherford Institute* (February 17, 2014). Online: www.rutherford.org/publications_resources/john_whiteheads_commentary/paranoia_surveillance_and_military_tactics_have_we_become_enemies_of_t

7   Mike Lofgren, *The Deep State* (New York: Viking, 2016).

8   See Henry A. Giroux, *America's Addiction to Terrorism* (New York: Monthly Review Press, 2016); Zygmunt Bauman, *Consuming Life* (London: Polity Press, 2007).

9   Zygmunt Bauman and Carlo Bordoni, *State of Crisis* (London: Polity Press, 2014).

10 For an excellent analysis of contemporary forms of neoliberalism, see Stuart Hall, "The Neo-Liberal Revolution," *Cultural Studies*, Vol. 25, No. 6 (November 2011), pp. 705–28; see also David Harvey, *A Brief History of Neoliberalism* (Oxford: Oxford University Press, 2005); Henry A. Giroux, *Against the Terror of Neoliberalism* (Boulder, CO: Paradigm Publishers, 2008).

11 Orville Schell, "Follies of Orthodoxy." In *What Orwell Didn't Know: Propaganda and the New Face of American Politics* (New York: Perseus Books Group, 2007), xviii.

12 Zoe Williams, "The Saturday Interview: Stuart Hall," *Guardian* (February 11, 2012). Online: www.guardian.co.uk/theguardian/2012/feb/11/saturday-interview-stuart-hall

13 Andy Thomason, "As Degrees Are Cut, Critics Continue to Decry Dismantling of U. of North Carolina," *Chronicle of Higher Education* (May 27, 2015). Online: http://chronicle.com/blogs/ticker/as-degrees-are-cut-critics-continue-to-decry-dismantling-of-u-of-north-carolina/99587

14 Monica Davey and Tamar Lewinjune, "Unions Subdued, Scott Walker Turns to Tenure at Wisconsin Colleges," *New York Times* (June 4, 2015). Online: www.nytimes.com/2015/06/05/us/politics/unions-subdued-scott-walker-turns-to-tenure-at-wisconsin-colleges.html?_r=0

15 Matt Egan, "5,300 Wells Fargo employees fired over 2 million phony accounts," *CNN Money* (September 9, 2016). http://money.cnn.com/2016/09/08/investing/wells-fargo-created-phony-accounts-bank-fees/

16 Joao Biehl, *Vita: Life in a Zone of Social Abandonment* (Berkeley: University of California Press, 2005).

17 Bill Boyarsky, "Go Directly to Jail: Punishing the Homeless for Being Homeless," *TruthDig* (September 10, 2015). Online: www.truthdig.com/report/item/go_directly_to_jail_punishing_the_homeless_for_beinghomeless_20150910

18 Zygmunt Bauman, *Wasted Lives* (London: Polity Press, 2004), pp. 76–7.

19 Therese J. Borchard. "Statistics about College Depression," *World of Psychology* (September 2, 2010). Online: http://psychcentral.com/blog/archives/2010/09/02/statistics-about-college-depression/; Allison Vuchnich and Carmen Chai, "Young Minds: Stress, Anxiety Plaguing Canadian Youth," *Global News* (May 6, 2013). Online: http://globalnews.ca/news/530141/young-minds-stress-anxiety-plaguing-canadian-youth/

20 Jonathan Turley, "10 Reasons the U.S. Is No Longer the Land of the Free," *Washington Post* (January 13, 2012). Online: http://articles.washingtonpost.com/2012-01-13/opinions/35440628_1_individual-rights-indefinite-detention-citizens

21 For a clear exposé of the emerging surveillance state, see Glenn Greenwald, *No Place to Hide* (New York: Signal, 2014); Julia Angwin, *Dragnet Nation: A Quest for Privacy, Security, and Freedom in a World of Relentless Surveillance* (New York: Times Books, 2014); Heidi Boghosian, *Spying on Democracy: Government Surveillance, Corporate Power, and Public Resistance* (San Francisco: City Lights Books, 2013).

22 Vanessa Schipani, "Trump on Torture," *FactCheck.Org* (July 28, 2016). Online: www.factcheck.org/2016/07/trump-torture/

23 Hannah Groch-Begley, "Fox Asks if Children Should Work for School Meals," *Media Matters* (April 25, 2013). Online: http://mediamatters.org/mobile/blog/2013/04/25/fox-asks-if-children-should-work-for-school-mea/193768

24 Jordan Weissmann, "Newt Gingrich Thinks School Children Should Work as Janitors," *Atlantic* (November 21, 2011). Online: www.theatlantic.com/business/archive/2011/11/newt-gingrich-thinks-school-children-should-work-as-janitors/248837/

25 Cited in Maggie Haberman, "Newt: Fire the Janitors, Hire Kids to Clean Schools," *Politico* (January 18, 2011). Online: www.politico.com/story/2011/11/newt-fire-the-janitors-hire-kids-to-clean-schools-068729#ixzz3o6Bz8bZU

26 Weissmann, "Newt Gingrich Thinks School Children Should Work as Janitors."

27 Editorial, "Housing Secretary Ben Carson calls poverty a 'state of mind'," BBC.Com (May 25, 2017). http://www.bbc.com/news/world-us-canada-40048192; Liam Stack, "Ben Carson Refers to Slaves as 'Immigrants' in First Remarks to HUD Staff." New York times (March 6, 2017). https://www.nytimes.com/2017/03/06/us/politics/ben-carson-refers-to-slaves-as-immigrants-in-first-remarks-to-hud-staff.html

28 Juan Cole, "GOP Finally Shocked as Trump Admits to Being Serial Groper of White Women on Hot Mic," *Informed Consent* (October 19, 2016). Online: www.juancole.com/2016/10/finally-shocked-admits.html

29 Eleanor Goldberg, "Andy Kessler, Former Hedge Fund Manager, Says Shelter Volunteers Cause Homelessness," *Huffington Post* (July 10, 2013). Online: www.huffingtonpost.com/2013/07/10/andy-kessler-homelessness_n_3568538.html

30 Ibid.

31 Catherine Lutz, "Making War at Home in the United States: Militarization and the Current Crisis," *American Anthropologist*, Vol. 104, No. 3 (2002), p. 723.

32 Editorial, "Cops or Soldiers: America's Police Have Become Too Militarised," *Economist* (May 22, 2014). Online: www.economist.com/news/united-states/21599349-americas-police-have-become-too-militarised-cops-or-soldiers

33 Michelle Alexander, "The Age of Obama as a Racial Nightmare," *TomDispatch* (March 25, 2012). Online: www.tomdispatch.com/post/175520/best_of_tomdispatch%3A_michelle_alexander,_the_age_of_obama_as_a_racial_nightmare/

34 Matt Taibbi, "The Police in America Are Becoming Illegitimate," *Rolling Stone* (December 5, 2015). Online: www.rollingstone.com/politics/news/the-police-in-america-are-becoming-illegitimate-20141205

35 Alice Ollstein, "Jeb Bush Says Unlike Others, He Won't Give African Americans 'Free Stuff,'" *ThinkProgress* (September 25, 2015). Online: http://thinkprogress.org/politics/2015/09/25/3705520/jeb-bush-says-hell-win-the-african-american-vote-with-hope-not-free-stuff/?utm_source=newsletter&utm_medium=email&utm_campaign=tptop3&utm_term=3&utm_content=5

36 Charles Blow, "Jeb Bush, 'Free Stuff' and Black Folks," *New York Times* (September 28, 2015). Online: www.nytimes.com/2015/09/28/opinion/charles-m-blow-jeb-bush-free-stuff-and-black-folks.html?_r=0

37 See, for instance, David Brooks, "The Nature of Poverty," *New York Times* (May 1, 2015). Online: www.nytimes.com/2015/05/01/opinion/david-brooks-the-nature-of-poverty.html?smid=tw-share&_r=0

38 Sean Illing, "Why David Brooks Shouldn't Talk about Poor People," *Salon* (May 1, 2015). Online: www.slate.com/articles/news_and_politics/politics/2015/05/david_brooks_shouldn_t_talk_about_the_poor_the_new_york_times_columnist.single.html?print

39 Keeanga-Yamahtta Taylor, *From #BlackLivesMatter to Black Liberation* (Chicago: Haymarket Books, 2016), pp. 24–5.

40 Blow, "Jeb Bush, 'Free Stuff' and Black Folks."

41 For an excellent rebuttal of the politics of resilience, see Brad Evans and Julien Reid, *Resilient Life: The Art of Living Dangerously* (London: Polity Press, 2014).

42 Paul Krugman, "Race, Class, and Neglect," *New York Times* (May 4, 2015). Online: www.nytimes.com/2015/05/04/opinion/paul-krugman-race-class-and-neglect.html?_r=0

43 I am borrowing this phrase from Varun Puri, an undergraduate student of mine who introduced it in one of his class papers.

44 David DeGraw, "Meet the Global Financial Elites Controlling $46 Trillion in Wealth," *AlterNet* (August 11, 2011). Online: www.alternet.org/story/151999/meet_the_global_financial_elites_controlling_$46_trillion_in_wealth

45 Robert Peston, "Richest 1% to Own More than Rest of World, Oxfam says," *BBC News* (January 19, 2015). Online: www.bbc.com/news/business-30875633

46 Robert Jensen, *Arguing for Our Lives* (San Francisco: City Lights Books, 2013), p. 95.

47 See, for instance, Evgeny Morozov, "The Rise of Data and the Death of Politics," *Guardian* (July 20, 2014). Online: www.theguardian.com/technology/2014/jul/20/rise-of-data-death-of-politics-evgeny-morozov-algorithmic-regulation

48 Personal correspondence with David Clark.

49 Chase Madar, "Everyone Is a Criminal: On the Over-Policing of America," *Huffington Post* (December 13, 2013). Online: www.huffingtonpost.com/chase-madar/over-policing-of-america_b_4412187.html

50 Cornel West, "American Neoliberalism: A New Neo-Fascist Era Is Here," *Guardian* (November 18, 2016). Online: http://readersupportednews.org/opinion2/277-75/40342-goodbye-american-neoliberalism-a-new-neo-fascist-era-is-here

51 See also, Zygmunt Bauman, "How Neoliberalism Prepared the Way for Donald Trump," *Social Europe* (November 16, 2016). Online: www.socialeurope.eu/2016/11/how-neoliberalism-prepared-the-way-for-donald-trump/#

52 Hedges, "The Last Gasp of American Democracy," *AlterNet* (January 6, 2014). Online: www.truthdig.com/report/page2/the_last_gasp_of_american_democracy_20140105

53 Stanley Aronowitz, "What Kind of Left Does America Need?" *Tikkun* (April 7, 1014). Online: www.tikkun.org/nextgen/what-kind-of-left-does-america-need

54 Ibid.

55 Gene R. Nichol, "Public Universities at Risk Abandoning Their Mission," *Chronicle of Higher Education* (October 31, 2008). Online: http://chronicle.com/weekly/v54/i30/30a02302.htm

56 I have taken the notion of grace in the pedagogical sense from Kristen Case, "The Other Public Humanities," *Chronicle of Higher Education* (January 13, 2014). Online: http://m.chronicle.com/article/Ahas-Ahead/143867/

57 Kristen Case, "The Other Public Humanities," *Chronicle of Higher Education* (January 13, 2014). Online: http://m.chronicle.com/article/Ahas-Ahead/143867/

58 Stanley Aronowitz, *Against Schooling* (Boulder, CO: Paradigm Publishers, 2008), p. 50.

59 Ibid.

60 Kelly Hayes, "To Baltimore with Love: Chicago's Freedom Dreams," *Truthout* (April 30, 2015). Online: www.truth-out.org/opinion/item/30531-to-baltimore-with-love-chicago-s-freedom-dreams

61 Andrew Benjamin, *Present Hope: Philosophy, Architecture, Judaism* (New York: Routledge, 1997), p. 10.

62 James Baldwin, "As Much Truth as One Can Bear," *New York Times Book Review* (January, 1962), p. 38.

11
RETHINKING RESISTANCE IN THE SECOND GILDED AGE

Whoever does not hope for the unhoped for will not find it.
(Ernst Bloch)

Living in a War Culture

History often repeats itself with a vengeance, signaling a crisis of memory, historical consciousness, and civic literacy. The dark ghosts of the past disappear in a comforting somnolence and a deadening market-driven culture of consumption, privatization, and individualization. As a mode of moral witnessing, memory wanes, lost in forms of historical and social amnesia that usher in the dark clouds of authoritarianism, albeit in updated forms.

With Donald Trump now heading the most powerful nation on earth, the scourge of authoritarianism has returned not only in the toxic language of hate, racism, and bigotry, but also in the emergence of a culture of war and violence that looms over society like a plague. War has been redefined in the age of global capitalism.[1] This is especially true for the United States. No longer defined exclusively as a military issue, it has expanded its boundaries and now shapes all aspects of society. As Ulrich Beck observes:

the language of war takes on a new and expansive meaning today
... The notions on which our worldviews are predicated and the
distinctions between war and peace, military and police, war and
crime, internal and external security; particularly between internal
and external in general have been magnified.[2]

As violence and politics merge to produce an accelerating and lethal
mix of bloodshed, pain, suffering, grief, and death, American culture
has been transformed into a culture of war. As Michael Hardt and
Antonio Negri point out, the veneration of war in the United States
has now reached a dangerous endpoint and has become the foundation
of politics itself. They write:

> What is specific to our era ... is that war has passed from the final
> element of the sequences of power—lethal force as a last resort—
> to the first and primary element, the foundation of politics itself.
> Imperial sovereignty creates ... a regime of disciplinary admin-
> istration and political control directly based on continuous war
> action. The constant and coordinated application of violence, in
> other words, becomes the necessary condition for the functioning
> of discipline and control. In order for war to occupy this funda-
> mental social and political role, war must be able to accomplish
> a constituent or regulative function: war must become both a
> procedural activity and an ordering, regulative activity that creates
> and maintains social hierarchies, a form of biopower aimed at the
> promotion and regulation of social life.[3]

The violence produced by a war culture has become a defining feature
of American society, providing a common ground for the deployment
and celebration of violence abroad and at home. At a policy level, an
arms industry fuels violence abroad while domestically a toxic gun
culture contributes to the endless maiming and deaths of individuals at
home. Similarly, a militaristic foreign policy has its domestic counterpart
in the growth of a carceral and punishing state used to enforce a hyped-
up brand of domestic terrorism, especially against Black youth and

various emerging protest movements in the United States.[4] A "political culture of hyper punitiveness"[5] serves to legitimate not only a neoliberal culture in which cruelty is viewed as virtue, but also a racist system of mass incarceration that functions as the default welfare program and chief mechanism to "institutionalize obedience."[6] The police state increasingly targets poor people of color turning their neighborhoods into war zones, all the while serving a corporate state that has no concern whatsoever for the social costs inflicted upon millions as a result of its predatory policies and practices. The persistent killing of Black youth testifies to a long history and domestic terrorism representing "an unbroken stream of racist violence, both official and extralegal, from slave patrols and the Ku Klux Klan to contemporary profiling practices and present-day vigilantes."[7] The historical backdrop to the current killing of Black youth, men, and women is coupled with the fact that "11 million Americans cycle through our jails and prisons each year," that the United States "imprisons the largest proportion of people in the world [and] that, with 4% of the global population, it holds 22% of the world's prisoners" and that 70 percent of these prisoners are people of color.[8] These figures testify not only to the emergence of a police state, but also to a justice system that has a long legacy of being driven by racism.

As police violence accelerates, the legacy of this tradition of terrorism reveals itself in a new form. Under such circumstances, important distinctions between war and civil society collapse as the police function as soldiers, cities are transformed into combat zones, shared responsibilities are replaced by shared fears, the boundaries disappear between innocent and guilty, and public safety is defined increasingly as a police matter. Neoliberal society has ceded any vestige of democratic ideals to a social formation saturated with fear, suspicion, and violence. At the same time, an unchecked gun culture and the extreme violence it produces no longer become a source of alarm but are privileged as a source of profit for the entertainment industry, extending from Hollywood films to the selling of violent video games to teenagers. Americans are terrified by the threat of terrorism and its ensuing violence; yet, they are more than willing to protect laws that privilege the largely unchecked circulation of guns and the toxic militarized culture of violence that amounts to "58 people who die a day because of firearms."[9]

Acts of intolerable violence have become America's longest-running, non-stop, cinematic production, overloading both the mainstream media and the entertainment industry. Representations of violence saturate American culture as unending coverage appears daily about mass shootings, children shot by gang members, people killed by gun-related injuries, and the police wantonly shooting and often killing unarmed Blacks with impunity. All the while, the distinction between moral repulsion and voyeuristic pleasure is blurred.

Violence now acts as both a monstrous political weapon in the service of oppressive relations of power and as a spectacle fueling an aesthetic that floods the culture with "a kind of hallucinatory form of entertainment in which violence provides one of the truly last possibilities for feeling passion, pleasure and a sense of control."[10] The line has become blurred between real acts of violence and mythical appeals to violence as cleansing and restorative, as is evident in Donald Trump's emotional appeal to his audience's rage and fear.

Dystopian violence is now legitimated at the highest level of politics both in its use as a spectacle fueling a presidential campaign and as a policy of terror, torture, and the killing of innocent people initiated most specifically in the murderous rampage of drone warfare. Politics is now an extension of the culture of war and violence, both as spectacle and real, is a generative force in the production of everyday life. What Trump and Obama share in spite of their ideological differences is a support for violence—both as a discourse and a material practice—as the organizing principle of politics. Both argue in different ways for what Achille Mbembe identifies as a "necropolitics"—a register of a war culture in which weapons are "deployed in the interest of the maximum destruction of persons and the creation of death worlds," especially against those considered to be America's enemies.[11]

Normalizing Violence

The normalization of violence in American society is not only about how it is lived and endured, but also about how it becomes the connective tissue for holding different modes of governance, policies, ideologies, and practices together through an assemblage of military activities. And it is precisely such activities that serve to legitimate the war on terror, the use of mass surveillance, the weaponizing of knowledge, and the merging of a war culture and warfare state. In the aftermath of the transition from the welfare state in the 1960s to the current warfare state, the appeal to fear on many political fronts became paramount in order to legitimate a carceral state that increasingly governed through what can be termed the war on crime, especially affecting marginalized citizens.[12]

Violence, however grotesque, has been relegated to the most powerful force mediating human relations and used to address pressing social problems. Violence is a habitual response by the state in almost every dilemma. Police violence is only one register of the landscape of everyday violence, but at the same time it is an important and visible indication of how violence has been "dragged into the heart of political life . . . turning [America] into a military state."[13] The hidden structure of violence is not always on full display in the killing of unarmed Blacks; it can also be found in a range of largely invisible sites of brutality that include debtors' prisons for children, racist juvenile courts, schools modeled after prisons, a systemic debt machine, and municipal governments that function as extortion factories and inflict misery and penury upon the poor.

At a more subtle level, the registers of militarization produce both armed knowledge through university research funded by the military-industrial-Pentagon complex and a growing culture of political purity in which the personal becomes the only politics there is housed within a discourse of "weaponized sensitivity" and "armed ignorance." Empathy for others only extends as far as recognizing those who mirror the self. Politics has collapsed into the privatized orbits of a crude essentialism that disdains forms of public discourse in which boundaries collapse and the exercise of public deliberation is viewed as fundamental to a substantive democracy.[14]

A sickening brutalism appears to have taken over American society and is partly reflected in various statistics that present a chilling measure of a society slipping into barbarism, if not sanctioned lunacy. The numbers are staggering and include "everything from homicides and multiple-victim gang assaults to incidents of self defense and accidental shootings."[15] In 2015, "36 Americans were killed by guns" on an average day, and "that excludes most suicides ... From 2005 to 2015 ... 301,797 people were killed by gun violence."[16] What is often not reported in the mainstream media is that more than half of American gun death victims are poor men of color, living in dilapidated segregated neighborhoods that represent zones of abandonment, rendered invisible and far from the gaze of the mainstream media, tourism, and the American public. Another largely unreported fact is that "Seventy-eight children under 5 died by guns in 2015—30 more than the 48 law enforcement officers killed by guns in the line of duty [and that] guns killed more preschoolers in one year than they did law-enforcement officers."[17] In Chicago alone in the first eight months of 2016, 12 people were shot daily. According to a Carnegie-Knight News21 investigation:

> For every U.S. soldier killed in Afghanistan during 11 years of war, at least 13 children were shot and killed in America. More than 450 kids didn't make it to kindergarten. Another 2,700 or more were killed by a firearm before they could sit behind the wheel of a car. Every day, on average, seven children were shot dead. A News21 investigation of child and youth deaths in America between 2002 and 2012 found that at least 28,000 children and teens 19-years-old and younger were killed with guns. Teenagers between the ages of 15 and 19 made up over two-thirds of all youth gun deaths in America.[18]

Children and the Politics of Disappearance

The killing of children in America has become part of a politics of willful disappearance in which a culture of cruelty, immediacy, and forgetting works in tandem with eliminating any trace of the factors behind the production of violence in the service of the unthinkable—a society willing to sacrifice its own children to the industries that trade and profit in the massive production and distribution of guns. Such extreme violence no longer appears to have a threshold that would make it intolerable. In part, because the business of violence has become standardized as part of the culture of business. Or, as Phil Wolfson puts it, "the business of violence has become a far too accepted part of the fabric of contemporary life in the United States."[19] If violence against children is part of a politics of disappearance, police brutality represents just the opposite and makes visible the most extreme of extreme violence as numerous shootings and the killings of unarmed Black men have been captured and distributed by bystanders who have recorded the violence on their cell phones and then put it on the internet and a variety of social media platforms. The new media has created a new form of moral witnessing, one that is viewed as dangerous to defenders of the punishing state. Recording such violence becomes especially important given the disproportionate rate at which the police shoot and kill people. For instance, by the end of September 2016, "697 people have been shot and killed by the police" including "161 Black men who have been fatally shot."[20]

Intolerable Violence in a Militarized Culture

Intolerable violence has become normalized. Uncritical support for a militarized culture now finds expression in a range of everyday events extending from the nightly news reports and the simulated violence of screen culture to sports events. One egregious instance often overlooked is evident in numerous military ceremonies that have become central to many sports events, a number of which are paid for by the Pentagon. For example, Eyder Peralta, a reporter for NPR, pointed out in a recent senate report released by Arizona Republican Senators John Flake and John McCain that:

> in the past few years, the Pentagon spent $6.8 million to pay for patriotic displays during the games of professional sports teams . . . For example, taxpayers paid $49,000 to the Milwaukee Brewers to allow the Wisconsin Army National Guard to sponsor the Sunday singing of "God Bless America." In another contract,

the New York Jets were paid $20,000 to "recognize one to two New Jersey Army National Guard soldiers as hometown heroes." *USA Today* reported that NFL teams received the biggest slice of the pie—$6 million, according to the report.[21]

Intolerable violence is also elevated to an everyday occurrence and legitimated in less evident ways through what Michael Schwalb has called instances of "micro militarism," which he defines as "pro-military practices squeezed into small cultural spaces."[22] Such instances are low-key advertisements for militarism, the "smallest of its cogs," that while largely unnoticed saturate the culture with militaristic values that celebrate war as the primary organizing principle of society and a general condition of the social order.[23] This is the small change of militarism and is present on some ATM receipts that post a "Support the Troops" message under the customer's bank balance. We encounter such messages when checkout clerks at gas stations and supermarkets ask for donations to "support our troops." Such messages function as military recruiting advertisements on the side of buses, cabs, and billboards. Higher-education institutions sponsor ads for graduate programs with pop-up images on their websites such as "Advance Your Military Career with an MBA." Inherent in all of these messages is that freedom and democracy are dependent upon the use of military force, state violence, and military service, the essence of which is "obedience, not courageous independence."[24]

These "small cultural spaces," when combined with various sites of militarism, ranging from public schools and sports events to popular culture and policymaking institutions, normalize war and violence and make it all the more difficult for the American public to question the merging of war and politics and the pathologizing of politics by a culture of violence. One consequence is that democratic idealism is replaced by the ethos of militarism and the use of military force and violence becomes the axiom by which everyday problems are both defined and mediated. Under such circumstances, the dominance of war-like values expands from the margins of society to become a powerful process by which civil society organizes itself, but coincides with what

Catherine Lutz describes as "the less visible deformation of human potentials into the hierarchies of race, class, gender, and sexuality."[25]

Reorganizing society in ways that support violence and discrimination, militarization not only undermines the memories of democratic struggles and possibility, it also criminalizes dissent and an increasing range of behaviors in a variety of sites such as schools and the streets of underserved neighborhoods. How else to explain the transformation of the police into SWAT teams or the endless practice of arresting students for trivial behaviors in schools, subjecting poor Blacks to fines for breaking rules that are petty and punitive, or the ongoing criminalization and assaults on Black people through policies of racial profiling that constitute practices of state harassment and violence. Aggressive policing is the underside of white supremacy because it is largely used in the service of whites against Blacks who have committed no crimes and who are targeted on the behalf of racist policies that amount to acts of terrorism.

War Machines and Intolerable Violence

War culture is a form of monstrous savagery that is often addressed through the extreme violence represented in videos of the police killing of both children such as 12-year-old Tamir Rice and adults such as Walter Scott, who was shot in the back as he was running away from his car by Michael Slager, a white North Charleston, South Carolina policeman. On an international level, such acts of intolerable violence are also denounced in images that show ISIS decapitating kidnapped civilians, shocking acts of terrorism in airports, night clubs, and congested urban centers carried out by a range of right-wing fundamentalists.

More recently, the vivid reminders of the horrors of war became painfully visible, once again, in the image of the lifeless body of Aylan Kurdi, a 3 year old who washed up on a beach face down while trying to reach with other refugees the Greek island of Kos. A second haunting image shows a toddler named Omran Daqneesh, bloodied and covered with dust, sitting silently in an ambulance after an airstrike on Aleppo, a city in northern Syria. Ordinarily, such images of dead, injured, and suffering children not only incite public outrage but also motivate people to act. As I mentioned in Chapter 6, one of the most powerful images to provoke moral outrage and public anger displayed the grossly mutilated body of Emmett Till that appeared in 1955 at his funeral. This representation of an act of brutalizing racist violence helped to galvanize the civil rights movement. Another image that changed the course of history was on display in 1972 when an anguished and terrified young girl was photographed running naked after a napalm bomb burned and disfigured her body. The picture not only became iconic, but also played a significant role in mobilizing protests that helped stop the Vietnam War. Reactions to such horrible images still exist, but the brutal and unimaginable acts of violence they portray produce short-lived outrage and now blend into the all-encompassing spectacle of violence and the fog of war.

The barbarism, scope, and visibility of such actions often promote policies further wedded to military solutions such as the suspension of civil liberties, the acceleration of the militarization of society, and the employment of counter-terrorism tactics that rely heavily on military force. As violence becomes both normalized and spectacularized in the media, the war machine becomes so deeply embedded in American society that "war has become . . . a form of rule aimed not only at controlling the population but producing and reproducing all aspects of social life."[26]

Yet, war machines do more than produce extreme forms of violence, they also designate whole categories of people as disposable, enemies, and force them into conditions of extreme precarity, if not danger. This is especially true of illegal immigrants, poor Black youth, Muslims, and those young people who now inhabit a neoliberal social order that has substituted precarity for social and economic protections. Young people today are told they are on their own and not to expect much from a society that offers them debasing employment, if any, poor health care, a terrain of uncertainty and insecurity, a crushing burden of debt, no hope for the future, and a market-based value system that tells them that their security and survival is no longer a social responsibility but a personal responsibility. If the future looks bleak for many young people, it is not because of their own doing. Yet, the ruling elite and mainstream media journalists continually label them as losers, suggesting that their failure is a character flaw rather than the outcome of wider structural and systemic forces over which they have no control. In this instance, intolerable violence is masked by a state that has been taken over by the ultra-rich, banks, and powerful hedge funds and has abandoned its social functions. Indifferent to its own criminality and "its allegiance to financial gain and market determinism over human lives and broad public values," the casino capitalism and financial elite that control it now inhabit the dark side of politics.[27]

Disposable Populations

Disposable populations increasingly cover more and more individuals and groups and represent the waste products of society. Etienne Balibar has argued that such populations are part of

> the cumulative effects of different forms of extreme violence or cruelty that are displayed in . . . the "death zones of humanity" and are subject to a poisonous form of neoliberalism that has become a mode of *production for elimination*, a reproduction of populations that are not likely to be productively used or exploited but are already *superfluous*, and therefore can be only eliminated either through "political" or "natural" means.

For Balibar, such practices of extreme violence represent "a triumph of *irrationality*" that threatens the very foundations of democracy.[28] Mbembe argues that such "*death-worlds*" represent new and "unique forms of social existence in which vast populations are subjected to conditions of life conferring upon them the status of *living dead*."[29] As a war culture shapes more and more of American society and life, fear and insecurity become workstations designed to trump any possibility or room for ideals, visions, and optimism. State violence in this case does more than impose insecurity, it also functions to undermine any viable form of dissent and create individuals who know how to obey. War culture not only creates a liminal space of insecurity and violence, it also functions as a kind of delegated vigilantism policing both bodies of the Other and boundaries of thought, while limiting the questions that can be raised about the use of power in the United States and its role in expanding the reach of a punishing state and domestic violence.

War culture is also legitimated ideologically by collapsing public issues into matters of taste, life-style, and fashion. This is a powerful pedagogical tool that functions to depoliticize people by decoupling social problems from the violence inherent in the structural, affective, and pedagogical dimensions of neoliberalism. Capitalism is about both winning at all costs and privileging what Zygmunt Bauman calls a "society of individual performance and a culture of sink-or-swim individualism [in which individuals are] doomed to seek individually designed and individually manageable solutions to problems generated by society."[30] Not only does the individualization of the social hide capitalism's structural violence, it also collapses politics into the realm of the personal substituting the discourse of power, racism, and class into the vocabulary of therapy, trauma, character, and lifestyles.

This mode of individualized politics functions as a weapon of fear that trades off conditions of precarity in order to amplify the personal anxieties, uncertainties, and misery produced through life-draining austerity measures and the destruction of the bonds of sociality and solidarity. Abandoned to their own resources, individuals turn to what Jennifer Silva calls a "mood economy" in which they "turn to emotional self-management and willful psychic transformation."[31] Trauma and pain become the start and endpoints for a politics that mimics a self-help culture in which the task of self-transformation and self-help replaces any attempt at structural transformation and political liberation.

The current regime of neoliberal pedagogy, which hides behind its anonymity, masks a structure of violence and a deeply anti-democratic ethos that maims and contains the critical modes of agency necessary for real change, while "the interaction between people and the state has been reduced to nothing but authority and obedience."[32] At the same time, poverty, patriarchy, structural racism, police violence, homophobia, and massive inequities in income and power are viewed as personal pathologies and shortcomings to be overcome by support groups, safe spaces, and other reforms that ignore fighting for what Robin D. G.

Kelley calls "models of social and economic justice."[33] This politics is an insidious form of learned helplessness that produces a depoliticized passivity and an absorption with the cruel and narcissistic dimensions of a consumer-based society that we see everywhere.

Towards a Comprehensive Politics

Any attempt to resist and restructure the war culture that dominates the United States necessitates a new language for politics. Such a discourse must be historical, relational, and as comprehensive as it is radical. Historically, the call for a comprehensive view of oppression, violence, and politics can be found in the connections that Martin Luther King, Jr. drew near the end of his life, particularly in his speech, "Beyond Vietnam: A Time to Break Silence."[34] King made it clear that the United States uses "massive doses of violence to solve its problems, to bring about the changes it wanted," and that such violence could not be clearly addressed if limited to an analysis of single issues such as the Vietnam War.[35] On the contrary, he argued that the war at home was an inextricable part of the war abroad and that matters of militarism, racism, poverty, and materialism mutually informed each other and cut across a variety of sites. For instance, he understood that poverty at home could not be abstracted from the money allotted to wars abroad and a death-dealing militarism. Nor could the racism at home be removed from those "others" that the United States demonized and objectified abroad, revealing in their mutual connection a racism that drove both domestic and foreign policy. For King, the "giant triplets of racism, extreme materialism, and militarism" had to be resisted both through a revolution of values and an expansive non-violent movement at home aimed at the radical restructuring of American society.[36] One ethical referent for King's notion of a radical restructuring was his moral and political abhorrence over the millions of children killed at home and abroad by a war culture and its ruthless machineries of militarism and violence.

Michelle Alexander more recently endorsed King's position by arguing that what we can learn from him is the need to connect the dots among diverse forms of oppression.[37] A totalizing view of oppression allows us to see the underlying ideological and structural forces of the new forms of domination at work in the United States. For instance, Alexander raises questions about the connection between "drones abroad and the War on Drugs at home."[38] In addition, she argues for modes of political inquiry that connect a variety of oppressive practices enacted in order to accumulate capital—such as the workings of a corrupt financial industry and Wall Street bankers, on the one hand, and the moving of jobs overseas, the foreclosing of homes, the increase in private prisons, and the caging of immigrants, on the other. Similarly, she calls for

> connecting the dots between the NSA spying on millions of Americans, the labeling of mosques as "terrorist organizations," and the spy programs of the 1960s and 70s—specifically the FBI and COINTELPRO programs that placed civil rights advocates under constant surveillance, infiltrated civil rights organizations, and assassinated racial justice leaders.[39]

More recently, we have seen the call for such connections emerge from the Black Lives Matter movement and a range of other grassroots movements whose politics go far beyond an agenda limited to single issues such as the curbing of Black violence. This type of comprehensive politics is exemplified in a policy document, "A Vision for Black Lives: Policy Demands for Black Power, Freedom and Justice," created by the Movement for Black Lives (M4BL), a coalition of over 60 organizations.[40] I have argued a similar position in my book, *America at War with Itself*, that I think is worth repeating:

> Yet, such struggles will only succeed if more progressives embrace an expansive understanding of politics, not fixating singularly on elections or any other issue but rather emphasizing the connections among diverse social movements. An expansive understanding such as this links the calls for a living wage and environmental justice to calls for access to quality healthcare and the elimination of the conditions fostering assaults by the state against people of color, immigrants, workers, and women. The movement against

mass incarceration and capital punishment cannot be separated from movements for racial justice, full employment, free quality healthcare and housing. In fact, Black Liberation struggles have strongly embraced this mode of politics by connecting police violence to poverty, under-resourced schools to the collapse of the welfare state, deportations to forms of racialized terrorism, and the death penalty to an analysis of the legacies of slavery. Such an analysis also suggests the merging of labor unions and social movements, and the development of progressive cultural operations such as alternative media, think tanks, and social services for those marginalized by race, class, and ethnicity. These alternative institutions must also embrace those who are angry at existing political parties and casino capitalism but who lack a critical frame of reference for understanding the conditions of their anger.[41]

Angela Davis has for years been calling for progressives to build links to other struggles and has talked about how what has happened in Ferguson must be related to what is happening in Palestine. This type of connective politics might raise questions about what the U.S. immigration policies and the racist discourses that inform them have in common with what is going on in authoritarian countries such as Hungary. Another example is illustrated in Davis' asking what happens to communities when the police who are supposed to serve and protect them are treated like soldiers who are trained to shoot and kill. How might such analyses bring various struggles for social and economic justice together across national boundaries? She argues that such connections have to "be made in the context of struggles themselves. So as you are organizing against police crimes, against police racism you always raise parallels and similarities in other parts of the world [including] structural connections."[42] Davis' politics embraces what she calls the larger context, and this is clearly exemplified in her commentary about prisons. She writes:

> We can't only think about the prison as a place of punishment for those who have committed crimes. We have to think about the

larger framework. That means asking: Why is there such a disproportionate number of Black people and people of color in prison? So we have to talk about racism. Abolishing the prison is about attempting to abolish racism. Why is there so much illiteracy? Why are so many prisoners illiterate? That means we have to attend to the educational system. Why is it that the three largest psychiatric institutions in the country are jails in New York, Chicago, Los Angeles: Rikers Island, Cook County Jail, and L.A. County Jail? That means we need to think about health care issues, and especially mental health care issues. We have to figure out how to abolish homelessness.[43]

I want to build upon a line of inquiry I have continually developed throughout this book by arguing that we need a new political vocabulary for capturing the scope and interconnections that comprise the matrix of permanent war and violence that shape a variety of experiences and spheres in American society. I argue that while the current focus on police killings, gun violence, mass shootings, and acts of individual bloodshed are important to analyze, it is crucial not to treat these events as isolated categories because by doing so we lose a larger understanding of the ways in which American society is being held hostage to often invisible but formative modes of intolerable violence that are distributed across a range of sites on a daily basis.

Intolerable violence is most visible when it attracts the attention of mainstream media and conforms to the production of what might be called the spectacle of violence, that is, violence that is put on public display in order to shock and entertain rather than inform.[44] Yet, such violence is just the tip of the iceberg and is dependent upon a foundation of lawlessness that takes place through a range of experiences, representations, and spaces that make up daily life across a variety of sites and public spaces.

In what follows, I highlight the terrible consequences such violence has on young people in diverse spaces, focusing on the often unacknowledged horror exacted on youth with the return of debtors' prisons and the modeling of public schools after prisons. The focus on young people is crucial because it is difficult to blame them for such violence while at the same time raising crucial questions about how any society could punish its own children. The fate of young people in a war culture also provides a crucial referent for analyzing the common thread of violence, particularly as it becomes the primary link connecting, for instance, public schools to juvenile detention centers and debtor prisons.

Youth in a Suspect Society

Young people, especially those considered the most suspect, provide a startling and eye-opening referent for analyzing how violence is not only represented and experienced, but also how it is distributed across a variety of interrelated sites. The daily violence experienced by youths, especially the most defenseless, does not often make news, because it exposes the harsh brutalizing reality that many face in such a racist, homophobic, carceral, and market-driven society. Such indifference is all the more tragic since one of the most unspoken acts of collective violence in the United States resides in the condition of its children.

Dietrich Bonhoeffer, the Protestant theologian, once argued that the ultimate test of morality, if not democracy, is how a society treats its children. If we take this principle seriously, America has failed its children, particularly those who are already underserved. In the current age of precarity, the usual causes of such violence point to a bleak future filled with low-paying jobs, the collapse of the welfare state, the threat of a lifetime of unemployment, the paralyzing burden of high levels of debt, and a political landscape that prioritized exchange relations over relationships built on trust, dignity, and compassion. All of these factors are important. Yet, there are still darker and more brutalizing forces at work that now bear down on many young people, forces that suggest that a distinctive type of hardness and culture of cruelty is now shaping American society.

In this instance, young people marginalized by class, race, and ethnicity have become waste products in a society in which the American Dream has been turned into an American nightmare. Young people now inhabit a landscape of permanent uncertainty and crisis, one in which they are spied on, incarcerated, criminalized, and written out of the discourse of democracy. No longer seen as a social investment, the most vulnerable youth have become a liability, subject to the harsh dictates of the neoliberal state, and a symbolic reminder of a social order that offers youth no promise of an alternative and democratic future. The dictates of precarity and austerity have become repackaged and weaponized under neoliberalism and the ongoing morphology of violence normalized as the only possible mode of life. America has arrived at a historical moment in which the war on children suggests "that the very notion of the future has been cancelled."[45] But the war on youth does more—it also reveals the raw reality of power politics and its willingness to crush all forms of resistance among young people. For many youth, the only spheres left for them to occupy seem to be the streets, prison, or the detention centers. Fortunately, many young people who are abandoned and disparaged refuse to buy into the false notion that the only form of agency left for them is to blame themselves, for this is not their only option. There is a growing sense of resistance among many young people, especially Black youth, that testifies to their determination to speak for themselves, embrace a liberated sense of collective identity, and take up the challenge to fight against the growing ecology of violence.

Zones of Social Death

Within the last few decades, it has become difficult to ignore how the criminal justice system has been transformed into a racist weapon.[46] Since the 1970s, the war on drugs has morphed into what can be called political hysteria and skyrocketing mass incarceration; essentially it has become a war on racial minorities, transforming many poor Black neighborhoods into spaces that resemble war zones.[47] Moreover, the war on terror has created a culture of fear and demonization largely aimed at minorities of color, while providing a rationale to put high-tech and powerful weapons from the battlefields of Iraq and Afghanistan into the hands of the increasingly para-militarized police departments.[48] The Department of Defense Excess Property Program now provides police departments in both local municipalities and on college campuses with military surplus including armored vehicles. Clearly, the lesson for poor Black and Brown communities is that force, rather than dialogue, is the first response of the police to the problems they confront.

As a recent Justice Department report on the Baltimore Police Department points out, the increasing militarization of the police and their use of zero-tolerance policies has resulted in "unconstitutional stops, searches, and arrests" that focus on African American men in poor neighborhoods.[49] The list of violations reads as if it were drawn from the pages of the Marquis de Sade's *120 Days of Sodom*. For example, the report documented cases of the police "jumping out" of their "vehicles and strip-searching individuals on public streets . . . In one of these incidents, a woman stopped for a missing highlight was ordered to remove her clothes."[50] A female officer "searched around her bra [and] then pulled down the woman's underwear and searched her anal cavity. This search again found no evidence of wrongdoing and the officers released the woman without charges."[51]

In another egregious and symptomatic case, in 2016 a teenage boy, while walking on the street with his girlfriend, was stopped by the police and forced to consent to a strip-search. The officer not only had the teenager pull down his "pants and boxer shorts," but humiliated the young man by strip-searching him in full view of the street and his girlfriend.[52] No contraband was found. The teenager later filed a complaint and in retaliation "was strip-searched again by the same officer who grabbed his genitals."[53] Such actions make up the day-to-day harassments, humiliations, and assaults waged against Black and Brown people in poor communities that often go unnoticed by outsiders and the mainstream press. In the eyes of the police, Black bodies are removed from broader historical and political contexts and reduced to things, objects, and abstractions, which make it all the easier for the police trained increasingly as soldiers to subject them to violent practices, even death. Yet, such practices amount to acts of domestic terrorism that would be unthinkable in middle-class white communities, and they also reinforce the notion that it is okay to treat Blacks as enemy combatants.[54]

Unconstitutional policing has become commonplace not only in highly publicized sites such as Ferguson, Missouri and Baltimore,

Maryland, but all over the country where Blacks in poor neighborhoods are targeted for trivial offenses such as spitting, panhandling, riding bicycles on sidewalks, and walking or driving their cars in white neighborhoods. Not only do officers often win awards for the number of arrests that they make, however unconstitutional, they increasingly act with impunity even when they kill weaponless Blacks including children and teenagers such as Michael Brown, Tamir Rice, Freddie Gray, and Tyre King. This is an updated version of a mode of policing that has become a kind of necropolitics in which entire populations of people are viewed as enemies, disposable, and subject to unimaginable acts of lawlessness and violence, representing the police state in its purest form.

At the same time, mass incarceration or what can be called the imprisonment binge has become the default disposability program for the racial punishing state and an incubator for intolerable violence, suffering, brutalizing punishment, torture, and social death. As Elizabeth Hinton observes, "there are 2.2 million citizens behind bars, representing a 943 percent increase over the past half century (costing) taxpayers $80 billion annually and [it] has become such a paramount component of domestic social policy that states like California and Michigan spend more money on imprisoning young people than on educating them."[55] Moreover, the punitive arm of the state produces especially severe consequences for "Black Americans and Latinos [who] together constitute 59 percent of the nation's prisoners, even though they make up roughly a quarter of the entire U.S. population."[56] The haunting and unanswered question for a country whose politicians argue is the greatest democracy in the world is why is it that "one in thirty-one people is under some form of penal control"?[57] No space appears to be immune from the punishment creep as the police occupy schools, health centers, airports, and sports events. What all this adds up to is that the police have become the first line of domestic defense in carrying out the dictates and policies of the warfare state, and the most vulnerable and most forgotten victims are children.

There is nothing new about the severity of the American government's attack on poor people, especially those on welfare, and both political parties have shared in this ignoble attack. What is often overlooked, however, is the degree to which children are part of the scorched earth policies that extend from cutting social provisions to the ongoing criminalization of a vast range of behaviors. It appears that when it comes to young people, especially poor and minority youth, society's obligation to justice and social responsibility disappears. Catherine Clement is right in stating that "Every culture has an imaginary zone for what it excludes, and it is that zone we must try to remember today."[58] That zone for children is a space where inscriptions of invisibility and misery are sanctioned by the rule of law. Such spaces constitute an endpoint in the dark ethic of a warfare culture, serving to accelerate the disappearance of the unwanted, a zone of abandonment where young people become unknowable, unrecognizable, and are subject to the machinery of social death. One such space that constitutes one of the most shameful attacks on young people is the rise of debtors' prisons for kids, whose aim is to punish young people when they or their families cannot pay for the harsh juvenile court costs, fines, fees, and other charges imposed on them by the criminal justice system. Such practices are particularly serious for youth who are poor and Black. One consequence is that "poor kids, who disproportionately are members of minority groups, enter the juvenile justice system earlier, more often, and stay in the system longer than more affluent children who have committed the same offense."[59]

Debtors' Prisons for Young People

Debtors' prisons for young people have not only become the dumping grounds for those youth considered disposable—the waste products of the American Dream—they are also a shameful source of profit for municipalities across the United States. These policies and practices operate as legalized extortion rackets and not only represent a tsunami of moral indifference and a lack of social responsibility among the American polity, but also point to a society "in which [the] political economy has become a criminal economy," one that places profits above the welfare of children.[60]

There are close to a million children who appear in juvenile courts each year. According to a recent report, "Debtors' Prison for Kids? The

High Cost of Fines and Fees in the Juvenile Justice System," many youths are incarcerated because they cannot pay an array of court costs and fines, services related to attorney fees, fees for room and board, clothing, probation, court-ordered evaluations, the cost of community-based programs, and restitution payments to victims.[61] According to the report, when a family can't pay these court fees and fines, the child is put in a juvenile detention facility. Such punitive measures are invoked without a measure of conscience or informed judgment, such as when children are fined for being truant from school. Nika Knight pointed to one case in which a child was fined $500 for being truant, and because he could not pay the fine "spent three months in a locked facility at age 13."[62] In many states, the parents are incarcerated if they cannot pay for their child's court fees.

For many parents, such fines represent a crushing financial burden, which they cannot meet, and consequently their children are subjected to the harsh confines of juvenile detention centers. Erik Eckholm has written about the case of Dequan Jackson, which resembles a story that merges the horrid violence suffered by the poor in a Dickensian novel with the mindless brutality and authoritarianism at the heart of one of Kafka's tales.[63] Eckholm is worth quoting at length:

> When Dequan Jackson had his only brush with the law, at 13, he tried to do everything right. Charged with battery for banging into a teacher while horsing around in a hallway, he pleaded guilty with the promise that after one year of successful probation, the conviction would be reduced to a misdemeanor. He worked 40 hours in a food bank. He met with an anger management counselor. He kept to an 8 p.m. curfew except when returning from football practice or church. And he kept out of trouble. But Dequan and his mother, who is struggling to raise two sons here on wisps of income, were unable to meet one final condition: payment of $200 in court and public defender fees. For that reason alone, his probation was extended for what turned out to be 14 more months, until they pulled together the money at a time when they had trouble finding quarters for the laundromat.[64]

Not only do such fines create a two-tier system of justice, which serves the wealthy and punishes the poor, they also subject young people to a prison system rife with incidents of violent assaults, rape, and suicide. In addition, many of these incarcerated youth have health needs and mental health problems that are not met in these detention centers and this has resulted in suicide rates that "are more than four times higher than for adolescents overall [and] between 50 and 75 percent of adolescents who have spent time in juvenile detention centers are incarcerated later in life."[65] Finally, as the Debtors' Prison for Kids report makes clear, young people are being sent to jail at increasing rates while youth crime is decreasing. In spite of this, the criminal justice system is mired in a form of casino capitalism that not only produces wide inequalities in wealth, income, and power, but it also corrupts municipal court systems that are underfunded and turn to unethical and corrupt practices in order to raise money, while creating new paths to prison, especially for children.[66]

I have spent some time on debtors' prisons for young people, because it is an exemplary site for understanding how a warfare culture can affect the most vulnerable populations in a society, exhibiting a degree of punitiveness and cruelty that indicts the most fundamental political, economic, and social structures of a society. Other sites of violence against youth can be found in many schools now modeled after prisons and organized around the enactment of zero-tolerance policies which as John W. Whitehead has pointed out put "youth in the bullseye of police violence." Whitehead argues rightfully that:

> The nation's public schools—extensions of the world beyond the schoolhouse gates, a world that is increasingly hostile to freedom—have become microcosms of the American police state, containing almost every aspect of the militarized, intolerant, senseless, over-criminalized, legalistic, surveillance-riddled, totalitarian landscape that plagues those of us on the "outside."[67]

Not only has there been an increase in the number of police in schools, but the behavior of kids is being criminalized in ways that legitimate what has been called the school-to-prison pipeline. School discipline has been transformed into a criminal matter now handled mostly by the police rather than by teachers and school administrators, especially in regard to the treatment of poor Black and Brown kids. But cops are doing more than arresting young people for trivial infractions, they are also handcuffing them, using Tasers and physical violence on them, and playing a crucial role in getting them suspended or expelled from schools every year.[68] The Civil Rights Project rightly argues that public schools are becoming "gateways to prisons."[69] One estimate suggests that one out of three young people will have been arrested by the time they finish high school. This is not surprising in schools that already look like quasi-prisons with their drug-sniffing dogs, surveillance systems, metal detectors, and a police presence, which in some cases resembles SWAT teams.

While there has been a great deal of publicity nationwide over police officers killing people, many of them Black, there has been too little scrutiny regarding the use of force by police in schools. Yet, as Jaeah Lee observes, the

> use of force by cops in schools . . . has drawn far less attention [in spite of the fact that] over the past five years at least 28 students have been seriously injured, and in one case shot to death, by so-called school resource officers—sworn, uniformed police assigned to provide security on k-12 campuses.[70]

There are over 17,000 school resource officers in more than half of the schools in the United States and only a small percentage have been trained to work in schools.[71] In spite of the fact that violence in schools has dropped precipitously, school resource officers are the fastest-growing segment of law enforcement and their presence has resulted in more kids being ticketed, fined, arrested, suspended, and pushed into the criminal justice system. Over half of public schools have school resource officers and the current number is just over 17,000.[72]

In 2014, over 92,000 students were subject to school-related arrests. In the last few years, videos have been aired showing extreme police brutality, such as a police officer inside Spring Valley High School in Columbia, South Carolina "slamming a teenage girl to the ground and dragging the student out of the classroom."[73] In Mississippi schools, a student was handcuffed for not wearing a belt, a Black female student was choked by the police, and one cop threatened to shoot students on a bus.[74] Neoliberal capital is not only obsessed with accumulating capital, it has also lowered the threshold for extreme violence to such a degree that it puts into place a law and order educational regime that criminalizes children who doodle on desks, bump into teachers in school corridors, throw peanuts at a bus, or fall asleep in class.[75] Fear, insecurity, humiliation, and the threat of imprisonment are the new structuring principles in schools that house our most vulnerable populations. The school has become a microcosm of the warfare state, designed to provide a profit for the security industries, while imposing a pedagogy of repression on young people.

According to the U.S. Department Office of Education for Civil Rights, a disproportionate number of students subject to such arrests are Black: it states that "While black students represent 16% of student enrollment, they represent 27% of students referred to law enforcement and 31% of students subjected to a school-related arrest."[76] Too many children in the United States confront violence in almost every space in which they find themselves—in the streets, public schools, parks, and wider culture. In schools, "more than 3 million students are suspended or expelled every year."[77] Violence has become central to America's identity both with regard to its foreign policy and increasingly in its domestic policies. How else to explain that

> the United States is the only country in the world that routinely sentences children to life in prison without parole, and, according to estimates from nonprofits and advocacy groups, there are between 2,300 and 2,500 people serving life without parole for crimes committed when they were minors.[78]

A predatory financial system reveals its obsession with violence when it targets poor, Black and Brown children instead of crooked bankers, hedge fund managers, and big corporations who engage in massive corruption and fraud while pushing untold numbers of people into bankruptcy, poverty, and even homelessness. For example, the international banking giant, HSBC, exposed the U.S. financial system to "a wide array of money laundering, drug trafficking, and terrorist financing . . . and channeled $7 billion into the U.S. between 2007 and 2008 which possibly included 'proceeds from illegal drug sales in the United States.'"[79] Yet, no major CEO went to jail. Even more astounding is that "the profligate and dishonest behavior of Wall Street bankers, traders, and executives in the years leading up to the 2008 financial crisis . . . went virtually unpunished."[80]

Violence against kids in various sites is generally addressed through specific reforms such as substituting detention centers for community service, eliminating zero-tolerance policies in schools, and substituting social workers for the police while creating supportive environments for young people. There have also been public demands that police wear body cameras and come under the jurisdiction of community. In addition, there has been a strong but failed attempt on the part of gun-reform advocates to establish policies and laws that would control the manufacture, sale, acquisition, circulation, transfer, modification, or use of firearms by private citizens. And while such reforms are crucial in the most immediate sense to protect young people and lessen the violence to which they are subjected, they do not go far enough. Violence has reached epidemic proportions in the United States and bears down egregiously on children, especially poor and minority youth. If such violence is to be stopped, a wholesale restructuring of the warfare state must be addressed. This suggests that not only must state violence be made visible, challenged, and dismantled, but also the underlying economic, political, and social conditions that it produces, including institutionalized racism and a class structure of inequality that breeds massive degrees of poverty, precarity, insecurity, misery, and anger.

The violence waged against children should become a flashpoint politically to point to the struggles that can be waged against the gun industry, the military-industrial-academic complex, and an entertainment culture, which revels in virtual and simulated violence, among other sites. Extreme simulated violence is an investment and millions appear willing to pay for it as a mode of entertainment that fuels what Dr. Phil Wolfson calls "fictive identifications" associated with "murderous combat illusions and delusions."[81] In addition, such violence, simulated and real, must be viewed as endemic to a regime of neoliberalism that breeds racism, class warfare, bigotry, and a culture of cruelty. Capitalism produces the warfare state and any reasonable struggle for a legitimate democracy must address both the institutions organized for the production of violence and the political, social, educational, and economic tools and strategies necessary for getting rid of it. What is crucial for progressives to remember is that power does not just inflict injury on the body through the practice of police violence, the tactics of the surveillance state, and mass incarceration. Violence also brutalizes subjectivity—the very notion of the self—as the threat of oppression is now coupled with the seductions of the market with its endless forms of passivity-inducing soma that is a defining feature of the wider commercialized culture. Undermining any notion of critical agency with state-sanctioned force and fear is now coupled with powerful corporate-controlled cultural apparatuses that infantilize the public by producing fake news, stripping meaning of any relevance, discrediting traditional sources of information, and promoting a dumbed-down culture of sensationalism, extreme violence, and sheer idiocy. At the same time, those public spheres such as schools, social services, alternative media, and higher education are under assault by powerful right-wing politicians and conservative funding sources such as the Koch brothers.

Violence has become normalized in the United States and mimics the worst dystopian fears of the writers George Orwell and Aldous Huxley. Orwell's surveillance and punishing state has merged with Huxley's version of a society drunk on the depoliticizing and infantil-izing pleasures of a celebrity and commodity-driven culture, which taken together effectively produce a mixture of hard and soft forms of repression. If the surveillance and tracking state represents one side of the authoritarian nightmare, the other side of such a dystopian vision is represented by a population chasing after the pleasures of instant gratification in a culture of consumer fantasies. Under such circumstances, Big Brother in the form of the authoritarian state and its heavy-handed repression and patrolling of borders serves not only as a subject of domestic terrorism but also as a reality TV show that turns surveillance into a form of entertainment. Repression now merges with entertainment and the reality of a nightmarish future simply becomes a script for an upcoming film, video game, or TV program.

Zygmunt Bauman is right in insisting that the bleakness and dystopian politics of our times necessitates the ability to dream otherwise, to imagine a society

> which thinks it is not just enough, which questions the sufficiency of any achieved level of justice and considers justice always to be a step or more ahead. Above all, it is a society which reacts angrily to any case of injustice and promptly sets about correcting it.[82]

It is precisely such a collective spirit informing a resurgent politics that is being rewritten in the discourse of critique and hope, emancipation, and transformation. The inimitable James Baldwin captures the debt which both burdens hope and inspires it. In *The Fire Next Time*, he writes "The impossible is the least that one can demand . . . Generations do not cease to be born, and we are responsible to them . . . the moment we break faith with one another, the sea engulfs us and the light goes out." Far from going out, the lights are burning with a feverish intensity, and once again, the left has a future and the future has a left.

Notes

1   On the origins of the warfare state, see Carl Boggs, *Origins of the Warfare States: World War II and the Transformation of American Politics* (New York: Routledge, 2017).
2   Ulrich Beck, "The Silence of Words and Political Dynamics in the World Risk Society," *Logos*, Vol. 1, No. 4 (Fall 2002), p. 1.
3   Michael Hardt and Antonio Negri, *Multitude: War and Democracy in the Age of Empire* (New York: Penguin Press, 2004), p. 2.
4   See, for instance, the section "End the War on Black People" in M4BL, "A Vision for Black Lives: Policy Demands for Black Power, Freedom and Justice" (August 1, 2016). Online: https://policy.m4bl.org/. Also, see Keeanga-Yamahtta Taylor, *From BlackLivesMatter to Black Liberation* (Chicago: Haymarket Books, 2016).
5   Steve Herbert and Elizabeth Brown, "Conceptions of Space and Crime in the Punitive Neoliberal City," *Antipode* (2006), p. 757.

6   Steve Martinot, "Police Torture and the Real Militarization of Society," *CounterPunch* (November 11, 2015). Online: www.counterpunch.org/2015/11/11/police-torture-and-the-real-militarization-of-society/

7   Angela Y. Davis, *Freedom Is a Constant Struggle: Ferguson, Palestine and the Foundations of a Movement*, ed. Frank Barat (Chicago: Haymarket Books, 2016), p. 77.

8   Rebecca Gordon, "Should Prison Really Be the American Way," *TomDispatch* (September 25, 2016). Online: www.tomdispatch.com/blog/176190/. For a vivid and searing portrayal of the racist nature of the carceral state, see Ava DuVernay's film, *13th*.

9   Cited in Marian Wright Edelman, "Why Are Children Less Valuable than Guns in America? It Is Time to Protect Children," *Children's Defense Fund* (December 8, 2015). Online: www.childrensdefense.org/newsroom/child-watch-columns/child-watch-documents/WhyAreChildrenLessValuableThanGuns.html?referrer=https://www.google.ca/

10 Brad Evans and Henry A. Giroux, "Intolerable Violence," *Symploke*, Vol. 23, No. 1 (2015), p. 201.

11 Achille Mbembe, "Necropolitics," trans. Libby Meintjes, *Public Culture*, Vol. 15, No. 1 (2003), pp. 39–40.

12 Jonathan Simon, *Governing through Crime: How the War on Crime Transformed American Democracy and Created a Culture of Fear* (New York: Oxford University Press, 2007).

13 George Monbiot, "States of War," *Common Dreams* (October 17, 2003). Online: www.commondreams.org/scriptfiles/views03/1014–09.htm

14 The notion of weaponized sensitivity is from Lionel Shriver, "Will the Left Survive the Millennials?" *New York Times* (September 23, 2016). Online: www.nytimes.com/2016/09/23/opinion/will-the-left-survive-the-millennials.html. Armed ignorance was coined by my colleague Brad Evans in a personal correspondence.

15 Jennifer Mascia, "15 Statistics that Tell the Story of Gun Violence This Year," *Trace* (December 23, 2015). Online: www.thetrace.org/2015/12/gun-violence-stats-2015/

16 Ibid.

17 Cited in Edelman, "Why Are Children Less Valuable than Guns in America?"

18 Kate Murphy and Jordan Rubio, "At Least 28,000 Children and Teens Were Killed by Guns over an 11-Year Period," *News21* (August 16, 2014). Online: http://gunwars.news21.com/2014/at-least-28000-children-and-teens-were-killed-by-guns-over-an-11-year-period/

19 Phil Wolfson, "Inciting Violence in This Culture of Violence," *Tikkun* (January 31, 2013). Online: www.tikkun.org/nextgen/inciting-violence-in-this-culture-of-violence

20 Editorial, "Terrence Crutcher," *Think Progress* (September 20, 2016). Online: https://mail.google.com/mail/u/0/?ui=2&ik=eaf3b5986f&view=pt&search=inbox&th=15748bc9e3ed0861&siml=15748bc9e3ed0861

21 Eyder Peralta, "Pentagon Paid Sports Teams Millions for 'Paid Patriotism' Events," *National Public Radio* (November 5, 2015). Online: www.npr.org/sections/thetwo-way/2015/11/05/454834662/pentagon-paid-sports-teams-millions-for-paid-patriotism-events

22 Michael Schwalbe, "Micro Militarism," *CounterPunch* (November 26, 2012). Online: www.counterpunch.org/2012/11/26/mico-militarism/

23 Michel Foucault, *Society Must Be Defended: Lectures at the College de France 1975–1976* (New York: Palgrave, 2003), p. 50.

24 All of the above examples are from Schwalbe, "Micro Militarism."

25 Catherine Lutz, "Making War at Home in the United States: Militarization and the Current Crisis," *American Anthropologist*, Vol. 104, No. 3 (September 2002), p. 723.

On the distinction between militarization and militarism, see John Gillis, ed., *The Militarization of the Western World* (New York: Rutgers University Press, 1989).

26 Hardt and Negri, *Multitude: War and Democracy in the Age of Empire*, p. 341.

27 William Greider, "Defining a New 'New Deal,'" *Nation* (September 21, 2005). Online: www.alternet.org/story/25745

28 Etienne Balibar, *We, the People of Europe? Reflections on Transnational Citizenship* (Princeton, NJ: Princeton University Press, 2004), p. 128.

29 Mbembe, "Necropolitics," pp. 39–40.

30 Zygmunt Bauman, *Strangers at Our Door* (London: Polity, 2016), pp. 58–9.

31 Jennifer M. Silva, *Coming Up Short: Working-Class Adulthood in an Age of Uncertainty* (New York: Oxford University Press, 2013), p. 10.

32 George Monbiot, "Neoliberalism—the Ideology at the Root of All Our Problems," *Guardian* (April 15, 2016). Online: www.theguardian.com/books/2016/apr/15/neo liberalism-ideology-problem-george-monbiot

33 Robin D. G. Kelley, "Black Study, Black Struggle," *Boston Review* (March 7, 2016). Online: https://bostonreview.net/forum/robin-d-g-kelley-black-study-black-struggle

34 Rev. Martin Luther King, "Beyond Vietnam: A Time to Break Silence," *American Rhetoric* (n.d.). Online: www.americanrhetoric.com/speeches/mlkatimetobreaksilence. htm

35 Ibid.

36 Ibid.

37 Michelle Alexander, "Michelle Alexander on 'Getting out of Your Lane,'" *War Times* (August 28, 2013). Online: www.war-times.org/michelle-alexander-getting-out-your-lane

38 Ibid.

39 Ibid.

40 See the statement online: https://policy.m4bl.org/

41 Henry A. Giroux, *America at War with Itself* (San Francisco: City Lights Books, 2017), pp. 260–1.

42 Davis, *Freedom Is a Constant Struggle*, p. 20.

43 Ibid., pp. 23–4.

44 Brad Evans and Henry A. Giroux, *Disposable Futures: The Seduction of Violence in the Age of the Spectacle* (San Francisco: City Lights Books, 2015).

45 Doreen Massey and Michael Rustin, "Displacing Neoliberalism." In Jonathan Rutherford and Sally Davison, eds, *The Neoliberal Crisis* (London: Lawrence Wishart, 2012), p. 205. Online: https://www.lwbooks.co.uk/sites/default/files/free-book/after_neoliberalism_complete_0.pdf

46 For instance, see Angela Davis, *Abolition Democracy* (New York: Seven Stories Press, 2005); Michelle Alexander, *The New Jim Crow* (New York: New Press, 2012); Maya Schenwar, *Locked Down, Locked Out: Why Prison Doesn't Work and How We Can Do Better* (San Francisco: Berrett-Koehler Publishers, 2014).

47 Elizabeth Hinton, *From the War on Poverty to the War on Crime: The Making of Mass Incarceration in America* (Cambridge, MA: Harvard University Press, 2016).

48 See, for instance, Radley Balko, *Rise of the Warrior Cop: The Militarization of America's Police Forces* (New York: Public Affairs, 2013).

49 U.S. Department of Justice, *Civil Rights Division, Investigation of the Baltimore City Police Department* (August 10, 2016). Online: www.justice.gov/opa/file/883366/download

50 Ibid.

51 Ibid.

52 Ibid.

53 Ibid.

54 Marc Lamont Hill, *Nobody: Casualties of America's War on the Vulnerable, from Ferguson to Flint and Beyond* (New York: Atria Books, 2016). See also Robin D. G. Kelley, "Why We Won't Wait," *CounterPunch* (November 25, 2014). Online: www.counterpunch.org/2014/11/25/75039/

55 Hinton, *From the War on Poverty to the War on Crime*, p. 5.

56 Ibid., p. 5.

57 Ibid, p. 6.

58 Catherine Clement, cited in Helene Cixous and Catherine Clement, *The Newly Born Woman*, trans. Betsy Wing, *Theory and History of Literature Series*, Vol. 24 (Minnesota: University of Minnesota Press, 1986), p. ix.

59 Michelle Oxman, "Debtors' Prison for Kids? Inability to Pay Juvenile Court Costs Leads to Jail Time," *Liberal America* (September 5, 2016). Online: www.liberalamerica.org/2016/09/05/debtors-prison-kids-inability-pay-juvenile-court-costs-leads-jail-time-video/

60 William Robinson, "In the Wake of Ayotzinapa, Adonde va Mexico?" *Truthout* (December 8, 2014). Online: http://truth-out.org/opinion/item/27862-in-the-wake-of-ayotzinapa-adonde-va-mexico

61 Jessica Feierman with Naomi Goldstein, Emily Haney-Caron, and Jaymes Fairfax Columbo, *Debtors' Prison for Kids? The High Cost of Fines and Fees in the Juvenile Justice System* (Philadelphia: Juvenile Law Center, 2016). Online: http://debtorsprison.jlc.org/documents/JLC-Debtors-Prison.pdf

62 Nika Knight, "Debtors' Prison for Kids: Poor Children Incarcerated When Families Can't Pay Juvenile Court Fees," *Common Dreams* (August 31, 2016). Online: www.commondreams.org/news/2016/08/31/debtors-prison-kids-poor-children-incarcerated-when-families-cant-pay-juvenile-court

63 Erik Eckholm, "Court Costs Entrap Nonwhite, Poor Juvenile Offenders," *New York Times* (August 31, 2016). Online: www.nytimes.com/2016/09/01/us/court-costs-entrap-nonwhite-poor-juvenile-offenders.html

64 Ibid.

65 See Child Trends Data Bank (2015). Online: www.childtrends.org/?indicators=juvenile-detention

66 Feierman et al., *Debtors' Prison for Kids?*

67 John W. Whitehead, "Another Brick in the Wall: Children of the American Police State," *Counterpunch* (August 25, 2016). Online: www.counterpunch.org/2016/08/25/another-brick-in-the-wall-children-of-the-american-police-state/

68 Ibid. See also, Henry A. Giroux, *Youth in a Suspect Society* (New York: Palgrave-Macmillan, 2010); Anthony J. Nocella II, Priya Parmar, David Stovall, eds, *From Education to Incarceration: Dismantling the School-to-Prison Pipeline* (New York: Peter Lang, 2014); Nancy A. Heitzeg, *The School-to-Prison Pipeline: Education, Discipline, and Racialized Double Standards* (New York: Praeger, 2016).

69 Cited in P. L. Thomas, "Education Reform in the New Jim Crow Era," *Truthout* (May 17, 2013). Online: http://truth-out.org/opinion/item/16406-education-reform-in-the-new-jim-crow-era

70 Jaeah Lee, "Chokeholds, Brain Injuries, Beatings: When School Cops Go Bad," *Mother Jones* (July 14, 2015). Online: www.motherjones.com/politics/2015/05/police-school-resource-officers-k-12-misconduct-violence

71 Amy Goodman, "When School Cops Go Bad: South Carolina Incident Highlights Growing Police Presence in Classrooms," *Democracy Now!* (October 27, 2015). Online: www.democracynow.org/2015/10/28/when_school_cops_go_bad_south

72   Ibid.

73   Ibid.

74   Nicole Flatow, "Report: Mississippi Children Handcuffed in School for Not Wearing a Belt," *Nation of Change* (January 30, 2013). Online: www.nationofchange.org/report-mississippi-children-handcuffed-school-not-wearing-belt-1358527224

75   See, for instance, Annette Fuentes, *Lockdown High: When the Schoolhouse Becomes a Jailhouse* (London: Verso, 2011).

76   See *Civil Rights Data Collection: Data Snapshot: School Discipline*, No. 1 (March 2014). Online: http://ocrdata.ed.gov/Downloads/CRDC-School-Discipline-Snapshot.pdf

77   Whitehead, "Another Brick in the Wall."

78   Lisa Armstrong, "The U.S. Is the Only Country that Routinely Sentences Children to Life in Prison without Parole," *Intercept* (June 3, 2016). Online: https://theintercept.com/2016/06/03/the-u-s-is-the-only-country-that-routinely-sentences-children-to-life-in-prison-without-parole/

79   Agustino Fontevecchia, "HSBC Helped Terrorists, Iran, Mexican Drug Cartels Launder Money, Senate Report Says," *Forbes* (July 12, 2012). Online: www.forbes.com/sites/afontevecchia/2012/07/16/hsbc-helped-terrorists-iran-mexican-drug-cartels-launder-money-senate-report-says/#1e15d7d44de4

80   William D. Cohan, "How Wall Street's Bankers Stayed out of Jail," *Atlantic* (September 2015). Online: www.theatlantic.com/magazine/archive/2015/09/how-wall-streets-bankers-stayed-out-of-jail/399368/

81   Wolfson, "Inciting Violence in This Culture of Violence."

82   Zygmunt Bauman and Keith Tester, *Conversations with Zygmunt Bauman* (London: Polity Press, 2001), p. 19.

EPILOGUE

Americans live at a time in which the destruction and violence waged by neoliberal capitalism is unapologetic and without pause. One consequence is that it has become more difficult to defend a system that punishes its children, destroys the lives of workers, derides public servants, plunders the planet, and abolishes public goods. Americans live in a new age of disposability in which the endless throwing away of goods is matched by a system that views an increasing number of people—poor Black and Brown youth, immigrants, Muslims, unemployed workers, and those unable to participate in the formal economy—as excess and banishes them to zones of social and economic abandonment. As Gayatri Spivak rightly observes, "When human beings are valued as less than human, violence begins to emerge as the only response."[1] At stake here is not just the crushing of the human spirit, mind, and body, but the abolition of democratic politics itself. Violence wages war against hope, obliterates the imagination, and cripples any sense of critical agency and collective struggle.

Yet, resistance cannot be obliterated, and we are seeing hopeful signs of it all over the world. In the U.S. Black youth are emerging from what are often viewed as conditions of impossibility and are challenging police and state violence, calling for widespread alliances among diverse groups of young people. This would include developing coalitions among groups such as the Movement for Black Lives (M4BL), worker-controlled labor movements, climate change advocates, movements against austerity, groups fighting for the abolition of the prison system, and many others. Such struggles are attempting to both invigorate and connect single-issue movements with an inclusive comprehensive politics, one that is capable of generating radical policy proposals that reach deep into demands for power, freedom, and justice.[2] Such proposals extend from reforming the criminal justice system to ending the exploitative privatization of natural resources. What these young people are producing is less a blueprint for short-term reform than a vision of the power of the radical imagination in addressing long-term, transformative organizing and a call for a radical restructuring of society.[3] What is important to remember is that calls for freedom cannot be limited to singular issues. Overcoming racism has little to do with the call for radical democracy, if it is not connected to calls for vanquishing sexism, homophobia, class exploitation, environmental plundering, and other modes of oppression that are as anti-democratic as they are dehumanizing and exploitative.

What we are seeing is the birth of a radical vision and a corresponding mode of politics that calls for the end of violence in all of its crude and militant death-dealing manifestations. Such movements are not only calling for the death of the two-party system and the distribution of wealth, power, and income, but also for a politics of civic memory and courage, one capable of analyzing the ideology, structures, and mechanisms of capitalism and other forms of oppression. For the first time since the 1960s, political unity is no longer a pejorative term, new visions matter, and coalitions arguing for a new democratic socialist party appear possible again. A new politics of insurrection is in the air, one that is challenging the values, policies, structure, and the relations of power rooted in a warfare society and war culture that propagates intolerable violence. State violence in both its hidden and visible forms is no longer a cause for despair but for informed and collective resistance. Donald Trump's election is the endpoint of an assault on public goods, community, and civic literacy that has been going on since the 1970s. Americans have lived through an ideological assault by the corporate and financial elite who have successfully inundated society with a hatred of community, an unchecked celebration of greed, self-interest, and a deep disdain for public morality. Ayn Rand's glorification of the self, hatred of altruism, and notion that compassion is a "morality for the immoral" supports not only a failed sociality and failed state, but also a social order that gives birth to monsters.[4] It is not surprising that Donald Trump has stacked his cabinet with followers of Rand's version of a social order devoid of any public morality.

Under the regime of Donald Trump, Americans are entering a period of counter-revolutionary change, one that foreshadows a dark and terrifying authoritarianism. As many critics have observed, it is not unreasonable to conclude that there is a thin line separating Trump's use of the rhetorical elements of authoritarianism—the demagogic use of fear, hatred, bigotry, ultra-nationalism, and demonization in order to blame others for America's problems—and his possible move towards implementing a number of hard-edged repressive policies that support a full-blown authoritarianism. Under the Trump administration, democracy appears to be on life support. Numerous polices are being implemented designed to dismantle crucial social provisions associated with health care, women's reproductive rights, and public and higher education. At the same time, the welfare state is being dismantled and all vestiges of the public good are under threat. All of these actions work to create a social order in which people are forced into what can be called survival mode, one that both inflicts massive injuries and prevents them from attending to the obligations of critical and informed modes of citizenship. Trump's disdain for critical media outlets, the poor, and journalists and intellectuals willing to make power accountable suggests a coming level of oppression that makes the unthinkable possible. As despairing as such events appear, it is crucial to remember that such historical moments are as hopeful as they are dangerous. Hope at the moment resides in the more general goal to reclaim the social imagination, bringing together an array of disparate, single-issue movements, while working to build an expansive social movement for real symbolic and structural change. Public spaces such as schools, alternative media, and other progressive spaces have to be defended against the neoliberal drive for privatization, deregulation, commodification, and disposability. Central to such a task is the need to build alternative public spaces that offer fresh educational opportunities to create a new language for political struggle along with new modes of solidarity. Worth repeating is the insistence that progressives make education central to politics itself in order to disrupt the force of a predatory public pedagogy and common sense produced in mainstream cultural apparatuses that serve as the cement for the rise of right-wing populism. This is not merely a call for a third political party. Any vision for this movement must reject the false notion that capitalism and democracy are synonymous. Democratic socialism is once again moving a generation of young people. We need to accelerate this movement for a radical democracy before it is too late.

More specifically, resistance has to take hold at the local level preventing the right-wing privatization of schools, health care, and the elimination of social provisions. Poverty, inequality, climate change, structural racism, xenophobia, the war on women, police violence against Black youth, mass incarceration, the threat of nuclear annihilation, and a ruthless persistent culture of cruelty, among other issues, all speak to those spaces and issues that inform everyday life and have to be reinvented as sites of education, consciousness raising, and collective struggle. These important sites provide the opportunity for progressives to construct a new and critical understanding of the social, community, and solidarity in order to invigorate and rethink politics and the promise of democracy itself.

Notes

1   Brad Evans and Gayatri Chakravorty Spivak, "When Law Is Not Justice," *New York Times* (July 13, 2016). Online: www.nytimes.com/2016/07/13/opinion/when-law-is-not-justice.html

2   See, for instance, M4BL, *A Vision for Black Lives: Policy Demands for Black Power, Freedom and Justice* (August 1, 2016). Online: https://policy.m4bl.org/

3   See, for instance, Robin D. G. Kelley, "What Does Black Lives Matter Want?" *CounterPunch* (September 2, 2016). Online: www.counterpunch.org/2016/09/02/what-does-black-lives-matter-want/

4   I have taken this term from an essay Gore Vidal wrote criticizing Rand. See, Gore Vidal, "Comment," *Esquire* (July 1961). Online: www.esquire.com/news-politics/a4595/comment-0761/

INDEX

Adorno, Theodor 51, 154
Advancement Project 106, 108–9
African Americans, derision against 59–60
Alexander, Michelle 239, 271–2
alienation, new forms of 217–21
America at War with Itself (Giroux, H.A.)
272–3
American fascism, Trump-like version of 69
Amnesia, United States of 78
anti-austerity movements 292
anti-democratic tendencies 26
anti-intellectualism: anti-politics,
democracy and 24–5, 31; illiteracy,
manufacture of 77
anti-other language 58
anti-politics, democracy and: anti-
democratic tendencies 26; anti-
intellectualism 24–5, 31;
authoritarianism, abyss of 22; Black
Lives Matter 40; Breitbart News
Network 24; capitalism, conscious
cruelty and 38; casino capitalism 24–5,
26–7; casino capitalism, visibility of
contradictions and brutality of 46–7;
change, origins of 45; civil disobedience
against authoritarian states, strategies
for 47; civil society 34–5; civil society,
fortunes of 32–8; civil society,
redefinition of 37–8; civilian control of
military, subversion of 24; collective

anger, new populism and 22;
Communication Power (Castells, M.) 23;
Crisis of the Republic (Arendt, H.) 31;
culture, power and politics, fusion of
41–2; democracy, need for new vision of
47; Democracy Movement 40;
depoliticization, rituals of 31;
disinformation, age of 30–1; domination
in age of Trump 41–2; electoral choice,
strategic illusions of 38; entrepreneurial
cooperation 37; ethnocidal violence 36;
forgetting and lies, culture of 23–32;
language as vehicle for violence 40;
liberation, new language of 38–40; lying,
politics of 29–30, 32; mass incarceration,
abolition of 47; neoliberal trade policies
22; neoliberal tyranny, self under
conditions of 36; *The Origins of
Totalitarianism* (Arendt, H.) 25–6;
performance, politics of 31; political
decision-making, structures of 33–4;
political framework, working beyond
"Lesser of Two Evils" 42–5; political
landscape 21–2; politics as entertainment
44; post-referential *jouissance* 46; post-
truth universe 30; power relations 35;
predatory capitalism 23–4; progressive
politics, new language of radical
transformation for 45–6; progressives,
vocabulary for 39–40; reactionary

of young people 234; disposability, politics of 234–5; Dream Defenders 253; education, politics and 245–6; education, role for 242–4; education as work of art 248–9; feedback loops, democracy and 243; global markets, power of 231; homeless people, criminalization of 234; hyper-consumption 243–4; ideas, institutional infrastructures and 246–7; left in politics, fragmentation of 249–50, 253; legal illegalities 235–6; militarization of American society 239; Military Commissions Act 235; National Defense Authorization Act 235; neo-Darwinist ethics 240–2; neoliberal authoritarianism, global threat of 244–5; neoliberal authoritarianism, new forms of 230–1; neoliberalism, products of 237; oppressive power 236; Patriot Act 235; pedagogy, democracy and 249; perpetual misery, fear of life of 231–2; possibility, discourse of 254; progressives, need for comprehensive education program for 251–4; public spaces, war zones of 229; radical democracy, promise of 244–7; radical imagination, revival of 247–54; social abandonment, zones of 233–4; social problems, criminalization of 243; social protection, neoliberal attitudes to 234; stupidity, induction of state of 246; totalitarianism, new forms of 229–30; totalitarianism, Orwell's vision of 228–9; violence, justice and 229; violence and cruelty, state sanctioning of 235–9; We Charge Genocide 253; winner-takes-all ethos 235

radical politics: development of, education and 81; education and 84–5; restructuring, King's notion of 271–2

radical vision, birth of 292

Rand, Ayn 293

Ravitch, Diane 105

reactionary populism: anti-politics, democracy and 35–6; defense against 293–4; isolation, loss and embrace of 215; normalization of 198

Reagan, Ronald 52, 76, 121–2, 142; society and the social, disavowal of 236

realist utopias, collective production of 190–1

refugee crisis, acceleration of 13

Reich, Robert 21, 80, 119

religious fundamentalism in American society 76

Remnick, David 177

repression: conformity and, pedagogies of 187–8; injustice and 4; pedagogies of 86; repression targets 80–1; state repression, orchestration of 200–1

Republican National Convention: fear mongering at 52; financial elite at 51

resistance: *America at War with Itself* (Giroux, H.A.) 272–3; authoritarianism, return of scourge of 259–60; Black incarceration, disproportionate nature of 283; Black Lives Matter 272; brutalism in American society 263–4, 268; children, violence against as catalyst for change 284–5; collective spirit, resurgent politics in 286; comprehensive politics, working towards 271–5; criminalization of behaviors 279, 281–2; culture of militarization, violence in 265–7; debtors' prisons for young people 279–86; disappearance, children and politics of 264–5; discrimination and violence, reorganization of society in support of 267; disposable populations 269–71; dystopian fears, proliferation of 285–6; dystopian violence 262; ear culture, legitimization of 270; financial system, predations of 283–4; hopeful signs of 291–2; hyper punitiveness, political culture of 261; incarcerated youth, problems for 281; intolerable violence, everyday occurrence of 266; Juvenile Justice System, Cost of Fines and Fees in 280; killing of children 264–5; Ku Klux Klan 261; local sites for 294; mainstream media, intolerable violence and 274; marginalization of youth 275–6; mass incarceration 278; militarism 260–1; militarization 265–7; militarization, registers of 263; Movement for Black Lives (M4BL) 272; necropolitics 262; neoliberal pedagogy, regime of 270–1; neoliberalism, production for elimination under 269; obedience, institutionalization of 261; penal control, punishment creep and

comments by 209–10; language of, notions of 'loser' and 213; language of bigotry and fear 129–30; law and order, emphasis on 130; law and order regime, promise of 230–1; legal illegalities, possible expansion under 235–6; "Make America Great Again" 56; media manipulation, master of 145–6; media strategy of 221–3; misogyny and acts of violence towards women 61; misrepresentation and disingenuousness within, momentum of 149–50; normalization of presidency of, threats from 74–5; peaceful transition to power, refusal to acknowledge necessity for 64; presence in American politics, effects of 199; presidential election, media coverage of 64–5; public schools and higher education under 166, 174; purging of facts and evidence of legitimacy 212; racial cleansing and white supremacy under 51, 52–3, 53–4, 56, 58, 59–60, 68; racial profiling call by 150; racism in age of 142–3; reality TV, adoption of practices of 151–2; right-wing extremists vying for power within 199; shame, trade in 211; torture methods, vow to reinstate 122–3; "Torture works, OK, folks?" 236; Trump-Clinton binary 33–4, 43–4; Twitter as weapon for 79–80; ultra-nationalism of 133; "uneducated," liking for 224; war culture of, dangers of 216

Tweets, weaponization of 79–80

ultra-nationalism, growing forms of 56

Vidal, Gore 78
violence: in America, characteristics of 100–1; cruelty and, state sanctioning of 235–9; cultural saturation in 13; daily spectacles of discourse of 91; ethnocidal violence 36; hate and, potential consequences of rhetoric of 64–5; institutional violence 99–100; intolerable violence, everyday occurrence of 266; justice and 229; language as tool of 62–3; language as vehicle for 40; militarization and 265–7, 267–9; normalization of

147–8, 262–4; organized culture of 151–2; political weaponization of 262; representations of, saturation by 262; society saturated in 57; state and institutional violence 104–5; state violence, collective resistance against 292–3; state violence, habit of 263; war culture and production of 260–1; against young people 120
voicelessness, promotion of 150

Walker, Governor Scott 232–3
Wall Street 1, 28, 30, 148, 152–3, 272, 284
war: hard war 126–36; horrors of 267–8; language of 260; militarization and, use of language of 85; permanent-war death machine, financial support for 172; veneration of 260; against youth 123–6
war culture: growth of seeds of 130–1; legitimization of 270; life in 259–62; savagery of 4–5; victims of 5
war machine: intolerable violence and 267–9; racial cleansing, white supremacy and 65
Ward, Olivia 30
Washington Consensus 37
Wayne, Lil (rapper) 142, 144, 146
We Charge Genocide 253
weaponized ignorance, lyrical fascism in time of: anti-Vietnam War movement 155; armed ignorance 146, 157; authoritarianism, reinforcement of 153–4; authoritarianism, return of 141–2; Black Freedom movement 155; bullying, vocabulary of 151–2; capitalist system, oppressions of 155; celebrity culture 144, 145; civil rights movement 140–1; cruelty, normalization of culture of 152; dangerous thought, crucial need for 154–5, 155–6, 158–9; democracy, tests for ideals of 141; disappearance and social abandonment, politics of 149; disconnection, politics of 156; empathy, waning of 158; exclusion and biology, discourses of 157; grievance, blindness and 157–8; historical memory, need for resources of 142; ignorance, manufacture of 148–9, 150–1; lies, mainstream media and proliferation of 151; media manipulation